Masterworks of Art
From Tutankhamun to Van Gogh

© 2007 by SCALA Group S.p.A., Florence
© 2007 Texts by E-ducation.it, Florence

This 2007 edition published by Barnes & Noble, Inc.
by arrangement with SCALA Group S.p.A.

Project Director: Cinzia Caiazzo
Editor-in-chief: Filippo Melli
Editorial staff: Francesca Bianchi, Carolina Orlandini,
Sibilla Pierallini
Graphic design: Studio Contri Toscano
Translation: Luisa Nitrato Izzo

ISBN-13: 978-0-7607-9284-1
ISBN-10: 0-7607-9284-4

Printed and bound in China

1 3 5 7 9 10 8 6 4 2

Masterworks of Art
From Tutankhamun to Van Gogh

Introduction by *Cristina Acidini*

BARNES & NOBLE

NEW YORK

TABLE OF CONTENTS

THE DREAM OF THE UNIVERSAL MUSEUM

If knowledge is akin to possession, then knowledge of art is a particularly valuable and rewarding possession: a gift for both mind and soul, widely available to us in the eminently reliable form of the book, the photographic archive, and the virtual database. Throughout our history, the desire to possess has often gone beyond the intangible realm of the mind and soul, manifesting itself in concrete terms in the fervent need to seek out, acquire and collect the most highly prized art and artifacts. As a result, countless works of art have traveled (and still travel) back and forth across the globe, often to places far from their original context: they have been uprooted and displaced, bought and donated, looted and carried off, and sometimes idolized abroad where they had been neglected at home. The removal of artworks and objects from their original context or resting place has provided the basis for many collections, and consequently, many museums. In this spirit, over the course of the centuries the human race has had a recurring dream, whose origins can be traced back to the ancient world and the museum and library of Alexandria in Egypt (perhaps the first instance of a collection of cultural artifacts made for the purpose of being preserved and handed down to future generations): the ambitious dream of the Universal Museum. Within the encyclopedic culture of the European Enlightenment, the idea of the Universal Museum became the motivating force behind the foundation and growth of some of the most important museums in Europe. Institutions such as the Hermitage in St Petersburg, the Kunsthistorisches Museum in Vienna and the Museo del Prado in Madrid owed their very existence to the vast and rich collections amassed by the ruling dynasties of the *ancien régime*;

while the Louvre in Paris was born out of the war spoils brought back to France after the Napoleonic military campaigns in Egypt and Italy, and the identity of the British Museum in London was founded on the Parthenon Marbles obtained from Athens by Lord Elgin. The model of the Universal Museum – exported to the United States in the 19th century, which saw the creation of the Metropolitan Museum in New York and its subsequent development in an ever more multiethnic direction – has attracted its fair share of criticism. The Greek claim to the "Elgin Marbles" has become an international *cause célèbre*, but museums also receive a regular flow of lesser known (yet equally contentious) restitution requests, particularly for the return of archeological treasures from countries "outside" the established network of European museums, such as the United States, Canada and Australia. The appeal of the Universal Museum was not lost on Adolf Hitler, who had grand designs for an international arts center in Linz to house the German and European masterpieces requisitioned from the countries he had invaded: a perverse and extreme interpretation of a vision of the museum which by then had already become outmoded, and which would have brought with it a raft of legal and ethical implications. The idea of the Universal Museum has not been entirely eclipsed, however; the Emirates, for example, are currently working closely with the Louvre on a project for their new national museum in Abu Dhabi. Indeed, if the international art world was already struggling with the moral dilemmas posed by works dubiously wrested from their (arguably) legitimate owners, the Second World War gave the question a modern urgency, as the stolen Jewish treasures which had resurfaced in museums and auction houses became the focus of increasingly frequent court-room battles. This complex web of ethical, museological, commercial and legal issues was the inspiration behind the "Declaration on the Importance and Value of Universal Museums" of 2002, formulated and signed by a group of major museum directors. The Declaration, which met with mixed reactions, included a statement on the subject of international art restitutions, asserting that the illegal traffic in archaeological, artistic, and ethnic objects should be firmly discouraged, while recognizing that "*objects acquired in earlier times must be viewed in the light of different sensitivities and values, reflective of that earlier era. The objects and monumental works that were installed decades and even centuries ago in museums throughout Europe and America were acquired under conditions that are not comparable with current ones.*" It went on to highlight the positive role played by the Universal Museum in the conservation, presentation, and interpretation of artifacts from different human civilizations for the benefit of the visiting public: "*Over time, objects [...] have become part of the museums that have cared for them, and by extension part of the heritage of the nations which house them. Today we are especially sensitive to the subject of a work's original context, but we should not lose sight of the fact that museums too provide a valid and valuable context for objects that were long ago displaced from their original source. The universal admiration for ancient civilizations would not be so deeply established today were it not for the influence exercised by the artifacts of these cultures, widely available to an international public in major museums.*" The Declaration thus offered a culturally sustainable explanation for existing Universal Museums, pronouncing itself in favor of maintaining their *status quo* while implicitly suggesting that this was a model which belonged firmly to the past. There remained the awkward question of "until when" that *status quo* should be maintained: and it was commonly accepted that the Second World War should mark the watershed period. In other words, restitution requests relating to the war period should be treated with the utmost seriousness, as should the prevention of illegal traffic in archeological and artistic objects.

THE UNIVERSAL BOOK

I have opened my introduction to *Masterworks of Art. From Tutankhamun to Van Gogh* with a brief survey of the origins, development and (perhaps) the end of the Universal Museum, and the thorny underlying issues which continue to pose problems for museums large and small, reverberating across exhibition halls and customs offices, gallery spaces and courtrooms.

However, it is worth stressing that the desire for a comprehensive knowledge of art is deep-rooted in anybody with an interest in the power of human creativity; particularly in an increasingly globalized society which, for better or worse, has forced us to expand our horizons and adopt a broader world view. To satisfy this desire we must move beyond the limits of the physical museum, and return to the virtual sphere. The book is the oldest, simplest and most authoritative solution; a universal guide which does not rely on the transportation of "real" objects, but instead gathers and organizes images and information, carefully selected by experts, offering the reader the chance to take a virtual "world tour" of artistic highlights, something that few people are able physically to do in the course of their lives.

What immediately attracted me to this book was its rigorously chronological structure, which enables it to present distant artistic phenomena simultaneously. Of course, the first contradictory element to the idea of total universal impartiality is the very choice of unit of time: of the many calendar systems in existence, ranging from solar and lunar, the Jewish calendar (beginning in 3761 BC), the Chinese calendar (invented in 2637 BC), the Buddhist calendar (starting from the death of the eighty-year-old Buddha in 544 BC), or the time before and after the Islamic hejira (adopted in 622 AD), it is the Western, Christian Gregorian calendar which, for practical reasons, has been adopted for the purposes of this book. Nonetheless, leafing through the stunning pages of this volume means taking a breathtaking journey through space and time, a journey of discovery of the finest expressions of human artistic achievement across two and a half millennia.

Head of Buddha, from Gandhara. Victoria and Albert Museum, London.

INTERPRETING ART: A FEW GUIDELINES

Perhaps the most natural and authentic way to "read" art, given the vast differences in its scope, purpose, style and content, is through our own individual emotional responses: the feelings aroused by a work of extraordinary originality or else by the repetition or reinterpretation of an existing model; the pleasure elicited by deeply harmonious forms, or indeed highly contrasting ones; the interest we have in the materials, precious or poor, used to create a particular work. A few examples: half a millennium after it was painted, Michelangelo's *Creation of Adam* on the Sistine Chapel ceiling continues to astonish us for the immense power and unique inventiveness of the climactic moment when God's finger meets Adam's. The *Chinese Terracotta Army* of Xi'an in the Chinese province of Shaanxi is equally thrilling for entirely different reasons: it is the visionary splendor of the multitude of warriors and horsemen, repeated in their hundreds and still standing guard over the grave of the emperor Qin Shi Huangdi at a distance of twenty-three centuries, that makes us catch our breath. We might compare the exquisitely balanced synthesis of draftsmanship, volumes and color in a Raphael painting such as the *Madonna of the Goldfinch* in the Uffizi, Florence, with the twisted, tragic greatness of Francisco Goya's nightmare visions, like the *Saturn* in the Prado, Madrid. And while some of the world's finest masterpieces have been created using valuable materials such as precious metals, bronze, gemstones and colored feathers, this does not diminish our admiration for the monumental fresco cycles of the Western and Eastern Worlds, executed with a humble palette of ground earth and natural substances and applied on plaster made from lime and sand.

Beyond pure emotion, the other guidelines I would suggest for interpreting art fall (with one exception) into pairs of opposing concepts; tools which, granted, are fairly limited when faced with the mystery and complexity of universal artistic creation, but that can still provide a useful departure point. The first pair, although somewhat awkward and archaic, is of fundamental importance: *iconic/anti-iconic*, in other words, with or without the human figure, from the Greek word *eikon* meaning image. From the ancient Middle Eastern and Mediterranean civilizations onwards – not forgetting the opulent female statuettes of Paleolithic Middle Europe exemplified by the "Woman of Willendorf" – the representation of the human form has been a recurring theme, for which the artists of Classical Greece elaborated a canon of proportions of such perfect harmony and beauty that it survived throughout the ages right up until the turn of the 20th century. In fact, the first examples of anti-iconic art to appear in Western Europe came as late as the end of the 19th century, when the prevailing spirit of Romanticism encouraged a more subjective artistic vision of the world which liberated forms of representation from the constraints of objective reality. During the 20th century, numerous artistic movements went on to transform the human figure: deconstructed and reassembled by the Cubists, it was eventually eliminated altogether by the Abstract artists, and reabsorbed into a non-figurative mode of expression composed of symbols, volumes and colors. Elsewhere, Islamic art developed in a completely different direction, dictated by the Koran which strictly forbade the realistic depiction of animate beings. (The obvious exception is the art of the Persian miniaturists under the 16th century Safavid Dynasty, whose flexible interpretation of the Koran permitted the creation of exquisite masterpieces of figurative art, concentrated in just a few decades). Islamic art thus expressed itself in a resolutely anti-iconic way through architecture, the decorative arts and calligraphy rather than painting and sculpture, reaching a supreme level of refinement and perfection. Its ornamental masterpieces featured pure geometric or highly stylized patterns applied to relief work, metal ware and ceramics; and it produced sophisticated works of calligraphy pertaining to both sacred and secular subjects (indeed, where Muslim history books omit the names of architects, painters or craftsmen, they record those of their calligraphers for posterity).

A second important contrast can be drawn between *sacred/profane*, within which further distinctions appear according to the subject (an individual image/moment or

Piero della Francesca, *Portrait of Federico da Montefeltro*, 1465-1466. Uffizi, Florence.

connected narrative episodes) and the destination of the artwork (places of worship or secular buildings, public or private areas). Entire cycles of religious narratives adorn the walls of churches and temples, just as secular allegories and historical events are found in the great halls of villas and palaces. Artists' imaginative representations of divinities (where this is permitted) can thus be juxtaposed with the realistic portraits of individuals: the vivid face of an ancient Roman, the features of a European aristocrat or merchant, an artist's self-portrait. Religions required artists to give form to the unknowable. Through their representation of the Greco-Roman gods, along with deified heroes such as those portrayed in the *Riace Bronzes*, they were able to formulate the canon of proportions. Christianity introduced the monotheistic concept of the Holy Trinity, and artists evolved a way of evoking God the Father and the Holy Spirit through the naturalistic symbolism of a venerable old man and a pure white dove, while Jesus came to be depicted with the features of a young man. Old and New Testament figures, particularly that of the Madonna, provided ample subject matter for centuries of painters, sculptors and miniaturists; although the most powerful and widely diffused image was undoubtedly that of Christ on the cross, whose suffering and physical death open the door to humanity's spiritual redemption from original sin. In direct contrast to this iconography of pain and violence, the sculpture of Gandhara, created centuries before Christ, offered a serene and detached vision of its own divinity, the Buddha, interpreting the beliefs and philosophy of his followers with exquisite abstraction.

From prehistoric times, funerary art has provided a bridge between the world of the living and the dead. Sacred images and objects were placed in the tombs of the dead to facilitate their passage into the afterlife and ensure that they were welcomed by the spirit world. Much of our knowledge of ancient civilizations such as the Egyptians and Etruscans stems from the discovery of burial chambers and necropolises. One of the most celebrated artifacts of the ancient world is the priceless golden funerary mask of Tutankhamun, a lesser Pharaoh of the 14th cen-

Crowned head of a Oni, from Ife (Nigeria), 12th-15th century. National Museum of Ife, Ife.

tury BC who died young and yet came to epitomize the lavish funerary art of the ancient Egyptians, whose daily lives were recorded for posterity in the tombs of the high priests and ruling aristocracy.

The third pair of opposites is *continuity/change*. Throughout the history of art, certain modes of iconographic representation have remained essentially unaltered; universal forms and subjects have been developed, fixed, repeated and handed down to successive generations; and stylistic solutions and techniques have become part of an established long-lived tradition. On the other hand, the artistic imagination has also experimented with and produced infinite variations and interpretations of these same recurring forms and subjects, as well as inventing brand new ones. A case in point is Byzantine art: stylistically evolving out of its Roman past (through Constantinople, former capital of the Eastern Roman Empire), it redirected its thematic focus entirely on the Christian story, which artists imbued with a transcendental dimension. In the period spanning the year 1000 AD, the elegant art of the Byzantine era – which had by then elaborated a number of archetypal Christian iconographic models such as the *Hodigitria*, the *Eleousa* and the *Glykophilousa*, all representations of the Madonna – reached a crossroads, from which two diverging artistic paths emerged, Western art and Eastern art. In Italy, Giotto and his successors developed a naturalism nourished by the study of the Classical art and remains diffuse across the length and breadth of the country; while conversely, in the major Russian cities of Moscow (the "third Rome" where the Tsars were modern caesars), Kiev, Novgorod and Pskov, the rigorously two-dimensional tradition of icon painting (more closely related to the Byzantine example) established itself as the prime mode through which the predetermined and immutable doctrines of the Christian faith could be symbolically expressed. For centuries the two diverse artistic cultures existed in parallel, only very occasionally meeting or crossing. From the Middle Ages to the Baroque period art and architecture in Italy flourished like never before, benefiting from the patronage of the popes and family dynasties such as the Medici and revel-

ing in the dynamic intellectual environments of the city states and courts. Inspired and spurred on by the study of nature and the ancient world, the invention of perspective and the wish to assert their strongly individualistic personalities, the innovative Italian artists experimented with a rich variety of styles and techniques which were in perpetual evolution. At the opposite end of the scale, Russian art, and especially icon painting, sought to maintain an iconographic and stylistic continuity which remained faithful to the eternal, unchangeable prototypes of religious artistic representation (effectively creating a "pictorial" doctrine to mirror the linguistic one of the bible), and also encouraged believers to turn their attention away from the corporeality of the physical world and achieve transcendence through the contemplation of sacred images which were often presented as *acheropite*, directly from God himself. Finally, at the start of the 18th century, Russia threw open its doors to Western European art at the behest of Peter the Great, and the icon painting tradition retreated to the monasteries, where it survives, unaltered, to this day.

Even if we widen our geographical and chronological scope, the opposing concepts of *continuity/change* remain useful. Over successive centuries, the art of Western Europe was in a continual state of flux, buffeted by groundbreaking innovations, new stylistic trends and emerging artistic movements; whereas in the East, particularly the Far East, the language of art was more constant. Correctly dating a wooden or bronze statue, a watercolor or ceramic jug thus becomes an impossible task for all but the most experienced experts. For example, the Gallery of Horyuji Treasures in the Tokyo National Museum contains a vast collection of art objects, including around fifty bronze figurines representing the Buddha, which to the average observer might appear very similar, yet have been reliably dated to the 7th and 8th centuries. When asked about their research methodology, the curators described the painstaking philological process by which every detail of each statuette – be it the folds of a garment, the curve of a finger or the angle of an eyebrow – had to be carefully examined for stylistic clues to their age or provenance.

Another distinguishing factor among different world art currents is the way *space* is represented. It is clear that the course of Western art was heavily determined by the introduction of spatial perspective. Taking his lead from the optical discoveries made by Arabic scientists, Filippo Brunelleschi first proposed his own theory of *perspectiva artificialis* in early 15th century Florence, which soon found its perfect figurative expression in Massaccio's *Trinity*; and a few decades later it was codified by Leon Battista Alberti. The intuitive rendering of spatial depth through the depiction of gradually decreasing forms was underpinned by a tight geometric control of the visual field, governed by a set of commensurate rules. The use of perspective ushered in a heightened illusionism, sometimes pushed to the virtuoso extremes exemplified by Mantegna's extraordinary *Dead Christ*; other artists delighted in experimenting with clever *trompe l'oeil* effects which fascinated viewers by blurring the boundaries of visual perception between the virtual and the real, the two-dimensional and the three-dimensional. The impact of perspective in the West was not only limited to the figurative arts and architecture; it altered the whole way the world was "measured", and with the development of cartography, heralded the age of discovery. In the East, meanwhile, space was conceptualized in a variety of ways, all different from that of the West. Often suppressed altogether, or else barely alluded to in essentially two-dimensional decorations, space could also assume a religious significance, as in Buddhism, where the soaring architecture of the stupa or the pictorial theme of a mountain summit alludes to the higher power of the cosmos. The figure of the dancing god Shiva (a type popularized from the 6th century onwards) inhabits his own purely symbolic space as he performs the cosmic dance of creation, existence and dissolution (*anandatandava*). Chinese art, especially of the Buddhist period, achieved a pinnacle of perfection well before the year 1000 AD. Li Cheng's masterpiece *A Solitary Temple Amid Clearing Peaks*, painted on fine silk using delicate veils of ink, depicts a mountain landscape formed by the interplay of alternating spaces and solids, with vertical lines which resolve the question of spatial depth without following the conventional rules of geometry. Japanese painting evokes a similar feeling for space: originally born out of the Chinese tradition, it developed along a different path from the 14th century onwards, when Japan grew increasingly hostile to external influences. Landscape was often represented in segments which recalled the essential harmony of nature and was dominated by elements such as trees and branches, but could also be interpreted using broken lines tending towards abstraction. In the illustrated manuscripts of the Islamic world, master calligraphers used ideograms, cursive elements and two-dimensional script which worked within the representational space to create further intricate conceptual interactions. The final "couplet" of opposites is *diffusion/isolation*. The influence of Classical Greek art was so widespread that its canons are still relevant to our modern-day aesthetic, two and a half millennia later. Yet Egyptian art, although it flourished for centuries, remained relatively self-contained, until the arrival of Roman art brought about its eventual demise. Buddhist art spread across an entire continent, from India to China; but its "Zen" offshoot, enclosed in isolationist Japan, only reached the West in the 19th century in the form of the Japanese print, which had an enormous impact on a number of European artistic movements, particularly in France. Other non-Western art forms exerted a similarly profound effect: African masks and art objects entered the Western artistic consciousness and accelerated the progress towards formal abstraction, and the huge monolithic *moai* heads and statues of Rapa Nui, Easter Island, "found" by Western explorers in 1722, were equally inspirational for their stark simplicity and quiet power. The exquisite art of certain distant civilizations only became known to the Western world when it was "discovered" by the *conquistadores*, colonialists, archaeologists or other groups, as in the case of the beautiful lintel reliefs of the Pre-Columbian Maya, the mysterious and captivating Mayan jadeite sculptures, the terracotta art of Djenné and the

bronzes of Ife and Benin. I could think of many more contrasting distinctions to be made in art: for example, the impassivity of Piero della Francesca (or some tribal art forms, or Gauguin) as opposed to the open expressiveness of the Flemish painters; or art which focuses on the nude figure as opposed to art which avoids or censures it; or the uniform light of Chinese and Japanese painting as opposed to the dramatic chiaroscuro effects of Caravaggio and his followers. However, it now remains for the reader to pick his or her own way through the vast array of images that only a book of this size and scope can bring together. The dizzying quantity, variety and quality of art in these pages can seem quite overwhelming; and yet its time span remains negligible, if we consider, as Dante put it, that a millennium is only the blink of an eye as compared with eternity: "*Before a thousand years have passed – a span / that, for eternity, is less space than / an eyeblink for the slowest sphere in heaven*" (Purgatory, XI, 106-108, trans. Allen Mandelbaum).
One thing is for sure: that as long as humans continue to exist, some works of art will remain fixed in our collective consciousness: masterpieces such as Leonardo's *Mona Lisa*, the *Taj Mahal*, Michelangelo's *David* and the frescos of the Sistine Chapel, the *Birth of Venus* and *Spring* by Botticelli, the *Mask of Tutankhamun*, the *Raft of the Medusa* by Géricault, Monet's series of *Rouen Cathedral*, Hokusai's *Great Wave*, Rodin's *Kiss*, Caravaggio's *Bacchus*…
examples which scale the heights of human artistic achievement and inspire almost universal feelings of admiration, respect and desire. This, after all is "Art for Eternity"; the art that we would want to save in the event of a planetary catastrophe, which would bear witness to what humanity was capable of.

Cristina Acidini
Director, The State Museums of Florence

Vincent van Gogh,
Self-portrait,
1887. Musée
d'Orsay, Paris.

22

TUTANKHAMUN AND THE VALLEY OF THE KINGS AND OF THE QUEENS

(EGYPT, 14TH CENTURY BC)

Tutankhamun and the pharaohs of the New Kingdom had themselves buried in the Valley of the Kings (Biban el-Muluk): an arid, rocky depression lying alongside the eastern bank of the Nile, facing Karnak and Luxor and overlooked by a mountain called Qurn ("Horn"), the highest summit in the valley, and immediately recognizable by its pyramid-like shape, which was probably significant for the ancient Egyptians. The area comprises the eastern valley – the most important, in which 58 tombs have been discovered – and a branch leading off it, the western valley, with four tombs.

Up until the decline of the XX Dynasty, the pharaohs generally chose long tunnels, sometimes penetrating deep into the mountain, for their burials. The entrances could be hidden, perhaps with stones, although some were more visible: inspections took place – these being well documented – and there was precise data on their location.

The internal structure of the tombs reveals three phases of elaboration, roughly corresponding to the three dynasties of the New Kingdom (XVIII, XIX, XX). During the XVIII Dynasty, the tombs were planned with a clear bending or curving of their axes.

With Horemheb, the last king of the XVIII Dynasty, there is a change. The plan becomes straighter, but the corridor is "split", continuing in parallel, with a "bayonet-like" junction. During the XX Dynasty, the plan tended to become simpler and was straight again. These were not showy sepulchres, attractive prey for robbers, but under-ground passages for the corpse of the pharaoh to lie in forever. Nevertheless, the majority of these tombs were ransacked in ancient times.

During the New Kingdom, the tombs were no longer considered places of worship and great funeral temples, such as those of Queen Hatshepsut (XVIII Dynasty) and the Ramesseum of Ramses II (XIX Dynasty), were constructed at other sites. In order to maintain secrecy, the workers were not housed in the immediate vicinity of the burial place, but some distance away at Deir el-Medina. Southeast of the Valley of the Kings, another valley opens out at the foot of a kind of open-air cave, recognizable from a distance by overhanging rocks, which appear about to tumble down. From time to time, rainwater forms a waterfall and collects in a basin. Perhaps because this suggested a female symbol, the valley was chosen as the "Seat of Beauty", nowadays known as the Valley of the Queens: a necropolis for queens and royal princes and princesses, especially of the XIX and XX Dynasties.

These tombs are similar to those of the pharaohs, but are simpler in their design, and decorated in a different manner, with images featuring the dead in front of the gods. That of the bride of Ramses II, Nefertari, has intensely contrasting chromatic scenes, and the tombs of two of the children of Ramses III are particularly notable for their bright colours. At the edge of the desert, following the cultivated land, there are the remains of temples of worship – "castles of millions of years" – corresponding to royal burial places.

Mask of Tutankhamun
Gold, stone, vitreous paste
h. 1.77 ft; l. 1.28 ft
c. 1330 BC (XVIII Dynasty)
Egyptian Museum, Cairo

The spectacular discovery of Tutankhamun's tomb, which bears the last number (62) in the Valley of the Kings, is perhaps the most famous adventure in archeology. The richness and splendor of the grave goods of the young pharaoh, who favored a return to traditional religion after Amenhotep IV-Akhenaten's attempt at

"monotheistic" reform, filled the pages of newspapers for a long time after that momentous day of November 4, 1922, stirring people's imagination and triggering a revival of enthusiasm for ancient Egypt.

That tomb with its abnormal layout was heaped with an incredible quantity of objects, the goods that were to accompany him on his journey of regeneration. A set of four gilded shrines held the sarcophagus, which was made of yellow quartzite and contained three anthropoid coffins, the last one of solid gold, the substance of which the flesh of the gods was made. Inside it lay the mummified body of Tutankhamun, its head covered by the mask.

Very hard to photograph because of its gleaming surfaces, the mask represents Tutankhamun's youthful face in an idealized style that indicates a return to tradition in the world of art as well. The *nemes* headdress, wrapped tightly under the nape of the neck, has blue

stripes. The diadem consists of goddesses in the form of a vulture and a cobra, representing Upper and Lower Egypt respectively; the gold is inlaid with cornelian, lapis lazuli, quartz and turquoise glass paste.

The eyebrows and outlines of the eyelids are made of lapis lazuli while the eyes are reproduced in obsidian and quartz, with a touch of red at the corners.

The divine beard, resembling that of the god Osiris, is an inlay of turquoise glass paste in gold; the collar is composed of elements of lapis lazuli, quartz and green feldspar. The text of a chapter from the *Book of the Dead*, specifically dedicated to protection of the head, is engraved in the gold on the back.

Equipement of the Burial Chamber of Tutankhamun
Valley of the Kings, Thebes

By mid-February, 1923, the antechamber had been cleared, and it was time to move on to the opening of the door, which, it was hoped, hid the mummy. On February 17, twenty people – members of the government and scientists – were admitted to the interior of the tomb to observe the great event. In absolute silence, Carter began to remove the upper layer of stone. As soon as the opening became large enough to allow an electric lamp to pass through, a marvellous vision appeared. It was a wall of solid gold, which turned out to be the anterior wall of the largest funerary coffin that has ever been discovered. After two hours of difficult work, they penetrated the interior of the burial chamber where a catafalque, completely

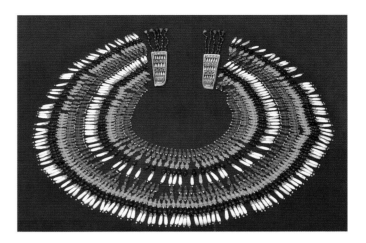

covered with gold, its sides inlaid with panels of azure majolica and covered with symbols, was revealed.

Its dimensions left the observers stunned: 17x10x9 ft. On November 29, 1923, work began on taking apart the catafalque, which consisted of four coffins placed one inside the other. The large, unsealed double doors on the western side opened easily, but the second coffin – which lay inside – still bore a seal: it was intact, and Tutankhamun rested in his tomb just as he had when placed there 33 centuries earlier.

The task of removal took 84 days, at the end of which the explorers found themselves in front of the enormous sarcophagus, carved from a single block of yellow quartz and covered with a granite slab. The opening of the sarcophagus took place on the February 12, 1924. Under linen bandages appeared the king: not the mummy but a portrait in gold of the young pharaoh. The completely rounded head had its face painted with gold, the eyes with aragonite and obsidian, and the eyelashes and eyebrows with lapis lazuli. The hands were fully formed, whilst the body was in *bas-relief*. Carnavon's death and

squabbles with the authorities interrupted further investigation and it was only in 1925 that Carter could get back to work and, removing the last casings, finally get to the mummy of the pharaoh.

Not only the mask and the sarcophagi or the gilded wooden throne, but also the smaller objects in the treasure are of extraordinary beauty and interest. Particularly striking are alabaster ointment jars, one featuring a lion, symbol of the god Bes, the other evoking the image of Semataouy or union of the two lands, and the ivory headrest, decorated with the figure of the god Shu. More suitable for everyday use are the numerous vases, lamps, chairs and stools, as well as the objects relating to the king's leisure, such as musical instruments and games tables.

Left and opposite:
Throne of Tutankhamun, and detail, *c.* 1330 BC. Egyptian Museum, Cairo.

Top: *Floral Funeral Collar*, from the Tomb of Tutankhamun, *c.* 1330 BC. Egyptian Museum, Cairo.

THE ASSYRIANS

(IRAQ, 7TH CENTURY BC)

During the Bronze Age, the kings of Assur gradually extended their power beyond their ancient national confines, and in a short space of time they conquered the whole of Mesopotamia, Syria and Palestine, finally subjugating Egypt. By developing a complex system of local administration overseen by a central power, the Assyrians were able to dominate and maintain their conquered territories through the control network they had established. The military exploits of the Assyrian kings are commemorated in the superb reliefs which decorated the interiors of the great palaces of Nimrud, Khorsabad and Nineveh. The Neo-Assyrian reliefs are one of the highest points of artistic expression in the Near East, and their innovations in form and concept represented a great step forward in the artistic culture of the ancient world.

From the beginning of the 1st millennium BC, a succession of Assyrian kings transformed this small northern Mesopotamian state into the first great and last-ing empire of the Near East. The kings, who styled themselves as high priests of the warrior god Assur, led numerous military campaigns in Babylon, Elam, Urartu, Syria, Palestine and Arabia, finally conquering Egypt in the 7th century BC. Between the 9th and 7th century BC the Assyrian nation, and with it the whole Mesopotamian civilization, experienced a period of unrivalled splendor, richly exemplified by the exceptional archaeological finds from the royal palaces.

As well as being shrewd rulers and military strategists, the Assyrian kings were undoubtedly excellent builders. They instigated a complex construction program which included both the restoration of ancient, venerated monuments and the creation of new temples, palaces and even entire cities, as in the case of Dur Sharrukin, the capital founded by Sargon II. The idea of the builder-king is an ancient one in Mesopotamian tradition, beginning with the kings of the Protodynastic and Neo-Sumerian periods, and continuing right up to the Assyrians and Babylonians of the 2nd millennium BC.

Relief of the Lion Hunt of Ashurbanipal
Stone panel, 3.51×2.33 ft
7th century BC
British Museum, London

The north palace of Nineveh contained some of the most famous and admired reliefs of the Neo-Assyrian period: the lion hunt of Ashurbanipal, unquestionably one of the finest examples of the skills and creative powers of the great Mesopotamian artists. In the lion hunt, the Assyrian king asserts his position as the one supreme guarantor of the terrestrial order; the act of hunting is in fact symbolic of man's power over the forces of nature. The principal duty

of the king was to maintain a steady control over both nature and enemies, who could threaten the confines and security of the Assyrian kingdom. The ancient theme of the royal lion hunt recalls the earliest examples of Mesopotamian art, in which the priest-king kills the ferocious beasts with his lance and bow and arrow. The lion hunt of Ashurbanipal is an event that involves the entire Assyrian population, who are pictured watching the king's feats from a hill-top vantage point. The king is accompanied by a series of assistants, who variously drive the carts, hold dogs on leads, or release the fierce lions from their cages. The king himself emerges from this setting, massacring the lions from his chariot. The drama of the scene is expressed with exceptional skill by the Assyrian stone carvers, for example in the way they have rendered the men's taut muscles and the king's dynamic movements. The different poses of the lions reveal the artists' close observation and knowledge of the animals: some roar menacingly as they try to attack Ashurbanipal's chariot, while others are wounded, in agony, or already dead. The skilful use of space and compositional technique is evident from the crowded group of felled lions and the central positioning of the king, making the lion hunt of Ashurbanipal a masterly example of the balance and expressive quality of great Neo-Assyrian relief art.

GREEK SCULPTURE OF THE 6TH CENTURY: *KOÙROI* AND *KÒRAI*

(GREECE, 590-520 BC)

Archaic Greek sculpture was initially characterized by rigidity, schematism and stateliness: sculptures were still conceived to be viewed from the front, and the musculature barely defined. The two principal types, the *koùros* and the *kòre*, were used as votive offerings in the shrines or funerary monuments of necropolises and did not have any distinguishing features, since they were meant to represent idealized male and female figures.

The *koùros*, inspired by Egyptian sculpture, is a young male nude with long hair down to his shoulders. The arms are held at the side of the body, with the hands closed into a fist at the hips; the left leg is placed slightly ahead of the right leg; the eyes are disproportionately large for the face and the lips are closed. There is a progression in the rendering of certain anatomical features such as the epigastric arch of the lower stomach and the knees, which are either engraved or in relief. In the earliest examples, the muscles, and in particular the hair and ears are depicted in a pure, stylized fashion. The oldest *koùroi* are much larger than life, such as the Sounion *koùros* (590-580 BC) which stands 9.8 ft high. The *Dipylon* head (*c.* 590 BC), discovered in Athens along

with a right hand, belonged to a colossal *koùros*, other fragments of which were found in the *agorà*. One original interpretation of the *koùros* type is the *Moskophoros* ("calf-bearer"), dedicated on the Acropolis of Athens by a man named Rhombos (*c.* 560 BC): the figure, who wears a close-fitting cloak, is constructed around the point where the man's arms and the animal's legs meet. The composition harks back to the traditional iconographic type of a figure carrying a ram, which was already known from representations of the god Hermes.

The *kòrai*, young female figures, wore either a woolen peplos or a linen chiton under a cloak or *himation*. One of the earliest examples from Attica is the larger than life size Berlin *Kòre* (570-560 BC), whose enormous hands and feet emphasize the statue's massive proportions. The figure's severity is almost at odds with the elegant hairstyle; she wears a *polos* on her head, earrings, a necklace and sandals. The solemnity of the *kòrai* of the Athens Acropolis contrasts with the fluid forms of the series from the Heraion of Samos. The rounded Ionic style is exemplified by the statue of around 560 BC dedicated by Cheramyes, which is now in the Louvre.

Peplos Kòre
Parian marble, h. 3.87 ft
530-520 BC
Acropolis Museum, Athens

The sculpture was found in 1886 to the west of the Erechtheum, where other *kòrai* were also discovered. All of these statues were votive offerings which had been buried around the Acropolis during the restoration work that was

carried out there following its destruction by Xerxes and his Persian army in 480 BC. The statues had been thrown into ditches which were rediscovered at the end of the 19th century, providing a valuable source for the study of Arcaic sculpture. Some scholars believe that the statue, of Parian marble, was made by the same sculptor responsible for the *Rampin Horseman*.

It is known as the *Peplos Kòre* after the heavy garment which conceals the chiton underneath. It has not been possible to trace the statue to an inscribed base, which means that the names of the person who commissioned her, and the sculptor, remain unknown, a problem for many of the Acropolis *kòrai*. Standing 3.87 ft high, the young woman is smaller than life size; she wears a pleated chiton, whose hems can be seen between the feet and at the right elbow; the peplos is worn over this, cinched at the waist by a belt, with a hem that falls around the stomach. Traces of a border painted with geometric designs and vegetation can be seen on the back and sleeves. The right arm is held at the side of the body with the hand closed around an attribute that has since been lost, while the left arm was stretched out in front of her, presumably to give an offering. The long hair is fastened at the nape with a band, and separates into three sections as it falls around the shoulders and chest. The hair on the forehead is split into three bands, and a number of holes suggest that there was once an ornament. The painted eyes are protruding and the lips are slightly parted in a smile. There are traces of a painted necklace, while holes in the earlobes indicate that she wore metal earrings.

CLASSICAL GREEK ART

(GREECE, 480-430 BC)

This period is characterized by the pursuit of the ideals of harmony and perfection, whose basis, in art as in nature, was the so-called "golden ratio", subsequently defined by Euclid in his *Elements*. The golden ratio is an irrational number whose decimal value can only be expressed as an approximation (1.618033). It is thought that Phidias used it both in his sculptures and for the construction of the Parthenon. The mathematical relationship can be found in the human body, as well as in the measurements of canonical beauty used by the Greek sculptors.

Phidias was the most renowned sculptor of the period, dominated by the figure of Pericles. At the start of his career, he was commissioned to sculpt the *Athena Pròmachos* (fighting), a bronze statue over seven meters high, of which only the base blocks survive. It was the first monument to grace the reconstruction of the Acropolis at Athens. The goddess carried a spear in her left hand, and a shield with relief decorations depicting a battle of the centaurs; her right arm, held out in front of her, may have carried a *Nike*. Another seminal work by Phidias, which may have been inspired by the *Pròmachos*, was the *Athena Parthènos* (or virgin), the colossal chryselephantine Parthenon statue known to us from various Roman copies. The armed goddess was depicted with an aegis, decorated at the center with a Medusa's head. She held a *Nike* in the palm of her right hand. Her shield, which protected the sacred serpent Erittonius, and her sandals featured scenes of battling Amazons, giants and centaurs, which alluded to the conflict between Greek and barbarian cultures. The base was decorated with the birth of Pandora, who was forged by Hephaestus and imbued with Athena's intelligence. Phidias left Athens after being accused of stealing some of the gold destined for the *Athena Parthènos*, as well as of irreverence for having dared to depict himself and Pericles on the goddess's shield. He subsequently made the colossal statue of Zeus at Olympia: the god is portrayed seated, holding a *Nike* in the palm of his hand. The *Wounded Amazon* is a later work, of which there are many surviving copies. Pliny writes of a competition which took place at Ephesus, possibly between 438-435 BC, between the sculptors Phidias, Polyclitus, Phradmon, Cresilas and Cydon, to make a statue of an Amazon for dedication to the temple of Artemis. Phidias's statue was admired for its unusual drapery, which flowed diagonally across the slender figure, while the winning statue, by Polyclitus, displayed a measured sense of proportion, with a facial expression that inspired pathos.

Polyclitus of Argos was another influential sculptor of the period, who worked in bronze. He also wrote a theoretical treatise significantly entitled the *Kanon* (Canon), of which few fragments survive. The title of the treatise also relates to one of the artist's statues, the *Doryphoros* (spear-carrier): the statue was designed using a precise system of proportional relationships between the different parts of the body which created a sense of balance and movement, and this solution was to become an integral part of the artistic canon. Polyclitus took his research further with the *Diadoumenos* of around 430 BC, the statue of an athlete in the act of tightening his headband. The figure, originally in bronze but known from marble copies, is rendered in a freer compositional style, with complex movement: the body flexes in a more accentuated manner than the norm, with the head inclined towards the forward-stretching leg. The musculature is more supple, and the curly locks of hair are colorfully rendered and more graceful than those of the *Doryphoros*, revealing the influence of the Phidian style.

Riace Bronzes

Statue A:
Bronze, h. 6.72 ft
460 BC
Statue B:
Bronze, h. 6.46 ft
430 BC
National Archaeological
Museum, Reggio Calabria

These famous statues were found in 1972 off the coast of Riace in Italy's Calabria region. They are thought to have belonged to the cargo of a Roman ship, possibly headed for Rome itself, when the vessel was shipwrecked in these waters. It is likely that the two statues were plundered from Greece at some point, for example when Corinth was captured by Mummius in 146 BC, or during Sulla's military campaign; or they may have been part of Nero's loot from Delphi, where he took over 200 statues of gods and male figures. Scholars still argue over the meaning and attribution of the statues, labeled A and B. What is certain is that they were not made at the same time: A is around thirty years older than B, which seems to be a more academic work. In spite of their different characteristics, some scholars have attempted to date the statues to a single period, suggesting, among other important works recorded by ancient literary sources, that they belonged to a group of votive works made by Phidias, and dedicated by the Athenians at Delphi for the Battle of Marathon. Statue A's hair is held in place by a headband; he has a curly beard, eyes of ivory and colored stone, copper lips and nipples, and silver teeth. The figure's left leg is extended forward, with the weight resting on the right, which raises the hip. The left arm originally bore a shield, of which the armband survives; the right hand is also thought to have carried something. The figure's stylistic and formal characteristics date it to around 460 BC. Statue B wears a helmet, fashioned onto an elongated skullcap. As with the first statue, the nipples, teeth, eyes and lips are rendered with colored elements. The fluid stance of the body and supple musculature, together with a greater attention paid to detail as opposed to form, indicate that the statue cannot have been made earlier than 430 BC.

Doryphoros

Marble, h. 6.95 ft
Roman copy from the
original by Polyclitus
of 450-440 BC
National Archaeological
Museum, Naples

This work by Polyclitus, lost in antiquity, was the physical transposition in bronze of his theoretical treatise, the *Kanon*. The figure was designed according to a strict principal of proportions based on the composition of multiples and submultiples of a fixed unit of measurement. The statue enjoyed widespread fame in antiquity, as testified by the numerous copies and the descriptions in ancient literary sources. It was also the inspiration for the sculptor of the *Prima Porta Augustus* statue in the Vatican Museums. A basalt torso at the Uffizi in Florence, a Berlin torso, and the whole copy found in Pompeii (now in the Naples Museum) give us an idea of what the original *Doryphoros* looked like. The statue depicts an armed young male nude, possibly representing Achilles, with a strong, taut body after the Peloponnese artistic tradition. The figure's pose suggests movement: the left leg is pushed back and bends at the knee, and the balance of weight shifts in diagonals down the body. The raised right hip is thus counterbalanced by the lowered left shoulder, while the head tilts towards the weight-bearing right leg. The musculature ripples with movement and instability. The left arm, which bends at the elbow and is held forward, carried a shield and spear, while the right arm held a second spear, which pointed downwards. The head is robustly modeled with tidy curling locks which flick upwards like little flames.

LYSIPPUS

(SICYON, GREECE *C.* 370-*C.* 300 BC)

Lysippus was the most influential artist of the period of Macedonian hegemony. Born in Sicyon, he enjoyed a long career, during which he became artist to the Macedonian court under the patronage of Philip II and then Alexander the Great. He is credited with devising a new canon of proportions for the human figure, itself a revision of the *Kanon* of Polyclitus: the head became proportionately smaller and the body more slender and lithe, with particular emphasis on the hair, composed of curly, voluminous locks. Lysippus thus surpassed the Polyclitan theory of ideal proportions: he claimed to represent men "as they appear" and not "as they are", placing more importance on what can be seen rather than on objective reality. He was commissioned by Dàochos II, an ally of Philip and lord of Thessaly, to execute a bronze group of his ancestors together with gods, which was erected at Pharsalus and copied in marble at Delphi. The monument was inspired by the devotional groups of numerous statues of the first half of the 5th century BC. Only one statue survives, the marble version of one of the ancestors, *Agìas*, a famous athlete who lived during the time of the Persian wars. The figure has slender proportions, with long legs and a small head; the balance of weight is fluid and unstable, suggesting a leftward turning motion. Further works by Lysippus trace the evolution of increasingly complex compositions: the outstretched arms of the *Apoxyómenos* ("the scraper") create a heightened sense of space, while the *Eros* is a study of opposing forces as he aims his bow and arrow. The statues are made to be viewed in the round, and this complete conquest of three-dimensional space marked the end of the single, privileged viewpoint.

Lysippus also seems to have played an important role in the development of portraiture: his integral approach enabled him to render faithfully the distinguishing physical features of his subjects, while at the same time bringing out their inner spirituality. The sculptor is said to have made a portrait of Socrates which provided the model for future philosophers' portraits; his portrait of Aristotle is known from Roman copies, and depicts the philosopher in old age, with a heavily lined forehead, small, deep-set eyes, and a short, tidy beard. Lysippus was the official portraitist of Alexander the Great, whose image became the standard for dynastic portraiture in the Hellenistic period. Among the numerous versions of Alexander's portrait, known through successive copies, it is very rare to find individual physical features, such as the jutting chin and the characteristic quiff over the forehead (*anastolè*); in general, the portrait is strongly idealized, deriving perhaps from the images of young gods and heroes like Achilles, whom Alexander idolized.

Apoxyómenos
Marble, h. 6.56 ft
Roman copy after the original by Lysippus of 320 BC
Museo Pio-Clementino, Vatican City

The *Apoxyómenos* (scraper) was brought to Rome to decorate the baths of Agrippa. Recorded in literary sources, it is only known through Roman copies, the best of which is in the Vatican Museums. The Polyclitan balance of weight has been superceded, and the figure seems to fill the surrounding space with the ample gesture of his arms. It is not known who the young athlete is, nor why the statue was made. Stylistic analysis of the sculpture dates it to the years immediately following the death of Alexander the Great.

The young athlete is depicted as he scrapes oil off his body with a small instrument the Romans called a strigil. The right arm, held at chest height and gently bent at the elbow, is outstretched into space; the left arm, bent into a right angle in front of the torso, scrapes under the right at the elbow with the strigil. The body is slender and lithe, with powerful musculature. The weight falls mainly over the straightened left leg, while the right leg is flexed forward, and appears tense from the way the foot is only half resting on the ground. The raised left hip is counterbalanced by the right shoulder blade and the slightly tilted head. The eyes, fixed on a distant point, and the small half-opened mouth reflect the youth's concentration. The locks of hair divide into a kind of vortex, following the round shape of the head.

THE CHINESE TERRACOTTA ARMY

(XI'AN, SHAANXI, CHINA, 3RD CENTURY BC)

In the summer of 1974, the chance discovery by some local farmers of a terracotta statue representing an ancient solder led to one of the most important archaeological finds of the 20th century: the Terracotta Army, created to guard over the eternal sleep of Qin Shi Huangdi. The army is just one part, albeit the most spectacular, of the imposing funerary complex ordered by the First Emperor to commemorate himself and his works for posterity. The funerary mausoleum is located to the east of Xi'an (Shaanxi province), in the Wei river valley, which runs to the north of the complex; a range of hills lie to the south of the valley, and one of these, Mount Li, has given its name to the whole archaeological complex, known as the "Mount Li necropolis". Work on the mausoleum was started in 246 BC, the year that the future First Emperor, Prince Zheng, acceded to the throne of the Qin State; and it was still unfinished by the time of his death in 210 BC.

The Terracotta Army is located almost a mile east of the tomb, at a site where three large ditches have so far been discovered containing the warrior statues, as well as a fourth, which is empty, and assumed to have been left uncompleted. The courage and ferocity of the Qin soldiers, to which ancient texts testify, were enough to give life to the spirit of these statues. The fear-inspiring appearance and physical features of the officers and their thousands of soldiers are vividly etched in the faces of the statues: these are genuine portraits, each individually sculpted to be different from the next. It is believed that the statues were meant to represent the different ethnic groups in China at that period, united for the first time under the command of a single man; by giving the soldiers individual distinguishing features, the army also appeared more "real", and therefore all the more suited to its task of accompanying and protecting the king in the afterlife.

The Terracotta Army is famous for the statues' surprising individualized facial features, but beyond this, a certain level of standardization was necessary in order to carry out a project on such an ambitious scale. This is evident from the treatment of the statues' bodies: the lower part is solid, while the torso is hollow, as is the head, which was placed in the gap between the shoulders and kept in position by a long neck. The heads, which were cast, were individually finished by hand, when details such as the facial features, ears, moustaches and hair were applied. The forearms and hands were made separately; the hands were originally designed to carry weapons, but these were removed during the popular revolt which led to the burning and subsequent destruction of the ditches, as well as the fall of the Qin Dynasty itself, with the accession to the imperial throne of Liu Bang, founder of the successive Han Dynasty (206 BC-220 AD).

Although the statues now appear gray, surviving traces of color are proof that that they were originally brightly painted. While this vast project was for the most part undertaken by thousands of anonymous craftsmen, Chinese archaeologists have identified signatures on some of the statues, thought to be by the masters who supervised the work.

Statue of a High Ranking Officer

Terracotta, h. 6.23 ft
3rd century BC
Museum of the Terracotta
Statues, Lintong, Xi'an
(Shaanxi province)

The officer's high rank is suggested by the sculpture's height, which is greater than that of the soldiers found in the ditches near to the tomb of the First Emperor, and also by the elaborate hair style and detailing on his uniform. The armored chest piece is particularly striking, and is made of thin metal plates threaded together with material, probably silk, and sewn onto a base of lacquered leather, examples of which have also been found elsewhere.

The neck has a scarf knotted around it, which some costume historians believe to be the earliest appearance of the tie. The thick pleating on the sleeves indicates that this was a winter uniform, and the legs are protected by leggings and square-toed shoes. The statue was one of seven high ranking officers discovered behind the remains of a cart, as if prepared to lead the army into battle. In spite of the high level of standardization required to make the statues, the first concrete example of mass production in Ancient China, the sculpture of the high ranking officer, which was discovered in fragments and subsequently reconstructed, is considered one of the oldest surviving examples of Chinese portrait art, particularly for the detailed way the facial features and the hair are rendered. These elements have also allowed Chinese scholars to identify which ranks the Terracotta Army soldiers belonged to, using the existing textual information as a reference.

Statue of an officer with a pleated skirt and, opposite, *Statue of a soldier*, detail of the head, Qin dynasty, 3rd century BC. Xi'an, Lintong (Shaanxi province).

ROMAN PAINTING

(ITALY, 2ND CENTURY BC - 4TH CENTURY AD)

Although a vast amount of Roman painting survives, there is only one known example of an official work: the recently discovered fragment of a fresco which was thought to have decorated a building, possibly the *praefectura Urbis*, before being incorporated into the baths of Trajan on the Colle Oppio. Most of the Roman paintings which exist today were made to decorate private houses, villas and tombs, and although some were commissioned by very important clients (for example Augustus, Livia, and Nero), they are nonetheless the work of decorators rather than genuine painters. As such, they document the history of taste more than the history of painting. In some ways, even the now well-established definition of the "Pompeian Styles", used to catalogue painting between the 2nd century BC-1st century AD, seems fundamentally misleading: firstly because it refers more to the different ways the decorative system was structured on the walls than to strictly stylistic characteristics; and secondly, because Pompeii was only a provincial town, albeit a relatively rich one, and these "Pompeian Styles" merely echoed fashions that had been invented, or widely accepted, in Rome.

The 1st century BC was characterized by a strong taste for illusionism: painting was used to decorate areas previously covered with stucco relief, and elaborate, theatrically-inspired scenes were defined using perspective (Second Pompeian Style). Columns, pillars, colonnades, podiums, plinths, overhanging ceilings, and open niches in the center of the walls disguised solid, two-dimensional walls and broke up the space, transforming it into porticos which opened wide onto a virtual exterior and were further decorated with masks, statues, human or mythological figures, birds, vases and plants.

This emphatic illusionism was abandoned during the reign of Augustus, and there was a return to the two-dimensional wall plane, divided into three large panels with a unified background; illustrated panels would be placed at the center, featuring relatively small numbers of figures against a light background, while the little landscape scenes were reduced to vignettes almost like miniatures in style (Third Pompeian Style). Decorative elements and figures of Egyptian origin became widespread, a reflection of the new province's influence on the Roman culture (Egypt was conquered by Augustus in 31 BC). During the Claudian period, this style was replaced by a new taste (Fourth Pompeian Style), for imaginatively exuberant, baroque compositions that were richly decorated, with scenes populated by allegorical figures whose illusionistic effects again broke up the wall plane.

In the centuries that followed, wall decoration increasingly veered away from complex, dramatic compositions and towards simpler, wide monochrome panels embellished with small pictures depicting scenes with animals, pastoral landscapes or seascapes, and still life. The spread of Christianity saw the rise of tomb painting (not just in the catacombs) characterized by soft brushstrokes and strong shading, depicting popular narrative scenes, episodes from the Old and New Testaments (such as Daniel in the lions' den; the stories of Jonah; Christ and the Samaritan woman; and the resurrection of Lazarus), involving solemn, composed figures. These paintings often translated classical iconography into a Christian context.

Portrait of Paquius Proculus and his Wife
Painted plaster, h. 2.13×1.90 ft
70-60 BC
National Archaeological Museum, Naples

There are few surviving examples of Roman portrait paintings, apart from the series of wood panel portraits found in the necropolises of Fayum in Egypt. Yet the genre must have been of prime importance, not least as a means of disseminating likenesses of the emperors across the provinces. This double portrait, almost unanimously thought to be of Paquius Proculus and his wife (although others believe it to be of the jurist Terentius Nero), came from a house in Pompeii. The man evidently held an office of the law, and had himself portrayed wearing the toga and holding a *rotulo* or scroll in his right

hand. His wife is depicted as an educated woman, with a stylus held to her chin as if deep in thought, and a diptych in her left hand. Despite their fixed, "posed" gazes, and a few other imperfections (the clumsy perspective of the woman's hand, for example), the portrait has considerable expressive strength, both in its obvious pursuit of realism (the woman's fashionable curls and large, made-up eyes framed by thick arched eyebrows, and the man's goatee beard), and in the way the artist has attempted to transform the two subjects' features, which are bourgeois and perhaps even a little plebeian, into those of the aristocratic class. The two busts are framed by a double brown and white border, and stand out against a neutral yellow background which may originally have alluded to precious marble.

Mysterious Scenes
Frescos
c. 50 BC
Villa of the Mysteries,
Pompeii

The frescos within the villa which bears their name are some of the most outstanding examples of Roman art, although their quality is perhaps not as high as their fame would suggest. The paintings are captivating for their sacred atmosphere, and for the grandeur of the imposing figures which stand out against the precious red background that imitates the most highly prized marble. Generally interpreted as scenes depicting Dionysiac initiation rites, the frescos are now considered (by Paul Veyne) to be copies of a painting made for the wedding of a Hellenistic dynast. This copy does not always achieve the high standards of the original, which emerges from the color palette and spatial arrangement of the figures, simplified in places by the Roman copyist. The narrative begins with a depiction of the morning of the wedding: the bride gets ready in the presence of her mother, the ritual bath is prepared, and the marriage contract is displayed under the auspices of the divine couple, Dionysus and Ariadne. On the left hand wall is a group consisting of a young boy reading and two matrons, followed by three female figures preparing a bath (which could be nuptial or ritual), a satyr-musician leaning against a pillar, a group of lovers and a female figure who runs away startled when she sees a satyr taking off a mask as young boys look on (a scene which takes place on the main wall at the end of the room). Next to this scene, in the middle of the wall, are Dionysus and Ariadne, pictured in a lover's embrace; semi-naked young girls uncover a phallus, watched over by a winged creature who is perhaps a kind of guardian. The last wall features a frightened female figure seeking comfort in the lap of a matron, and finally a bathing scene with Eros and a bejeweled matron.

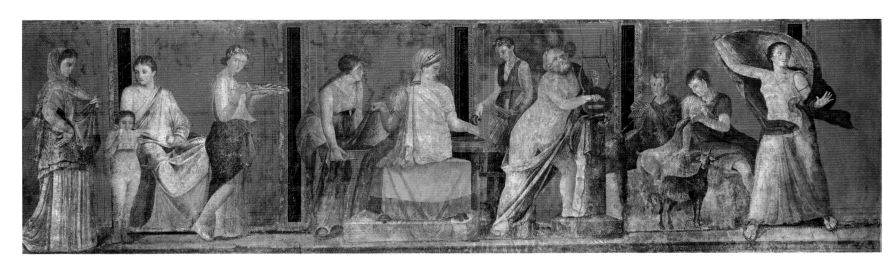

Garden Paintings from the Villa of Livia

Frescos, h. 9.84 ft
20-10 BC
National Roman Museum, Palazzo Massimo, Rome

Entering the great underground hall of the Villa of Livia near the Prima Porta, *ad galinas albas* on the Via Flaminia, must have been like being immersed in the dream-like atmosphere of a garden. The series of plants includes rare and precious species which are perfectly recognizable; but the paintings' significance lies in the way they allude to the owner's pleasurable lifestyle, her knowledge, and her ability to organize nature, which is essentially chaotic, according to the rules of civilized society, transforming it into a perfectly kept garden.

Although Roman art has naturalistic elements, there is no genuine tradition of landscape painting. Even the belvederes in villas which looked out over the surrounding countryside framed it between colonnaded porticos. A cane fence runs

the entire length of the hall, and beyond it are the paintings of large trees loaded with fruit, rare plants and exotic flowers, which are all arranged behind a low marble balustrade featuring niches and exedra. Colorful birds fly between the branches and enliven the scene, which is set against a clear blue sky. The chaos is only apparent: in reality, everything is the result of careful planning by a skilful gardener, accustomed to the exquisite elegance of the *ars topiaria* (art of the garden). The realistic depiction of the flora and fauna creates a perfect illusionism which recalls the refined architectural compositions of gardens that graced suburban *domus* and *villae*, essential to the culture of easy living of the upper classes. The paintings referenced not only the gardens which surrounded the villa (and the rare and precious plants that beautified the fences and garden paths in the Villa of Poppea at Oplontis, in the Gulf of Naples), but also, and above all, the parks and gardens of the palaces of Alexandria and Pergamum.

Art of the First Millenium AD

NOK ART

(NIGERIA, 6TH CENTURY BC - 5TH CENTURY AD)

Evidence of the Nok culture was first discovered in 1928 near the Nigerian village of Nok in the southern Savannah, where artifacts dating to a period between the 6th century BC and 5th century AD were found.

The objects were unearthed by chance during the excavation of tin mines near a river: water erosion along the banks had carried sculptures, stone and iron works downstream, and deposited them away from their original resting place.

In 1969, the discovery of a forge at another site at Taruga (dating between 805 BC and 25 AD) confirmed that the Nok people knew the process of iron smelting. Scholars believe this to have been an indigenous invention, rather than one brought in from elsewhere. Nonetheless, the process did not appear to have revolutionized the way of life or culture of this agricultural people, who continued to work with stone alongside iron.

In the majority of cases, the heads of the statues (usually hollow) were found separated from their bodies, which had broken into fragments. More recently, whole figures and relief work have also come to light. The objects range in size from a few centimeters to almost life size.

One characteristic feature is the stylistic treatment of the heads, which are spherical, or elongated cone and cylindrical shapes, with elaborate hairstyles. The large eyes are a focal point, framed by wide arching eyebrows and curving lower eyelids. The pupils are bored holes, as are the navel, ears, nostrils and sometimes the mouth.

The figures are depicted in a range of poses – standing, kneeling, sitting or squatting – with their heads and limbs also taking a variety of positions. They wear loincloths or longer garments at the waist, and are often decorated with bracelets, anklets, and long beaded necklaces.

In addition to the human figures, animal representations have also been found.

The findings from a number of tombs at the site of Yelwa seem to have ruled out the possibility of the statues having a funerary function: while copper bracelets and ivory jewelry were uncovered, there were no terracotta statues in the tombs. It is therefore thought that they were designed to be placed on altars, and had a ritual use.

Sitting Female Figure
Terracotta, h. 22.80 in
Private collection

The facial features are clearly defined, with full lips and wide nostrils made from bored holes; the large almond-shaped eyes gaze out intensely from their bored pupils, and are emphasized by the curved lids and lashes. The sitting stance, long beaded necklace and elaborate looped hairstyle indicate that this was a person of high social standing. The figure's calm pose and the symmetrical arrangement of the body, with hands resting on the knees, combine to give the statue an air of dignity.

The large oval head is the most important element, its oversized proportions accentuated by the hairstyle and sitting position (which contracts the height of the body). The enlarged head reflects the fact that the artist did not intend this to be a realistic portrait of an individual, but a symbolic representation based on the role the person had within the community.

By comparing these figures with modern Nigerian sculptures, and referring to ethnological studies, scholars of Nok art have been able to develop their own theories on this aspect. The large size and detailed rendering of the head visibly highlights its central importance to the characterization of the person portrayed, while the rest of the body is intentionally left in a much rougher state.

Kneeling figure and, opposite, *Head*. National Museum, Lagos (Nigeria).

GANDHARA ART

(AFGHANISTAN/PAKISTAN, 2ND-3RD CENTURY AD)

In antiquity, Gandhara was the region which covered the lower basin of the Kabul river, or the Peshawar Valley (formerly Purushapura), today part of northern Pakistan. In art, however, the term has assumed a wider meaning, and is generally used to designate the vast collection of works produced in this and the surrounding regions of north-western Asia, roughly spanning modern-day north-eastern Afghanistan and northern Pakistan, including the Swat Valley, the region known as Kapisha in antiquity, and Bactria. Throughout the first centuries AD, this art developed the themes and principles of Buddhism using modes of expression substantially borrowed from Hellenic art.

During the reign of Darius, around 500 BC, Gandhara became a satrapy of the Persian empire, and later on Alexander the Great would fight across the region and found his cities; kings with Greek names were thought to have ruled in Bactria in the 2nd century BC, and there were said to be "Greek" remains at Ai Khanum. The art discussed here evolved later, however, when the region fell into the hands of the Shaka and Parsi; the results, still uncertain, were tinged with elements that recalled both Iranian and Indian art. When the Kushana established their empire there was a decisive move to adopt the artistic models derived from Hellenism.

Beyond the fact that this is a frontier region with a complex history, there are other factors which make the study of this art problematic. It is only in the last few decades that excavation work has been carried out in an organized fashion: in the past, the sculptures of Gandhara ended up in numerous different museums, when they were not stolen, and in these cases it is difficult to establish the exact provenance of the pieces, which prevents them from being studied within their own regional context. However, in spite of the difficulty of dating the works, the best art of Gandhara is considered to have been produced during the period of the great Kushana kings. Kushana rulers continued to reign in the region after the fall of their immense Indian empire; but although Gandhara art may have survived the invasion of the Eftalites, it was finished by the 7th century, when the Chinese traveler Xuanzang wrote that the majority of the Buddhist buildings were in ruins.

The monuments are essentially sacred areas, places of worship, and monasteries. There is an enormous number of findings: the Buddhist clergy undoubtedly exerted huge power across the region. The focal point of the sacred area was the *stupa* monument, whose architecture was directed upwards. Typically, the main *stupa* in a place of worship was surrounded by minor *stupa*, in the center of an enclosure overlooked by a series of chapels; the monastery would be next to it, designed on a square plan, with the monks' cells arranged around a central courtyard.

Stele Depicting the Amitabha Buddha

Stone, h. *c.* 3. 60 ft
2nd-3rd century AD
Lahore Museum, Lahore
(Pakistan)

While the monks' residences were characterized by extreme austerity, the religious monuments were richly embellished with sculptures, steles, reliefs and friezes. The Buddhas and Bodhisattvas are portrayed wearing heavy drapery of Greco-Roman inspiration, with features that have been described as "apollonian" because of their similarity to the ideals of beauty of the ancient Mediterranean. Some figures follow western iconography, like the Bodhisattva Vajrapani, who is sometimes represented as a Hercules or Zeus. Some of the compositional arrangements in the reliefs also reflect western influences, along with architectural elements which evoke the Doric and Corinthian orders. On the other hand, the representation of figures according to hierarchical proportions is typically Indian; the ideology informing this art, and its aims, come from India, and certainly not from the West. Gandhara art is thus a product of the collision of different worlds; and it went on to demonstrate its international flavor in a different way. Together with Buddhism, its influence would travel along the Silk Route towards central Asia and the Far East.

Bodhisattva Head,
2nd-3rd century AD.
Philadelphia Museum
of Art, Philadelphia.

Opposite left, *Statue
of Bodhisattva*, 2nd-3rd
century AD. Museum
of Fine Arts, Boston.

Opposite right,
Statue of Bodhisattva Maitreya,
2nd-3rd century AD. National
Museum, New Delhi.

PALEOCHRISTIAN ART IN ROME

(ROME, 3RD-5TH CENTURY AD)

When Constantine's edict of 313 allowed Christians to practise their religion openly, the Church developed its own liturgy and built public places of worship for the faithful. The new buildings were not innovative in design, but based on typical Roman structures, favoring those which could best be adapted to the needs of the Church. The architectural model was therefore not the pagan temple but the basilica, originally intended for public meetings, and the mausoleum, characterized by a centralized structure. The basilica was able to hold large numbers of worshippers, to whom separate areas were designated: the catechumens witnessed mass from the quadriporticus (a courtyard porticoed on four sides), the faithful from the naves, and the women from the women's gallery, while the presbytery was reserved for the clergy. Mausoleums and baptisteries, on the other hand, adopted a central architectural plan. The builders also looked to Roman art for technical solutions and stylistic elements: columns, capitals and lintels were even taken from the ruins of classical buildings, and mosaics only differed from their secular counterparts in their religious subject matter.

Rome's most famous basilicas were constructed shortly after the edict of Constantine. The city had been the scene of numerous Christian martyrdoms, and places of worship were often erected on the spots where the faithful had met their deaths. The ancient basilica of St Peter, for example, was built on the site of Peter's crucifixion during the Neronian persecution. Begun in 324 and consecrated in 326 by Pope Sylvester, it underwent a number of alterations until the 15th century, when Nicholas V ordered it to be completely rebuilt. The restructuring program was only carried out during the pontificate of Julius II, however, who decided to have the ancient basilica demolished at the start of the 16th century.

The paleochristian church was based on a basilican plan and divided into five naves of four rows and twenty-four columns surmounted by a perpendicular lintel. The roofing was made of wooden trusses and was preceded by a quadriporticus set aside for the catechumens. These buildings changed the physical character of Rome, and although it gradually lost its role as political capital of the world, it was to become the center of the Christian faith. The events of the 5th century hastened its decline, and other cities took control of the empire.

Basilica of Santa Maria Maggiore

3rd-5th century AD
Rome

The basilica of Santa Maria Maggiore is one of the most magnificent examples of paleochristian architecture in Rome. It was built in the middle of the 4th century in the popular quarter of the Suburra, and was more centrally located than earlier basilicas which had been erected by the empire to immortalize the early Christian martyrs' tombs. The basilica was the first church in Rome to be dedicated to the Virgin. Behind its 18th century façade, the church has kept its original character, barely disturbed by subsequent additions (the gilded coffered ceiling and the two arches bisecting the columns along the transept, added in the 13th century along with the polygonal apse). It is built on a basilican plan divided by columns crowned with Ionic capitals, supporting a horizontal trabeation similar to the one originally found in the ancient basilica of St Peter. High pilasters rise up to the ceiling from the trabeation, framing panels with mosaics and windows. A rich mosaic decoration covers the interior walls of the building, drawing on a vast iconographic repertoire which brings together stories from the Old and New Testaments and other passages from the apocryphal Gospels. The work is exceptionally lavish, its elements combining to create a striking whole: the luxurious garments, the shining golden background, and the compositional arrangement of the holy figures seated on precious thrones, surrounded by choruses of angels. The numerous episodes depicted along the nave relate to the lives of Abraham, Jacob, Moses and Joshua. The figures are rendered in relief, moving freely within their naturalistic settings of green fields and blue skies, and there is a lively interplay of looks and gestures between them.

The Hospitality of Abraham

Mosaic
5th century AD
Santa Maria Maggiore, Rome

The *Hospitality of Abraham* brings together two different biblical episodes, elaborated over two overlapping levels within a shared setting. The upper register illustrates the prologue to the episode, and the figures appear smaller and more distant: Abraham runs towards the angels, who appear as visions against a blazing sky. Below, the patriarch appears twice in the same scene: on one side he gives orders to his wife, who is preparing lunch in front of the house decorated with a cross on the gable; on the other side, he attentively serves the three mysterious guests who have come to announce the birth of his son. The artificial nature of the composition actually gives clarity to the story. However, there are elements of naturalism in the mosaic: the green fields and clear, bright skies punctuated with clouds, and the solid, substantial forms of the figures who cast long shadows onto the ground. The artist of the mosaic did not find it necessary to separate the different scenes with architectonic or decorative frames: some elements even cross over into the scene above, such as the fronds of the tree and the roof of the house, although this does not disturb the overall spatial coherence of the composition. The area of pictorial representation of the *Hospitality of Abraham* is carefully constructed in each scene, and is bounded and defined by the planes of two slanting panels, which guide the composition's lines of perspective. This creates a realistic space, inhabited by figures who move freely and are arranged in depth.

PALEOCHRISTIAN ART IN RAVENNA

(RAVENNA, EMILIA-ROMAGNA, 5TH CENTURY AD)

In 402 the emperor Honorius left Milan and transferred the capital of the Western Roman Empire to Ravenna, a small harbor city on the Adriatic coast of Italy. The city remained the capital until 476, when the Empire, having been ravaged by internal fighting and the barbarian invasions, finally fell. In the intervening years, however, the city was enriched with magnificent new Byzantine architecture fitting for its role as capital of the Empire. Buildings such as the Orthodox Baptistery and the Mausoleum of Galla Placidia, sister of Honorius, bear witness to the extraordinary artistic flowering of the period. Galla Placidia was also thought to have been responsible for the building of the basilica of St John the Evangelist. The church was divided into three naves by rows of columns, with architectural elements that would provide a model for other Ravennese basilicas: namely the apse and the "pulvino", a feature which took the form of an upturned truncated pyramid, placed on top of the capitals. In mosaic decoration, there was a gradual evolution from the concrete realism which had its roots in western art, to a more abstract artistic language of eastern origin, which was better adapted to expressing the symbolic elements of Christianity.

Mausoleum of Galla Placidia

5th century AD
Ravenna

The building of the mausoleum is traditionally attributed to the sister of Honorius, Galla Placidia, who ruled the Empire between 425 and 450 on behalf of her son Valentinian. Galla Placidia was an enthusiastic supporter of the arts, continuing the patronage initiated by her father Theodosius I in Rome. The structure (now partially below ground) is designed on the plan of a Greek cross, whose arms describe the barrel vaulted ceiling, with a dome at the center. The exterior of the dome is covered with quadrangular cladding, and rises above the lateral parts of the building whose gables are enclosed within a heavy cornice. The building's external appearance is characterized by a geometric symmetry underpinned by the sober brick façade, itself modulated by a series of blind arches. The architectural lines of the interior are transformed by the stunning mosaic decoration covering the area above the high marble band. Light filters softly through the alabaster windows, illuminating the great golden cross, symbol of Christ's death and resurrection, which dominates the center of the dome. The cross is set against a blue sky studded with stars arranged in concentric circles; the attributes of the Evangelists also float among the clouds. The apostles, dressed in pure white tunics, hail the cross from the large lunettes beneath, under gigantic shell-shaped bowers. Among these are St Peter, identified by the key he is holding, and St Paul, who is depicted with an elongated face, pointed beard and bald head. The mosaics in the lunettes at the end of the main arm of the building feature a more complex design: the artist has attempted a narrative representation within a naturalistic setting. Christ appears above the entrance in the guise of Good Shepherd. His divinity is represented by his golden tunic, purple mantle, halo and cross, which replaces the typical shepherd's crook. The figure of Christ moves freely within the surrounding space and plays a pivotal role in the whole composition, gathering together the groups of sheep beside him, which are intentionally arranged to break the rigid symmetry. The naturalistic rendering of their wooly coats, along with the depiction of the rocky landscape punctuated here and there by tufts of grass, reveals the careful attention with which the artist has tried to imitate nature. The lunette opposite is executed in the same naturalistic style: St Lawrence walks bravely and purposefully towards the gridiron of his martyrdom, in the name of the Evangelist whose four books can be seen in the open cabinet.

Orthodox Baptistery

5th century AD
Ravenna

The baptistery was erected next to the original Ursine basilica which was destroyed in the 5th century. Its proportions have considerably altered over the centuries, with the rise of the level of the city. The building is also known as the "Neon Baptistery" after the Bishop Neon who founded it, and was called the Orthodox Baptistery to distinguish is from the Arian Baptistery, built by a group of heretics who followed the doctrine of Arius and denied the divine nature of Christ. As with the mausoleum of Galla Placidia, the building's richly decorated interior of marble and mosaics is in sharp contrast with the simple lines of the exterior. The bare outer brick walls are modulated on the upper level by a succession of small suspended arches linked together and punctuated by pilasters. The octagonal building features eight large windows, one for each side, on the lower level; below these, the semicircular outlines of the four apses protrude from the sides of the building, alternating with four doors which today are almost entirely buried below ground level. Inside, the octagonal space is completely covered with a polychrome decoration: marble intarsia and stucco work combine with two levels of blind arches and culminate in the magnificent mosaic of the dome (made using a system of clay tubes which help to reduce the weight of the decoration significantly). The dome mosaic is divided into three concentric zones. The physical and symbolic center of the composition is the *Baptism of Christ*: Christ's naked figure emerges from a golden background, half-immersed in the waters of the River Jordan which is personified by the old, bearded man to his right. The mosaic artist has given the faces individual features, in a portrait style, and the different colors of the garment and pallium contribute to the flowing rhythm of the composition. A stucco decoration covers the area at window level: this appears to be a trompe-l'oeil representation of the women's galleries found in paleochristian churches. Between the lateral arches are stucco niches, crowned with coping which is alternately semicircular and triangular, bearing a shell at the center. These frame a number of male figures, depicted strictly from the front; they each carry an open book and rolled-up scroll, by which they can be identified as Old Testament prophets. Apart from their hands and heads, whose wide eyes stare outwards, the figures are extremely flat; even the folds of their garments do not follow the bodies' contours, instead covering their surfaces with fine incisions. This effect would originally have been tempered by the polychrome covering, which was an integral part of this type of sculpture: the stucco figures were in fact modeled taking into account the subsequent addition of color, which disguised the imperfections of the reliefs.

MAYAN
LINTEL RELIEFS

(MEXICO/CENTRAL AMERICA, 7TH-9TH CENTURY AD)

Stone lintel reliefs are the best preserved of the Mayan art forms. The sculptures which adorned many of the Mayan buildings and public squares are not only works of art but important documents on the life and customs of the Mayan rulers: the way they dressed, their rituals, and their military conquests. The reliefs are often accompanied by long written texts which record important events, the names of individuals, cities and honorary titles, providing further valuable information to improve our knowledge of the ancient Mayan culture. mayan artists reached an exceptional level of mastery in lintel relief work which decorated the doorways of important buildings. The lintels were only for the eyes of the privileged few who were allowed to enter the rooms where they were located. This explains the relatively small size of the figures and glyphs, as compared with the much larger ones found on the altars and steles, designed to be seen from a distance. The Mayan artistic style which produced the most beautiful stone lintels is the Usumacinta style: there are spectacular examples of lintel relief work from this period at Piedras Negras, Yaxchilán, El Cayo and Bonampak. The Maya also carved lintels from softer materials, such as wood, which unfortunately have been less well preserved than the stone ones. The few surviving examples come from the temples of Tikal.

Lintel 25
From Yaxchilán (Mexico)
Limestone, h. 4.25 ft
Late Classical period,
723 AD
British Museum, London

Yaxchilán lintel 25 is rare in precolombian Mayan art in that it has a female protagonist.
It is part of a cycle of three lintels which decorated the entrance to the internal rooms of Temple 23 in Yaxchilán, dedicated to the Lady K'ab' al Xook. The Lady was the wife of Shield Jaguar II, and came from a very high ranking family herself. She probably held an important role at court, and although her sons did not succeed their father to the throne, she was compensated by being depicted in one of the finest sculptures of the site, in fact of the whole Mayan period.
The Lady K'ab' al Xook is represented at the bottom right of the lintel; the focal point of the scene, at the center, shows a god emerging from the jaws of a serpent to offer her the symbols of power. This is actually a vision provoked by the woman's sacrificial blood letting ritual, commonly performed by the Maya in order to communicate with their gods and ancestors. The ritual, which involved passing a rope through a hole made in the tongue, is also depicted elsewhere: in another Yaxchilán lintel relief representing a woman named Balam de Ix Witz, as well as in the wall paintings of Bonampak, where it is performed by a woman believed to be the mother of the heir to the throne. Following her sacrificial ritual, K'ab' al Xook places the rope, along with the paper used to collect the blood, in a bowl resting by her feet. In her hands is another bowl, also containing paper, which she offers up to the god in front of her. Every detail is exquisitely rendered, and the clothing, jewelry, and feathers on her outer garment are particularly outstanding.
The first lintel of the cycle (26) commemorates the marriage of the Lady K'ab' to King Shield Jaguar II, while the second (24) depicts the lady as she performs the sacrificial ritual in front of the king, passing the rope through her tongue.

Lintel 24,
from Yaxchilán,
Late Classic
Period,
c. 600-900 AD.
British Museum,
London

Opposite,
Lintel 26,
from Yaxchilán,
Late Classic
Period. Museo
Nacional de
Antropología,
Mexico City.

MAYAN JADEITE ART
(MEXICO/CENTRAL AMERICA, 7TH-9TH CENTURY AD)

Among the finest surviving gemstone objects of the Mayan period are the items of jewelry originally worn by the kings who ruled over the major cities during the Late Classical era. Many of these are made from jadeite, particularly prized since the time of the Olmecs both for its green color which was associated with water, and for its rarity and "exoticism". Votive jadeite axes were also fashioned in the Olmec tradition, although the stone was most commonly made into grains, which were thrown in high quantities into the sacred *Cenote* of Chichén Itzá, and left as offerings in the tombs. The grains symbolized life, and when depicted in front of the rulers' noses, they represented the "royal breath". One of these small beads was found at Copán, inside a *Spondylus* shell,

representing a child inside the womb: the shell was emblematic of women and childbirth in Mayan culture. Other jadeite objects include earrings, necklaces, bracelets and figurines of gods, such as those depicting the sun god Kinich Ahau in the tomb of the Lord of Altún Ha in Belize. The most spectacular examples of jadeite art are undoubtedly the funerary masks, both for their ritual function and for their beauty. These have been found in different Mayan sites, and were made out of mosaic tiles tied to a wooden base to create the image of the dead person's face. The eyes and mouth were generally of obsidian and shells.

Jadeite mosaics were also used to decorate objects such as the wooden vase of Tikal, which display a highly skilful rendering of detail.

Jade Plaque of a Maya King, from Teotihuacán (Mexico), Classic Period, *c.* 600-900. British Museum, London.

Vase from Tikal

Jadeite, h. 9.53 in
Late Classical Period,
after 734 AD
Museo Nacional de
Arquelogìa y Etnologìa,
Guatemala City

This cylindrical vase made with jadeite mosaic tiles was part of the funerary cache of the tomb of Yik'in Chan K'awil (also known as Ah Cacau), found in the Temple of the Great Jaguar (5-73 AD) at Tikal. The lid of the vase is decorated with a human head, probably a portrait of the king as a youth, bedecked in the jewelry he must have worn when alive: a necklace of jadeite grains and circular earrings with tubular shaped pendants. The Mayan craftsmen made other superb works from jadeite mosaic tiles, as exemplified by the funerary masks found in Calakmul and Tikal, but this vase is one of the highest expressions of their skill. The mosaic tiles which form the lid are tiny, and finely worked. Each one is different from the next, and they combine to create the face and hairstyle of the king, the grains of the necklace, and the earrings. The vase is all the more extraordinary for the fact that it was made using only abrasives, rope and stone tools, rather than metal instruments. A zoomorphic head emerges from one of the tiles, probably a stylized representation of the head of the monster Xooc, a shark which more commonly decorated the belt of the young corn god, whose facial features are evoked in the face of the young Yik'in Chan K'awil.

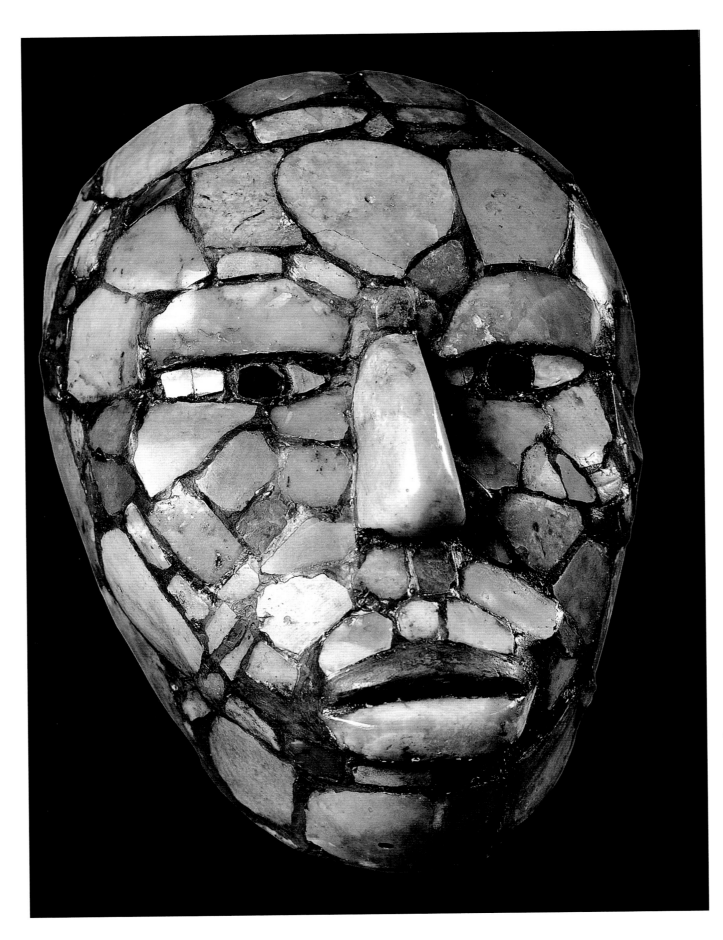

Jadeite Mask,
from Dzibanché
(Mexico),
Temple II,
Kinichná group,
Late Classic
Period.
INAH Center,
Campeche.

Opposite,
Jadeite Mask,
from Calakmul
(Mexico), Tomb I,
Ancient Classic
Period.
INAH Center,
Campeche.

ART AFTER THE YEAR 1000

THE CHOLA KINGS AND BRONZE ART

(INDIA, 9ᵀᴴ-13ᵀᴴ CENTURY)

The Chola Dynasty (middle of the 9th century-13th century) was one of the most powerful ever to have emerged on Indian soil. It originated in the far south of Tamil Nadu, in the valley of the Kaveri, the sacred river of southern India. From here, the great Chola kings expanded their empire north, conquering large parts of the Deccan and even venturing overseas. The art of southern India achieved its pinnacle under these kings, reflecting their enormous power. Around one hundred temples are ascribed to this period, the majority dedicated to the cult of Shiva. Some of these were built to epic proportions never before seen, marking a decisive turning point in the temple architecture of the south.

The modest early Chola temples gave way to buildings of grandiose dimensions like the temple of Shiva Nataraja ("Lord of the Dance") at Cidambaram, where according to mythology, Shiva danced his cosmic dance. This temple's gigantic size would provide a model for all the temples that were to follow. Founded by King Kulottunga, who ruled from around 1070-1122, the majority of work on it was carried out by his immediate successors in the 12th and 13th centuries. Rather than having just one outer wall, the temple was gradually encircled by a number of rectangular and concentric walls of increasing width; in its definitive form, it had four walls totaling around 1148 by 1033 ft, with the outer one probably dating to a much later time (the 16th century).

The Chola period is also renowned for its splendid bronze statues, an art form which represented an important corollary to the lavish temples they were created for. The bronzes depicted the gods and saints of the Tamil tradition, and were "moveable" figures (*chala*, in contrast to *achala*, "fixed") used primarily for celebrations and a variety of other increasingly complex rituals associated with the cult. Generally measuring between 23-35 inches in height (sometimes taller), they were made using the traditional "lost wax" technique, which produced solid metal figures. The statues display an exquisite formal elegance and technical refinement, and represent the various forms of Shiva and his wives Uma and Parvati, or episodes involving the god with other figures. The most elaborate symbolic depiction, and also the most celebrated creation of Chola sculpture, is Shiva dancing the *anandatandava*, the "cosmic dance" which beats out the rhythm of life and death for all creation.

Shiva, Lord of the Dance
Bronze, h. *c.* 26.77 in
10ᵗʰ century
Temple of Shiva Nataraja,
Cidambaram (India)

The dancing figure of Shiva started to appear in a number of Indian regions from the 6ᵗʰ century onwards. This particular pose, representing the so-called *anandatandava*, the "cosmic dance", was developed in the Tamil area during the 10ᵗʰ century, and became a classic. According to mythology, Shiva danced his cosmic dance in Cidambaram, and the city was therefore placed at the symbolic center of the universe. The god dances to the rhythm of time, guiding life in its cyclical process of creation, existence and dissolution. His right foot rests on the demon Oblivion, while his raised left leg and long flowing hair (symbolizing his creative force) express powerful movement. The first of his right hands beats on the hourglass-shaped tambourine (*damaru*), which represents sound, the first act

of creation; while the upper left hand, in symmetry with the right, holds the flame of destruction towards which the world is moving. The second right hand gestures "do not fear" (*abhayamudra*) to the worshipper, and the remaining left hand indicates the raised foot, showing that the way to salvation lies in devotion to Him. A halo of flames encircles the figure: according to different allegorical interpretations, this evokes either the supreme light of knowledge, or the purifying fire of the funeral pyre. The flames also blaze symbolically in the hearts of the worshippers, consuming their ego, and the illusion that makes them believe they are separate entities from the god Shiva. The whole composition is a synthesis of the processes that govern the life of both the world and the individual: the image is a terrifying one, since the god's dance leads inexorably to death, but it also holds the promise of rebirth, and the possibility of liberation from the endless cycle of destruction. The interplay of space and volumes draws the eye in towards the precious detailing; the bronze god's lithe body, exquisitely modeled in the characteristic Chola style, expresses the perfect balance on which the universe rests.

DJENNÉ ART

(MALI, 9TH-15TH CENTURY)

Ancient Djenné (today Djenné-Jeno) was founded in 250 BC in Africa, Mali, and developed during the 9th-15th century an important sculptural tradition.

According to archaeologists Susan and Roderick McIntosh, who studied the site of Djenné-Jeno, the Djenné sculptural tradition and its widely ranging iconography may have evolved out of the people's need to reaffirm their own cultural identity in a visual form, given the strong competition among the different ethnic groups who shared the same urban environment. On the one hand, the art would thus have enabled the inhabitants of Djenné to differentiate themselves from each other, and on the other, it would have unified them in the face of the growing Muslim threat to their land and way of life.

The sculptures vary in height from between 11.80-19.70 inches, and are usually solid (and sometimes reinforced with iron); in some cases traces of red paint can still be seen on the surface, or, more rarely, other colors.

Perhaps the most striking aspect of Djenné art is the way it differs from the more common style of wooden African art: while the latter is characterized by frontal poses, the symmetrical arrangement of limbs, and the division of the body into geometric forms, the varied postures of the Djenné display an organic fluidity.

Since these figures were found in domestic settings, it is believed that they were originally placed on family altars as offerings during the propitiatory rites performed when a new building was erected, or else that they were made as votive offerings to the gods to ensure the recovery of a sick person. It is probable that they represented people in the act of supplication, or the figures of leaders or ancestors from different family lines.

In iconographic terms, the sculptures can be grouped into distinct types: bearded, armed male figures, often on horseback and wearing garments and jewelry which probably had a ritual function; and more simply dressed figures, often in just a loincloth and sometimes kneeling with their hands folded over their bodies, or in freer poses. Another peculiarity is the fact that they also appear in couples, or in larger groups of interacting figures to create a tableau, uncommon in African art where lone figures predominate.

There are a number of characteristics typical to the Djenné style (although they are not always present in the sculptures from this area). The human figures have oval heads which flatten out towards the jaw; their protruding eyes are emphasized by a horizontal median profile and the multiple lines of the almond-shaped lids, or the incised vertical lines of the lashes. The nose is triangular and the mouth is made from two parallel forms which are either rounded or slightly triangular; sometimes the figure has a beard, which frames the face and increases its size.

Horse and Rider

Terracotta, h. 17.32 in
9th-15th century
Entwistle Gallery, London

The profusion of ornaments (helmet, bracelets, anklets and the horse's tack), along with the composed, solemn posture, suggest that this was a person of high social rank. In terms of detailing, the accent firmly falls on the upper parts of the two figures, particularly the heads of both horse and rider. Conversely, little attention is paid to the legs and horse's hooves, which are only summarily modeled into cylindrical shapes.
The difference in treatment probably corresponds to the difference in importance placed on the various parts of the body.
The rider's head tilts upwards, perhaps to look at the sky, or else to express his superiority in a pose of dignified detachment. His nose, mouth and ears are rendered with triangulating forms which mirror the overall shape of the face.
The beard assumes great

significance, and probably symbolizes authority and wisdom: its semidiscoidal form frames the face from ear to ear and juts it forwards, elongating it and increasing its prominence.

Linear incisions on the headdress, nose, ears, beard, and especially around the eyes, draw the viewer's attention and also connect the various elements to each other. The same is true of the criss-cross pattern along the garment's hem, the horse's tack, and the stripes of red paint on the bodies of both horse and rider.

The different handling of the figurative elements according to their differing symbolic importance may also explain why the human figure's body is disproportionately large to that of the animal: the horse, in fact, is not represented as an autonomous figure, but as an attribute of the human being, indicative of his social standing.

In this case, the horse is a particularly effective measure of status: these animals were rare in sub-Saharan Africa, where it was difficult for them to survive the harsh conditions, so only the most important people could keep them.

THE ABBEY OF CLUNY
AND EUROPEAN ROMANESQUE

(EUROPE, 10TH-12TH CENTURY)

In 910 William of Aquitaine founded the Abbey of Cluny in Burgundy, a pivotal moment in the religious and artistic history of the West during the middle ages. The new abbey promoted the reform of the Benedictine order, and over a short period it created a wide network of subsidiary monastic houses, becoming one of the richest and most powerful monasteries in the entire Christian world. The need to find new architectural solutions developed as a response to the specific liturgical requirements of the Benedictine order; and in time, these solutions would come to be reused and adapted to buildings across Europe, over a period when Romanesque architecture was constantly redefining its own characteristics. While nothing remains of the first church at Cluny (consecrated in 927), modern-day excavation work has uncovered the plan of the second building, erected between 948 and 981. Measuring 180 ft in length, the church of Cluny II was notably large for the time. Little remains of the third church, founded in 1088 and destroyed during the French Revolution: a part of the southern transept, along with an octagonal bell tower. However, contemporary sources testify that the church was famed throughout Europe for its majestic architecture and the magnificent sculptures, paintings and mosaics which adorned the interior. At 561 ft long, the monumental size of Cluny III made it the largest church in Christendom. The complex plan bears witness to the exceptional nature of the building, with five naves, a double transept, and a choir with an ambulatory encircled by side chapels and five towers. The surviving capitals of the ambulatory, now preserved in the museum (converted from the 14th century flour store), also provide a clue to the lavishness of the original decorations: the large capitals' delicate, fluid relief work and elegant decorative style reveal an outstanding technical mastery on the part of the sculptors who carved them. They depict the eight tones of the Gregorian octave, the seasons, the cardinal and theological Virtues, original sin and the rivers of paradise. Other capitals feature biblical scenes, such as the *Fall of Man* and the *Sacrifice of Isaac*, while some are carved in the Corinthian style.

Capitel with the Four Rivers of Paradise, from the abbey of Cluny, beginning of the 12th century. Musée du Farinier, Cluny.

Church of Sainte-Madeleine
12th century
Vézelay (Bourgogne)

The church of Vézelay Abbey was an important stopping point for pilgrims on the road to Compostela, and was believed to contain the relics of St Mary Magdalene. It came under the jurisdiction of Cluny III, whose influence can be felt in the architecture. Rebuilt around 1100, it fell into ruin during the French Revolution, and was subsequently heavily restored between 1840 and 1859 by the architect Viollet-le-Duc. Although the imposing façade, with its great window and tower, was almost completely rebuilt, and the apse at the far end of the long nave underwent a Gothic renovation between 1171 and 1198, the rest of the church has preserved its Romanesque character. The sculptures, completed between 1120 and 1150, can be ascribed to a number of different workshops, and hence lack the stylistic unity of the decorations in the Cathedral of Saint-Lazare in Autun. The tympanum above the portal between the porch and the central

nave of the church features a rare iconographic theme, which is not to be found in other churches. Christ is represented at the center, as he sends his apostles away to preach the gospels to the world; the figures in the architrave and side sections of the archivolt all relate to this scene. The inhabitants of distant, exotic lands, among them the pygmies of central Africa and the people of the Indian subcontinent, are depicted with a certain naturalism, particularly around their faces. The two archivolts carry representations of the zodiac and the labors of the months, with plant motifs decorating the exterior. The work is typical of Burgundian sculpture, and similar in style to those executed by Gislebertus at Autun. Inside the church, the decorative program continues with ornamental garlands which follow the architectural lines of the building, and with the capitals of the nave. These are carved with spirit and confidence, and depict various subjects which do not appear to belong to a single iconographic program.

Gislebertus, Last Judgement
Stone
12th century
Cathedral of Saint-Lazare,
Autun (Bourgogne)

The Cathedral of Saint-Lazare in Autun, consecrated in 1132 by Pope Innocent II, was clearly influenced by the architecture of Cluny III. This is not surprising given the strict ties between Bishop Stephen of Autun, who founded the church, and the Abbey of Cluny, where he retired to lead a monastic life in 1132. Saint-Lazare is renowned for the superb sculptures which decorate its façade and interior: these constitute one of the most important sculpted cycles of Romanesque art in general, and of the Burgundian school in particular. The tympanum over the portal features one of the earliest surviving signatures of a medieval artist: the name of the sculptor Gislebertus, inscribed beneath the feet of Christ. The stylistic unity of the majority of the church's decorations, executed between 1125 and 1145, suggests that Gislebertus carried out, or at least oversaw, the entire program. The *Last Judgement* in the tympanum was intended to induce terror in sinners so that they would turn to God. The composition is dominated by the central image of Christ in Judgement, grave and impassive.

His enormous figure is framed in a mandorla surrounded by four angels and two medallions depicting the sun and moon; according to medieval beliefs, the latter presided over the most important events in human history. At Christ's side, in the upper register, are the Virgin (to the left) who is seated next to a trumpeting angel, and a second angel (to the right) flanked by apostles. Underneath are the representations of Heaven and Hell. St Peter appears in Heaven, surrounded by the blessed, while on the opposite side St Michael weighs the souls, along with a large devil and other demonic figures. The *Resurrection of the Dead* is depicted in the architrave: at the center of the scene, beneath the feet of Christ, is an angel who repels the damned and welcomes the blessed, among them two pilgrims.

The internal archivolt features a splendid decoration with plant motifs, while the external one depicts the signs of the zodiac along with the labors of the months. Gislebertus imbues his marble sculptures with an unmistakable style: the slender, elongated bodies, wrapped in rich, fine drapery, are portrayed with a moving realism that profoundly expresses the desperation of the damned and the serenity of the blessed.

Canterbury textile factory, Bayeux Tapestry
Linen, 230 ft × 20 in
1066-1082
Centre Guillaume le Conquérant, Bayeux

The famous *Bayeux Tapestry* was woven in Canterbury between 1066 and 1082, following the Norman conquest of England. The tapestry was commissioned by Odo, the Bishop of Bayeux (and a relative of William the Conqueror) to celebrate the Normans' victory. It was thought to have hung for a long period in the bishop's palace, until it was donated to the Cathedral of Bayeux, where it remained for centuries before being transferred to the museum which is now dedicated to it. The narrative technique recalls the epic and literary traditions. The scenes are represented in a single register, bordered above and below by stylized ornamental and animal motifs, and accompanied by an inscription with a didactic function.
The story of the island conquest begins with a prologue to the events, and continues until the Battle of

Hastings (1066), to which a considerable part of the tapestry is dedicated. William the Conqueror was the architect of a model feudal state in Normandy, and had been elected successor to Edward the Confessor, the Anglo-Saxon king of England, who had no heir. Upon Edward's death, however, the Anglo-Saxon noblemen nominated Harold, Count of Sussex, to the throne. This sparked the subsequent events: the expedition of William, Harold's defeat, and the conquering of England. The tapestry culminates in the Norman landing, the preparations for battle, the depiction of the two armies, the appearance of Bishop Odo, and the final clash: the numerous battle scenes between the Normans and Anglo-Saxons are skilfully rendered with realistic dynamism. The defeat of the Anglo-Saxons is obviously shown from the perspective of the Norman victors, but the representation of details, customs, objects, weapons and modes of transport make the piece a unique source of historical evidence, and an outstanding contribution to our knowledge of daily life at that time.

IFE ART

(NIGERIA, 10TH-15TH CENTURY)

If art takes its name from the city of Ile-Ife, which in Yoruba mythology was located in the region southwest of Nigeria. There are close parallels between the Ife art produced during the 10th-15th centuries and the present-day culture of the Yoruba who inhabit the region between Benin and Nigeria.

The Yoruba have never had their own unified state, and the name "Yoruba" is itself foreign and relatively recent (it was the term the Muslim Hausa people gave to the Kingdom of Oyo, which was only one of many Yoruba kingdoms); nonetheless, it is the Yoruba themselves who have traced a link connecting them (through their mythology) to ancient Ife.

The first Ife bronze sculptures were discovered in 1910 by the anthropologist Leo Frobenius. The unexpected naturalism of these figures perplexed European scholars at the time, who at first denied their African origin and improbably ascribed them to the Etruscan, Egyptian or Portuguese cultures.

More terracotta vases and heads, together with around thirty "bronzes" (actually made from copper alloy containing tin and zinc) were found by chance near the royal palace (1938) and close to one of the ancient city gates (1959).

A later excavation of 1971 brought to light a number of artworks of a very different character, uncovered in a sacrificial area along with human bones and skulls: terracotta heads with frowning, tense faces and anguished expressions, which seemed to show signs of illness or violence. The Ife aesthetic seemed therefore to hinge on the polarity between "peace and violence, calm and terror, health and disease"; and the statues appear to have met with the same fate as the human beings they were buried with.

Naturalism was thus not the only stylistic current running through Ife art: on the altars, alongside the more realistic heads, were found other more schematic, almost abstract representations, whose facial features were barely suggested by small bore holes on a terracotta cone. This stylistic diversity has been interpreted as two different yet complementary ways of expressing the relationship between the head's external, physical dimension, and the internal one, a concept of humanity which is also found among the modern-day Yoruba.

Head of Oni
Bronze, h. 12 in
12th-15th century
National Museum,
Ife (Nigeria)

The homogenous style of the bronze heads suggests that they were produced in a relatively short period of time and by a small number of artists, who may even have belonged to the same workshop. The heads represented the Oni, the sacred king of Ife, whose dignified portrayal did not bear any individual distinguishing features. It is thought that they were placed on altars and used as stands for the king's crown during public ceremonies; or they may have been an outward, visible symbol of the monarchy's stability during the transition from one king to another. The series of bore holes which appear on various heads around the mouth and along the hairline are believed to have originally carried a layer of beading, like the beads which decorate the crowns of present-day Yoruba kings. The lines may also represent shadows cast by the beading, as well as ritual scarification. The function of these crowns was to screen the face of the king and so contain his mystic power (*ase*), preventing it from being unleashed in a dangerous, uncontrolled way. The composure of the head could have been a manifestation of the king's ability to control the flow of cosmic energy, which was particularly concentrated in him, and was expressed in his good character (*iwa*), calm attitude, and circumspection. The scarifications, a permanent body modification, may have symbolized the irreversible transformation from man to god which occurred upon the king's accession to the throne.

Bust of Oni,
and opposite,
*Crowned Head
of Oni,*
15th century.
National Museum,
Ife (Nigeria).

97

Russian Icons

(Russia, from the 12ᵀᴴ century)

The word "icon" derives from the ancient Greek *eikon*, meaning "image". Passed down to the Byzantine culture who in turn kept it alive from the 5th century AD onwards, the term's meaning expanded and developed over time to define the archetypal religious or sacred image painted on wood: a representation of the divine which perfectly expressed the Christian message. After the fall of the Eastern Roman Empire in 1453, the Balkan peoples continued to produce and diffuse icons throughout the orthodox world, and particularly across Russia. Here, the icon assumed a special significance, both for its religious symbolism and for the revered centuries-old tradition it was born out of. Historically, the icon was considered to be the work of God himself, a manifestation of his perfection: the iconographer or artist was merely the mortal intermediary through whom God communicated his message, and as such it would have been unthinkable for the artist to stamp his own identity on the work by adding his signature. The images themselves appear timeless: the sacred figures, eternal, are represented from a purely spiritual perspective, with fixed gazes which are abstract and absorbed in concentration, indicating their elevation from the world of terrestrial passions into a spiritual dimension beyond space and time. Technically, the icons were painted on panels of varying sizes pre-prepared with a base of chalk and glue followed by red bolus, onto which the paint itself would be applied, highlighted by precious gold leaf gilding. The iconography was repeated over the centuries without any change or attempt at originality, and thus itself came to signify purification and direct contact with the divine. Russia is the home of the quintessential icon, and to this day Russian artists are still producing icon paintings using age-old skills and formulas. Having assimilated the Greek tradition, Russian iconographers enriched it, rigorously handing their knowledge down from generation to generation. The icon painting tradition has always embodied devotion, and provided the artist with a tight framework on which to project his own experience. In the modern era, the philosopher and mystic Pavel Alexandrovich Florensky (1882-1937) was one of the most respected scholars of icon painting, interpreting and exploring its symbolic meaning and precious spiritual value. Essentially, the icon is like a conduit, a window onto the spiritual world for all those true believers capable of discerning its real significance. Even so, some retain it inappropriate to define the icon as a simple artistic representation, given that every aspect of the painting, including the colors themselves, has a symbolic value that goes beyond pure aesthetics: blue for transcendency, red for the blood of the martyrs, green for nature and fertility, and white and gold for harmony, peace, and divine light.

Virgin of Tenderness (Mother of God of Tenderness) of Vladimir
Tempera on wood,
30.70×21.65 in
Beginning of the 12th century
Tretyakov Gallery, Moscow

This panel is Russian's oldest icon painting, and was originally brought to the country from Constantinople. The figures of the Virgin and child, framed within the panel, stand out against their orange setting. Traces of the earlier golden background and fragments of inscriptions can still be made out here and there. The Virgin is enshrouded in a black veil flecked with golden lines and studded with two stars. She holds the Christ child in her arms and tilts her head gently towards him: the sweet tenderness of her gaze is masterfully expressed by the painter with a few simple strokes. The child turns his face completely towards his mother, and stretches his arms out to hug her. His red clothing helps to define him against the background; the golden highlights, symbolic of his holiness, are also the means by which the painter gives substance to the otherwise two-dimensional figure.

NICOLA PISANO

(PUGLIA ? 1215/1220 - ? 1278/1284)

Nicola was the head of a family of Italian sculptors active throughout the 13th and 14th centuries, and is considered to be the father of Italian Gothic sculpture. One of the chief protagonists of 13th century European art, Nicola revolutionized sculpture in much the same way that Giotto would revolutionize painting a few decades later. His Classicism was never merely imitative; it was a means of reintroducing narrative structure and achieving a more naturalistic representation of space and human figures, informed by the grave composure of ancient sculpture. His forms are solid and compact, with contours described by monumental drapery; they emerge powerfully from the background plane, and move naturally within the space of representation, often displaying a subtle restlessness which gives them a marked Gothic quality.

Known in documentary sources as "Nicholas Petri de Apulia" or simply "Nicholas de Apulia", Nicola was probably born in Puglia between 1215 and 1220. He completed his training in southern Italy, assimilating the classical language of southern statuary produced during the reign of Frederick II (1228-1250). Following his move to Tuscany (1245?), he continued his investigation into Classical sculpture with a close study of the Late Classical sarcophagi which had been preserved in the city of Pisa.

Nicola's first signed work was the pulpit of the Baptistery of Pisa, dated 1260. Between 1265 and 1268 he executed the pulpit of Siena Cathedral, along with his son Giovanni, Arnolfo di Cambio and other assistants. In 1273 he was active in Pistoia, and at the same time involved in decorating the exterior of the Baptistery of Pisa. Other important works include the tomb of St Dominic in Bologna (begun in 1264) and the main fountain of Perugia (1277-1278). Nicola and his workshop are also credited with the lunette of the *Deposition of Christ from the Cross* and the architrave beneath in Lucca Cathedral. Nothing is known of Pisano after 1278, until his death was reported in a document of 1284.

Pulpit

Marble, h. 15.20 ft
1257-1260
Baptistery, Pisa

This is the first signed work by Nicola Pisano, and was executed between 1257 and 1260, probably for Filippo Visconti, the Archbishop of Pisa. Breaking away from the established tradition, the master conceived the pulpit as an architectural structure in its own right, independent from the building it was designed for. The hexagonal-shaped pulpit features five marble reliefs, representing the *Nativity, Adoration of the Magi, Presentation in the Temple, Crucifixion* and *Last Judgement.* The upper part of the structure rests on seven columns symbolizing the Seven Sacraments, three of which are supported by lions. Above the classicizing capitals are statues representing the Archangel Michael, St John the Baptist and the four cardinal Virtues (Justice, Fortitude, Temperance and Prudence). The columns are connected by trilobed arches, on whose sides are sculpted the figures of the prophets and sibyls. The architecture of the pulpit is skilfully gauged: the vertical columns perfectly balance the horizontal decorative reliefs. Nicola creates spatial depth in the relief scenes by arranging his many figures on receding parallel planes, with buildings relegated to the background. Each scene is striking for the harmonious proportions of the figures, and the overall symmetry. The group of prophets integrated into the pendentives follow and adapt to their architectural context, and the small statues on top of the capitals are sculpted in the round, linking them perfectly to the columns below.

Pulpit

Marble, h. 15 ft
1265-1268
Cathedral, Siena

Between 1265 and 1268, Nicola sculpted the pulpit of Siena Cathedral aided by a well-documented group of assistants: his son Giovanni, Arnolfo di Cambio, Lapo di Ricevuto and a certain Donato. This work characterizes Nicola's mature style, as compared with the Pisan pulpit: the narrative of the reliefs is conveyed with greater pace and drama, and the individual scenes are more complex. The octagonal pulpit rests on columns of African granite alternately supported by lions, while the statues which punctuate the trilobed arches are sculpted almost entirely in the round. Above these are eight consecutive relief scenes depicting major episodes from the Gospels, with a particular focus on the stories of Christ's childhood, the Passion and the apocalyptic visions of the end of the world: the *Nativity, Adoration of the Magi, Presentation in the Temple, Massacre of the Innocents, Crucifixion* and the *Last Judgement*, which is split into two panels with *Christ in Judgement* at the center. The sculptor has concentrated on the expression of movement, which pervades each scene and is communicated to the next via the figures on the corners. The narrative clarity of the Pisan pulpit reliefs, framed within a solid architectural structure, has been superceded here by panels crowded with figures which move fluidly, accentuating the drama of the episodes they represent. In the *Crucifixion*, the body of Christ represents a powerful caesura between the two scenes at either side: two contrasting veins flow away from the scene to high dramatic effect, translated in the opposing directions of the bystanders' heads. In the scene of the *Last Judgement*, the compositional arrangement of the numerous figures, and their strongly individualized facial features, reveal the master's in depth enquiry into the expressive possibilities of the human body.

ARNOLFO DI CAMBIO

(COLLE VAL D'ELSA, SIENA, TUSCANY C. 1245 - FLORENCE 1302/1310)

Arnolfo di Cambio is documented as having worked in the studio of Nicola Pisano between 1265 and 1267, when both the pulpit of Siena Cathedral and the tomb of St Dominic in Bologna were being executed. Arnolfo's taste for substantial volumes, Gothic "naturalism" and the reinterpretation of Classical forms probably derived from his master Pisano; however, he would soon evolve his own original style which rearticulated Classicism in a modern language. The sculptor moved to Umbria in the late 1270s, where in 1281 he completed the smaller fountain at Perugia (subsequently disassembled). It is probable that Arnolfo came to Perugia with the workshop of Nicola and Giovanni Pisano, who had been commissioned to sculpt the main fountain in 1275. Arnolfo was also often in Rome, where he had his own studio; it was here that his art matured as a result of his direct contact with the statuary of Classical and Late Classical antiquity. The master was extremely open to the influence of cultures past and present, finding inspiration in a wide variety of artistic movements, from Etruscan to Romanesque, Roman to Gothic. One of the earliest of his Roman works was the large marble portrait of Charles

of Anjou (Capitoline Museums, Rome), part of a commemorative monument which is now lost. At the same time, the sculptor received important commissions from the Church in Rome: one example is the tomb monument he executed for Pope Boniface VIII (some of which is still preserved in the Vatican Grottoes). While in the service of Charles of Anjou, Arnolfo was able to build on the experience gained in his youth and develop a personal style characterized by the rigorous definition of geometric forms. To these he added colorful inlaid backgrounds, inspired by the work of the Roman marble sculptors, clothing the sculptures in an abstract splendor and precious chromatic effects. The contemporary Gothic taste also informed and contributed to Arnolfo's sculptural style, breathing life into the figures' compact forms whose sinuous movements quiver with vital energy. His growing interest in architecture led him to sculpt the two elaborate *ciboria* (altar canopies) in the churches of St Paul-Without-the-Walls and St Cecilia in Trastevere (the latter signed and dated 1293), works whose sculptural elements were designed and integrated into an architectural setting. In the late 1290s Arnolfo returned to Florence, where he became director of the project for the building of Florence Cathedral (Santa Maria del Fiore), founded in 1296; he also executed a number of sculptural groups for the façade (now in the Museo dell'Opera del Duomo, Florence). Arnolfo, who died between 1302 and 1310, is traditionally credited as architect of the Florentine church of Santa Croce and the Palazzo dei Priori, now better known as Palazzo Vecchio, as well as several other buildings in the region of Tuscany.

**Tomb Monument
of Cardinal de Braye**
Marble
1282
St Dominic, Orvieto

Only a part of the original sculptural ensemble survives today in the church of St Dominic in Orvieto. Completed by Arnolfo in 1282, much of it was lost after the monument was disassembled and the various pieces carried off to different locations. The present-day reconstruction is not faithful to the original tomb monument: scholars believe that it would have been framed within a large cuspidated canopy, while the stucco volute supports which now separate the sarcophagus from the three sculptural groups above are thought to be have been a much later addition (17th century). Arnolfo pioneered a number of innovative ideas in this work, which subsequently provided a model for much of the tomb sculpture of the 14th century. Combining architectural and sculptural elements, he commemorated a contemporary historical figure with a narrative depicting his death and eternal salvation achieved through the interventions of St Dominic and St Mark. The figure of Cardinal de Braye appears below, behind a curtain held open by two imperious members of the clergy. The cardinal's dead body is rendered with detailed realism: the eyes are closed, the face sunken, the features stiff and the flesh limp and lifeless. Above, he reappears kneeling at the feet of St Mark as he contemplates the Madonna, who sits on a throne holding the Christ child: this figure represents the physical and symbolic apex of the whole composition. While the statue's solid forms and detached gaze are informed by Classicism, it is also infused with a Gothic tension and energy. Small details break the apparent stillness of the sculpture: the hand, which rests on the smooth knob of the throne's arm, is light and nervous, the feet are parted, and the head turns suddenly to the right.

Ciborium
Marble
1293
St Cecilia in Trastevere, Rome

The ciborium, which can be dated to 1293, reveals a strong Gothic influence in its vigorous forms, and the combined effect of the cubes above the capitals, the cuspidated crowning and the system of spires and pinnacles. This effect is tempered, however, by the thin marble slabs on top of the cubes, which project horizontally outwards, breaking the vertical lines of the ensemble and isolating the canopy from the structure beneath. The marble slabs support four corner sculptures, whose robust forms stand out confidently from their architectural setting to occupy the surrounding space. St Cecilia's still, rigid stance gives the statue an archaic quality. She wears a crown and long pendant earrings with pearls, and holds a coronet in her hand which, according to legend, was given to her by an angel; the saint lifts her cloak to show her richly decorated garment. Her husband Valerian is animated by an internal dynamism, reflected in the vibrant, soft drapery, while a powerful energy emanates from the brother-in-law Tiburzio, culminating in the violent torsion of his horse's neck; conversely, their spiritual master St Hubert is characterized by a solemn composure. The ciborium is further embellished with bas-relief decorations depicting prophets, angels and the Evangelists, which combine superbly with mosaic motifs. Color dominates the whole work, especially the marble columns and the golden capitals.

GIOTTO

GIOTTO DI BONDONE
(VESPIGNANO, VICCHIO DI MUGELLO, FLORENCE *c.* 1267 - FLORENCE 1337)

Giotto was one of the leading exponents of International Gothic, and along with the sculptors Nicola and Giovanni Pisano and Arnolfo di Cambio he revolutionized Italian artistic culture in the 13th and 14th centuries. This historical role was already recognized by his contemporaries, from Dante to the 14th century author Cennino Cennini, who wrote that "Giotto translated the art of painting from Greek to Latin" and was thus a modernizing force: in other words, he abandoned the pictorial language of the Byzantine (Greek) culture and created a new (modern) visual style whose roots were in the Gothic (Latin) art of the West. Giotto's early life and work remain obscure and are still open to debate. He is believed to have served his apprenticeship in the studio of Cimabue, and following this he may possibly have traveled to Rome; by 1290 he was definitely in Assisi. During his formative years he would have come into contact with the work of contemporary Roman painters, whose classically inspired style had a significant influence on his own artistic development. The *Scenes from the Life of St Francis* in the Upper Basilica of Assisi are regarded as his most important youthful work; some art historians have also attributed the Old and New Testament episodes on the upper register to the master, but this is disputed. In 1300 Giotto was summoned to Rome by Pope Boniface VIII for the Jubilee. Although there is very little surviving evidence of his work in the capital, the painter clearly left a deep impression on the local artists. By the early 1300s, Giotto was a rich and established artist with a large workshop in Florence, where he executed a number of works including the *Badia Polyptych* (Uffizi, Florence) and the *Enthroned Madonna* for the church of San Giorgio alla Costa. From Florence he traveled to Rimini, where his influence led to the birth of an important local school of painting; the exquisite *Crucifix* in the church of St Francis is the only surviving work from his stay. Between 1303 and 1305 Giotto painted the fresco cycle in the Scrovegni Chapel of Padua, considered to be his masterpiece and one of the prime works of International Gothic painting. By 1311 he was back in Florence. Two more masterpieces can be dated to this period: the *Madonna and Child Enthroned with Saints* (or *Ognissanti Madonna*, now in the Uffizi, Florence), and the *Crucifix* for the church of Santa Maria Novella: in this work, Giotto breaks away from the accentuated pathos of the Byzantine tradition exemplified by the *Crucifixes* of Cimabue (such as the *Crucifix* of St Dominic in Arezzo). The frescoes of the Chapel of St Mary Magdalene and those decorating the transept of the Lower Basilica of Assisi are believed to have been executed during the first and second decades of the 14th century, mostly by Giotto's pupils. Immediately before his second stay in Padua (1317), when he completed the *Crucifix* for the Scrovegni Chapel, Giotto was in Florence again, where he painted the fresco cycle of *Scenes from the Lives of St John the Baptist and St John the Evangelist* in the Peruzzi Chapel in Santa Croce. The *Dormitio Virginis*, originally for the Florentine Church of Ognissanti (now in Berlin), can also be dated to this period, and is almost entirely by Giotto's own hand. The frescoes of *Scenes from the Life of St Francis* in the Bardi Chapel in Santa Croce were completed before 1328, and again were predominantly executed by the master himself. Between 1328 and 1333 Giotto was in Naples, working with his pupils on a number of commissions for Robert of Anjou, but very little survives from this period. The signed polyptych in the Bologna Pinacoteca (only partly by Giotto) is thought to have been finished shortly after the Naples period, as is the *Baroncelli Polyptych* in Santa Croce, the majority of which was probably painted by Taddeo Gaddi. In 1334 Giotto was assigned to direct the works at Florence Cathedral, and he founded his eponymous bell tower in the same year (subsequently completed by successive artists). The master seems to have been active right up to his death in 1337: in 1335 he was summoned to Milan to execute works in the Azzone Visconti palace (subsequently lost).

Presentation of Jesus in the Temple

Fresco, 78.74×72.83 in
1303-1305
Scrovegni Chapel, Padua

The frescoes were commissioned by Enrico Scrovegni, the son of Reginaldo, a notorious usurer whom Dante mentioned in the *Divine Comedy* (*Inferno*, XVII, 64-75). This was not the only chapel Giotto decorated for rich clients: he also painted frescoes for the bankers Bardi and Peruzzi in their family mortuary chapels in the Florentine church of Santa Croce. One of the reasons that prompted these people to decorate their family chapels was the idea that the redemption of the soul could be attained through donations, which would finance the embellishment of places of worship and the celebration of masses. It is significant that the formula used in wills for these donations was "for the redemption of souls." Social status was another important factor for the wealthier members of the rising classes: owning a mortuary chapel and having it decorated by a celebrated artist certainly conferred great prestige.

Painted between 1303 and 1305, the frescoes were mentioned in the writings of the contemporary chronicler Riccobaldo Ferrarese (*Compilatio Chronologica*, 1312-13) and the poet Francesco da Barberino (*Documenti d'Amore*, 1313) just a few years after their completion. Still in a good state of preservation, the recently restored paintings are one of Giotto's finest achievements, in which he

shows himself not just to be a master of composition, as he had already demonstrated at Assisi, but also an excellent colorist.

The scene represented here is based on a passage from the Gospel of St Luke (2: 21-38). On the left St Joseph is holding the turtledoves or pigeons to be offered in sacrifice. Jesus is in the arms of Simeon, who has been told by the Holy Spirit that he will see Christ before he dies: the elderly priest of the temple recognizes him as the Savior and communicates this to his mother. On the right is the prophetess Anna, who also recognizes the child as the bringer of salvation. The inscription on the scroll she holds alludes to the child's destiny (with the abbreviations filled in): *Quoniam in isto erit redemptio seculi* ("*For in him will be the redemption of the world*").

Madonna Ognissanti
Tempera on wood, 11×7.5 ft
c. 1310
Uffizi, Florence

In the first hall of the
Uffizi there are three large
altar-pieces which depict
the enthroned Virgin
surrounded by angels, or
Maestà as this iconography
was known, painted by
the most important artists
working in Tuscany between
the end of the thirteenth
century and the beginning
of the fourteenth century:
Cimabue, Giotto and
Duccio di Buoninsegna.
Giotto's altar-piece, now
conserved in the Uffizi,
dates to the first decade of
the fourteenth century and
had originally been made
for the church of Ognissanti
(All Saints) in Florence. It
was one of the most famous
works by the sublime
Tuscan artist, painted in
Florence after the great
fresco cycles of Assisi and
Padua had made him famous
in his own time. The solid
structure of the Madonna,
depicted frontally and
surrounded by the Gothic
architecture of her throne, is
full-bodied and realistic as
a result of the monumental
realism created by powerful
chiaroscuro effects.
The aedicule which
surrounds the figure
reveals a revolutionary and
innovative concept of spatial
depth. In this sense, the
artist has gone beyond the
Byzantine iconography of
his early training to arrive
at a new representation
of space, despite the gold
background which is still
in the Byzantine tradition.
The angels that surround
the Madonna are in fact
depicted at different depths,
covering one another,
in a modern vision that
intensifies the sense of space.

Stefaneschi Polyptych

Tempera on wood,
86.6×96.4 in
c. 1330
Vatican Picture Gallery,
Vatican City

When Cardinal Jacopo Caetani degli Stefaneschi decided to commission an altarpiece for the main altar of the Basilica of St Peter, he naturally chose the most revered artist of the era: Giotto di Bondone. Giotto's rapid rise to fame can be ascribed to his innovative pictorial language, which resonated with life and emotion in contrast to the fixed formulas of contemporary Byzantine icon painting. Giotto's many admirers included the literary giants Dante, Petrarch and Boccaccio, whose writing helped spread the painter's name throughout Italy and elevated him to legendary status. Dante was just two years older than Giotto, and celebrated the painter's absolute supremacy in a verse of the *Divine Comedy* (in *Purgatory*), which records Giotto as having exceeded the fame of his master Cimabue. In one of the stories of the *Decameron*, Boccaccio explains the reason for Giotto's widespread renown: his genius enabled him not just to imitate nature in his art, but to surpass it. The *Stefaneschi Polyptych* provides an example of the artist's much lauded realism, particularly in the central panel, which is entirely by Giotto. This panel, like the rest of the polyptych, is painted on both sides for reasons relating to the work's original location on the main altar of St Peter's. The principal side, which faced the nave and congregation, depicts St Peter enthroned with Cardinal Stefaneschi and the

canonized pope St Celestine I at his feet. The back of the altarpiece represents Christ enthroned, and features a second portrait of the cardinal: this side could only be viewed by the pope and his court, who would traditionally celebrate mass behind the altar.

DECORATIVE ARTS OF THE MAMELUKES

(EGYPT/SYRIA, 13TH-14TH CENTURY)

Lorenzo de' Medici ("the Magnificent") loved to dress up as a "Saracen", which at that time in the 15th century meant a "Mameluke". Alexandria and Cairo had many Western communities, who were completely integrated into the life of the realm, and profited handsomely from the commercial trade links. In Venice, the merchants knew exactly when the annual caravan left Mecca, and when the goods would start appearing in the markets of the West: the carpets and rugs, metalwork objects, fabrics and ivory were common sights in the ports of the Mediterranean. Metalwork was highly prized during the Mameluke era, as attested by the Florentine traveler Simone Sigoli, who was in Damascus in 1384: "*They still produce large numbers of brass basins and vessels, which look like they are made out of gold, and on the basins and vessels they engrave figures and foliage and other intricate work in silver, which is a most beautiful thing to see*". The description corresponds perfectly to the figurative work of the first Mameluke period. On the other hand, the metalwork objects of the late Mameluke era are characterized by elaborate inscriptions in the *thuluth* style and rarely include figurative representations. Occasionally, couples of birds in flight were inserted into the arabesque roundels, but this is unusual; writing was increasingly used as the main decorative element, with the addition of fleur-de-lys and peony motifs demonstrating the influence of the Far East. The most common objects were jugs, large basins, plates and candelabra, predominantly worked in brass, which tended to replace bronze.

Muhammad ibn al-Zayn, Basin

Brass inlaid with gold
and silver, diam. 19.7 in (rim)
1290-1310
Louvre, Paris

This is one of the most famous metalwork basins of Islamic art, signed by the artist Muhammad ibn al-Zayn. The piece is a masterpiece of its kind, both for its size and the exceptional quality of the craftsmanship. The principal external decoration, which is exquisitely detailed, is arranged within a large central band featuring panels and roundels. The roundels depict riders on horseback clothed in different garments, perhaps denoting their rank: the first set of riders attack a bear or dragon with their

lances, while a second rider battles with a lion and a third holds a polo mallet. The panels contain standing figures, which have been identified as court dignitaries assigned different functions depending on their position within the Mameluke court hierarchy. The large central band is bordered at the top and bottom by two smaller bands featuring running animals (unicorns, bears, leopards, elephants, griffins, gazelles, panthers, rabbits, deer, camels and sphinxes), set against a florid arabesque background which is punctuated by small roundels decorated with fleur-de-lys (added when the basin arrived in France). The exterior decoration continues in the area above the upper band, towards the rim, with a

frieze of lanceolate leaves. The thick rim of the basin is also decorated, again with running animals. The interior of the basin is rendered in a similar fashion, with seated figures in the roundels and hunting and battle scenes in the panels. Even the bottom of the basin inside is richly ornate, with concentric motifs featuring aquatic animals (fish, frogs, alligators, turtles, crabs and lizards). Traditionally the splendid basin was known as the *Baptistère de Saint-Louis*, after St Louis IX of France, who was very active in the Crusades; in fact, the saint died some fifty years before the basin was made. The piece was first documented in 1742, and in 1856 it was used to baptize Prince Napoleon Eugene.

Bronze censer,
from Syria,
14ᵗʰ century.
Bargello,
Florence.

Opposite,
Bronze Jug,
1363-1377.
Bargello,
Florence.

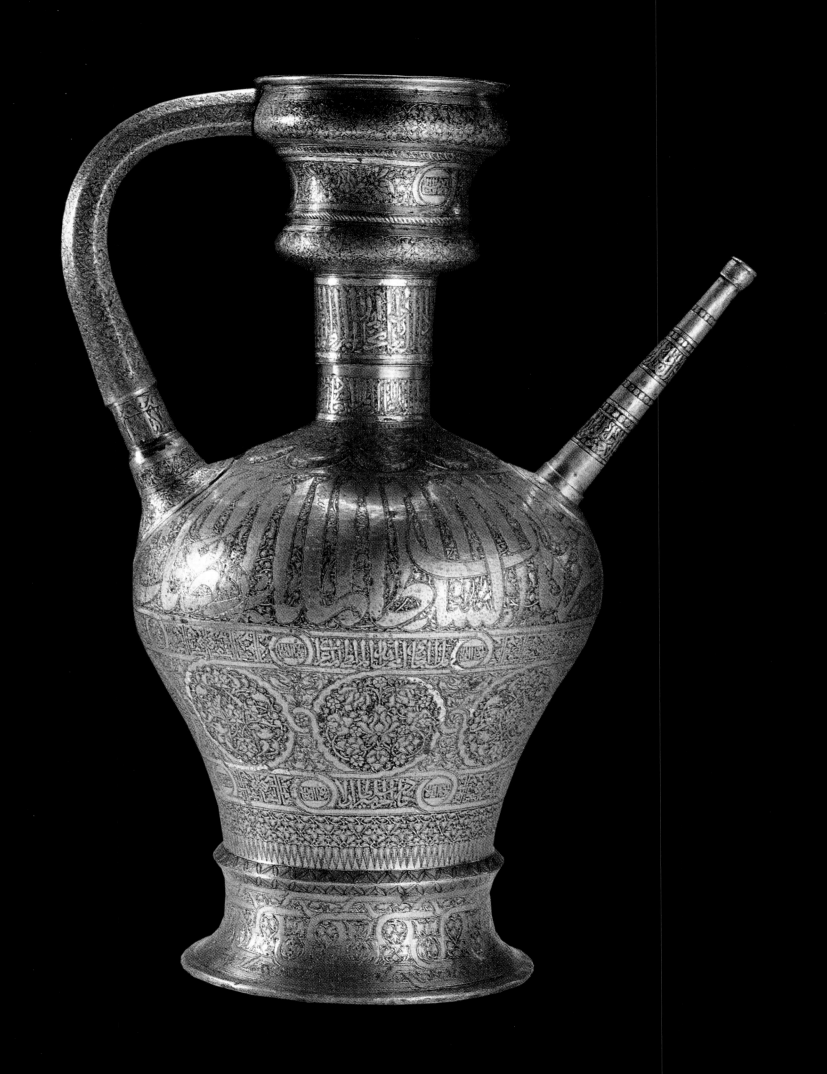

SIMONE MARTINI

(SIENA, TUSCANY C. 1284 - AVIGNON, PROVENCE-ALPES-CÔTE D'AZUR 1344)

Regarded as "most noble painter and most famous" by the 15ᵗʰ century artist Ghiberti, Simone Martini's personality and confidence come across from his earliest major work, the *Maestà* in the Palazzo Pubblico of Siena (1315). The young painter was profoundly influenced by Duccio di Buoninsegna, master of the Sienese school, by the sculptures of Giovanni Pisano in the Siena Cathedral, and by the elegance of the French Gothic artists. His sophisticated interpretations of religious and secular subjects exploited the expressive potential of the linear style.

Other than in his native city of Siena, the master worked in Naples for the Court of Anjou, and in the Lower Basilica of St Francis of Assisi, where he painted the images of various saints in the right arm of the transept. During the 1320s and 1330s Simone completed some of his most celebrated works: in 1328, the equestrian portrait in fresco of the soldier *Guidoriccio da Fogliano* in the Palazzo Pubblico of Siena (whose attribution has, however, recently been thrown into doubt); and in 1333 the altarpiece of the *Annunciation*, originally for Siena Cathedral and now in the Uffizi in Florence, in which his Gothic linearism found an exquisite expression. In 1340 the artist transferred to Avignon where he executed frescoes in the Papal Palace which unfortunately deteriorated with time. At the papal court he met and became close friends with the Italian poet Petrarch, who commissioned at least two treasured works from him: a full page miniature which Simone painted in the poet's most prized manuscript from his library (now in the Biblioteca Ambrosiana in Milan), and a portrait of Laura, Petrarch's muse and lifelong love, who died in her youth. The portrait was lost, but its astonishing quality was recorded by Petrarch in two moving sonnets.

Saint Louis of Toulouse Crowning His Brother Robert of Anjou

Tempera on panel,
78.74×54.33 in;
predella 22×14.96 in
(each scene)
1317
National Gallery of
Capodimonte, Naples

The work, dated to 1317, constitutes a genuine political manifesto of the House of Anjou. On the death of Charles II, the King of Sicily, in 1296, his son Louis renounced the crown of Naples in favor of his brother Robert, and took monastic vows, entering the Franciscan order. The succession caused a great deal of controversy and Robert was accused of usurping the throne, even though the pope, to whom he had appealed, had recognized his right to rule. The canonization of Louis in 1317 was therefore welcomed by the king as an invaluable opportunity to strengthen his own position and confirm the legitimacy of his reign. The work which was immediately commissioned from Simone Martini, almost as an act of propaganda, translates Robert of Anjou's political conception into visual terms: the saint, seated on a throne, receives the heavenly crown from angels. The pluvial, miter and crosier recall his episcopal rank, and the habit his membership of the Franciscan order. On his breast, however, is set a large brooch with the Anjou crest, underlining the fact that he belongs to the royal family of Naples. With one hand Louis places the crown on the head of his kneeling brother: this is thus a double coronation, of the bishop saint by God, and of Robert by the saint. So the king derives his authority from a legitimate succession, through the renunciation of Louis, and is in a way included, again through his brother, in a celestial investiture. The principal episodes in the saint's life are depicted in the predella: his acceptance of the appointment as bishop of Toulouse in exchange for the possibility of entering the Franciscan order, the repetition of his vows in public, Louis serving the poor at table, his funeral and a miracle worked after his death.

125

Annunciation

Tempera on wood, 6×6.8 ft
1333
Uffizi, Florence

The Archangel Gabriel has just landed from Heaven, his fine cloak still delicately fluttering in the air, to bring his message to the Virgin. The words float out of his small mouth and materialize into letters of gold, but the Virgin, taken by surprise, shrinks away in fear with a sudden movement that has all the grace of an arabesque. Simone Martini painted this panel in 1333 with his brother in law Lippo Memmi, with whom he ran a flourishing studio in Siena. The names of the two painters and the date appear on the one surviving fragment of the old frame, inserted in the current one (added in the 19th century). It is almost impossible to distinguish which parts of the work were executed by which of the artists, although some art historians attribute the central section to Simone and the two side sections to Lippo, along with the four prophets in the tondi.

The picture was purposely commissioned to be placed on the altar of Saint Ansano in the Siena Cathedral: the saint, one of the four patron saints of Siena, is represented on the left panel, while the saint on the right is believed by most scholars to be Margaret. In 1799 the Grand Duke Pietro Leopoldo ordered the work to be transferred to Florence, where it was displayed in the Uffizi that same year. The splendor of the gold leaf and brilliance of the colors, which also glint with golden highlights, create an atmosphere of austere abstraction, which is impossibly elegant and almost inscrutable. To the Goncourt brothers in the late 19th century, the angel appeared "*almost satanic [...] with his long serpent's neck [...] and the strangeness of his perverse beauty*"; while the respected art critic Bernard Berenson likened Simone's elegant lines to the Persian, Chinese and Japanese miniaturists.

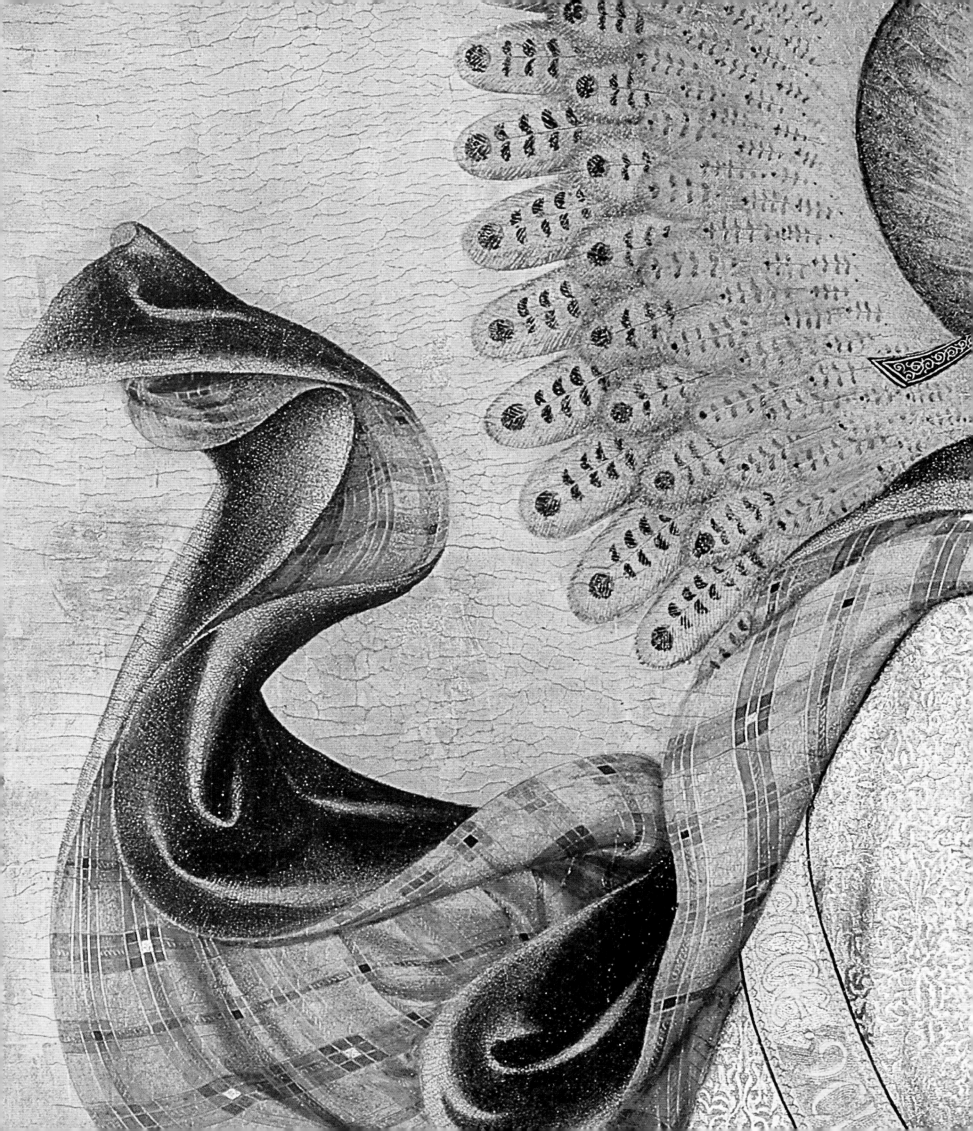

THE ALHAMBRA IN GRANADA

(GRANADA, ANDALUSIA, 13ᵀᴴ-14ᵀᴴ CENTURY)

The Alhambra in Granada is regarded as one of the most outstanding monuments of Islamic art. Originally a fortified administrative citadel, it was gradually transformed into an extraordinary royal residence. Following the fall from power of the Almohads in Spain, the emergence of the Nasrid Dynasty, in the 13ᵗʰ century, signalled the beginning of the Alhambra's most glorious period. The citadel of the Alhambra began life as administrative center independent from the surrounding properties and holdings, and was initially built to accommodate a garrison; the palace was erected subsequently and progressively, although the most important core elements were constructed under Yusef I

(1333-1354) and his son Mohammed V (1354-1391). The architectural plan is relatively simple and linear, with the space organized around two large courtyards: the public reception areas look onto the Court of the Myrtles, while the residential quarters are arranged around the Court of Lions, named for the fountain with twelve lions set among orange trees). The areas alternate between intimate (such as the Patio of the Cuarto Dorado, or the Gilded Room) and expansive, with connecting corridors and small rooms emphasizing the sudden explosions of light and space. The two main courtyards feature water fountains and pools, considered an essential element of palatine architecture. Given the fact that

the Alhambra was a relatively small provincial court, the decoration surpasses all expectations. A wainscot of polychrome ceramic tiles introduces the true protagonist of the decorative program: the gilded polychrome stucco work, featuring intricate geometric and floral patterns along with inscriptions in cursive and Cuphic script. The private residential area around the Court of Lions is the most stunning, particularly thanks to the two halls which stand opposite each other in perfect architectural symmetry: the Hall of the Two Sisters and the Hall of the Abenserrajes. Following a classical architectural design, the square floor plan of each hall is topped by a dome: in the Two Sisters the design is masterfully and seamlessly articulated from floor to ceiling, while in the Abenserrajes the architecture displays a more obvious transition from the square floor plan to the stellar eight-point "canopy", created by the interplay of niches *a muqarnas* integral to the brilliant structure. A series of sixteen windows divides the area. Architecture is a fusion of mathematics, geometry, design and technical expertise; and the planning and execution of the Alhambra complex is an almost perfect example of the integration of structure and decoration. Unfortunately much of the original color of the stucco work was lost.

ANDREI RUBLEV

(REGION OF MOSCOW C. 1360 - MOSCOW 1430)

There is little reliable evidence on the life and artistic production of this painter. He worked almost exclusively alongside other artists, which has led to conflicting opinions on the attribution of numerous works. Although few of his paintings have survived, it is certain that he was active mainly in Moscow and the surrounding cities and monasteries. He served his apprenticeship in the most cultured and refined environment of the period, the court of the Prince of Vladimir. Rublev's strict adherence to the Byzantine style only serves to highlight the contrasting vein of nascent humanism also present in his art. The earliest written mention of him is in a source of 1405, which states that he participated in the decoration of the Cathedral of the Annunciation in the Moscow Kremlin. In 1408 he painted the frescoes and icons for the pulpit of the Assumption Cathedral in Vladimir, together with the great icon painter Daniil Cherni; sadly little remains of this monumental work. From this point onwards there is scant evidence of Rublev's activity, until the late 1420s when he is known to have painted at the Monastery of the Trinity in Sergievsky (where he had spent his youth as a novice): between 1427 and 1428 he frescoed the entire conventual church, although once again there are few traces of his original work as they were repainted on successive occasions after 1635. However, the icons painted for the same monastery have survived, including the artist's masterpiece, the *Trinity*. Prized for its originality at the time, the painting came to be considered a model of representation of human beauty and nature, and in 1551 was singled out by the Synod as the exemplary masterpiece all painters should try to imitate.

Trinity

Tempera on panel,
4.65×3.74 ft
Early 15ᵗʰ century
Tretyakov Gallery, Moscow

The subject of Rublev's icon painting is inspired by the biblical text of Genesis 18, 1-16: the painter has synthesized the narrative into a single image, choosing to depict the moment in which three mysterious pilgrims, guests of Abraham, are seated at a table in front of the Patriarch's tent, near the oaks of Mamre. This episode of the Holy Scriptures has always been interpreted by the Fathers of the Church as a presage of the mystery of the Holy Trinity, since in the text, the pilgrims are alternately referred to in the singular (as if they were as one) and the plural. A close examination of the icon reveals the rich symbolism employed by the painter to underline the three figures' common identity and divine nature. They are all represented as winged angels, sitting around a table with a chalice at the center. Their faces are practically identical, and all three appear to be the same age: in God, there is no past or future, but an eternal present. The three pilgrims each hold a wayfarer's walking stick, emblematic of their authority; and even their brilliant yellow halos are the same, with no distinction made between them. All wear a blue garment (more or less visible), the blue of divinity, and all sit on identical thrones which emphasize their dignity and status. There are some distinguishing elements, however, identifiable by the pilgrims' different stances, gestures, and the varying colors of their garments (beyond the blue common to all). The angel on the left is wrapped in a light orange-red cloak, whose faint bluish shading alludes to the pleats, in direct contrast with the red-brown garment of the central figure. The third angel sits awkwardly to the right of the painting, and wears a thin cloak. The figures are rendered with a light, sinuous line which animates the scene. An urban landscape was originally painted behind them in the background, of which only a few traces now remain. None of the bodies' contours are realistically rendered, but their flat outlines combine with the elegant use of color to give the picture an abstract quality fundamental to the representation of the subject matter. The *Trinity* was executed by Rublev in the pursuit of interior purity, a purity held to be necessary for the painting of a perfect icon (since it was considered to be a message directly handed down from God himself through the artist), and for contemplating the divine; as such, Rublev's icon represents a theological revelation in the truest sense.

LORENZO GHIBERTI

(FLORENCE 1378-1455)

Although Ghiberti trained as a goldsmith, it is recorded in his journal that he left Florence in 1400 to work as a painter in Pesaro. On returning to his native Florence, he won the competition of 1401 to decorate the north door of the Baptistery with his trial relief of the *Sacrifice of Isaac* (Bargello, Florence). The door, divided into twenty quatrefoil panels depicting *Stories from the New Testament* and eight representing the Four Evangelists and Fathers of the Church, was finally completed in 1424. During this period, Ghiberti also belonged to one of the most important artists' workshops in Florence, and sculpted the bronze statues of *St John the Baptist* (1414), *St Matthew* (1420) and *St Stephen* (1427-1428) for the external niches of the church of Orsanmichele. In 1424 he made a trip to Venice, and around 1430 he traveled to Rome.

Lorenzo also worked in Siena, carving reliefs of the *Baptism of Christ* and *St John the Baptist Before Herod* (1427) for the baptismal font of the city's famous Baptistery. In 1425 he was awarded the task of decorating the third door of the Florence Baptistery, subsequently given the grand epithet of the *Porta del Paradiso* or *Gate of Paradise*, which he only finished in 1452: the ten square panels represent *Stories from the Old Testament*. At the same time, he also worked for the Opera del Duomo, the official body in charge of the artistic program for Florence Cathedral, and executed the *Shrine of the Three Martyrs* (1428; now in the Bargello, Florence) and the *Shrine of St Zanobius* (1442). In his later years the master wrote three books of *Commentaries*, a journal containing historical notes, biographical memoirs and theoretical reflections on art.

The Sacrifice of Isaac
Partially gilted bronze,
17.7×14.9 in
1401
Bargello, Florence

With this trial piece, the 23-year-old Lorenzo Ghiberti swept away his competition, beating older and more experienced masters for the commission to decorate the north door of the Florence Baptistery. Seven sculptors took part in the challenge (including Jacopo della Quercia), from which only two trial pieces survive: that of Lorenzo and the runner-up, Filippo Brunelleschi. The comparison between the two has become a classic in art history. His relief belongs emphatically to the International Gothic style which dominated Europe at the start of the 15ᵗʰ century, and its elements recall the most fashionable sculptural work being produced at the time in France, Bohemia and Burgundy: the rock that looms up to create a diagonal break in the composition, the elegantly flowing drapery, the graceful arch of Abraham's figure as he prepares for the sacrifice, and the delicacy of Isaac's polished nude body. The figure of the servant, elegantly wrapped in a light cape and standing with his back to the viewer, displays a confident use of space which lends naturalism to the scene; Lorenzo was so pleased with the pose that he repeated it in subsequent works.
It was not just the beauty and lyricism of the composition that convinced the judges to award him the competition, however: Lorenzo's casting technique was unquestionably superior to Brunelleschi's. The master's bronze, produced from a single cast, weighed a full seven kilos less than his rival Brunelleschi's, whose own relief had to be created by soldering the separately cast parts together.

139

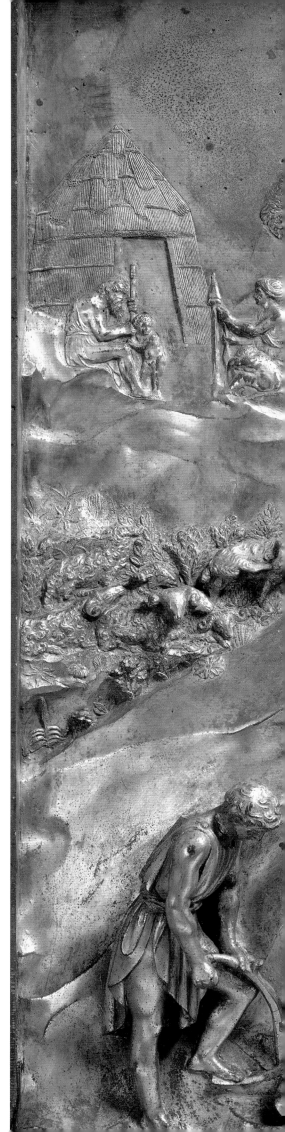

Gate of Paradise
1425-1452
Baptistery, Florence

Scenes from the story of Cain and Abel
and
Solomon Receiving the Queen of Sheba
Panels of the Gate of Paradise
1425-1452
Museo dell'Opera
del Duomo, Florence

In 1425, Lorenzo was also entrusted with decorating the east door opposite the cathedral, which Michelangelo was later to dub the *Gate of Paradise* for its incomparable beauty. He worked on it for twenty-seven years, producing one of the great masterpieces of bronze sculpture, and was so satisfied with the results that he commented: "I carried out this work with great diligence and great love". For the east door, Lorenzo was allowed to abandon Andrea Pisano's medieval quatrefoil scheme, and instead produced ten square panels in gilded bronze which represented *Stories from the Old Testament*. The scenes are characterized by their masterful use of perspective and refined linear style.

DONATELLO

DONATO DI NICCOLÒ DI BETTO BARDI
(FLORENCE 1386-1466)

After serving his apprenticeship in the studio of Lorenzo Ghiberti, Donatello joined the Opera del Duomo in 1407. Here he worked alongside Nanni di Banco on a series of sculptures which attempted to rearticulate the Gothic artistic language, including the marble *David* (Bargello, Florence) and the *St John the Baptist* (Museo dell'Opera del Duomo, Florence). A trip to Rome with Filippo Brunelleschi left Donatello with a first profound impression of the art of antiquity. In 1416 he started work on the statue of *St George* for one of the exterior niches of the Florentine church of Orsanmichele (now in the Bargello), which together with the relief of *St George and the Dragon*, has come to be an archetypal symbol of the Renaissance civilization. From 1425-1433 Donatello collaborated with Michelozzo on another series of works, including the funerary monuments of the Antipope John XXIII (Baptistery, Florence) and Cardinal Brancacci in Naples. At the same time, he also executed one of the first important bronze works made using the innovative *stiacciato* (low relief) technique: the *Feast of Herod* relief for the baptismal font of Siena Baptistery. Between 1430 and 1432 Donatello was in Rome again, and made the *Tabernacle of the Sacrament* for St Peter's Basilica, possibly with the help of Michelozzo. Upon his return to Florence, he created one of his finest masterpieces, the bronze *David* now in the Bargello. This period also saw him carry out the prestigious commissions of the *Pulpit* for Prato Cathedral and the *Cantoria* (choir or singing gallery) for Florence Cathedral (now in the Museo dell'Opera del Duomo, Florence), two works in which Donatello unleashed an exuberant repertoire of motifs directly inspired by Classical sculpture, with dancing *putti* which were much imitated by successive artists. In 1443 the sculptor was summoned to Padua, where he executed the *Equestrian Monument to Gattamelata*, as well as decorating the altar of the Basilica del Santo with a series of reliefs dedicated to the *Miracles of St Anthony* and a statue of the *Madonna with Child and Saints*. The Padua projects would keep him there until 1454, when he returned to Florence and rented a house with a studio in the Piazza del Duomo. The group of *Judith and Holofernes* for the garden of the Medici Palace, and the *Mary Magdalene* in polychrome wood (Museo dell'Opera del Duomo, Florence) have both been dated to this period. As the pioneer and one of the finest exponents of Florentine Classical humanism, Donatello interpreted his culture and times with extraordinary freedom, creating seminal works which would become a fundamental reference point in the history of Italian and European sculpture.

St George

Marble, h. 7 ft
1416-1417
Bargello, Florence

"*He made a sculpture of St George in his armor for the Art of the armorers, very lifelike, in which the beauty of youth, the spirit and courage of the soldier, pride and the vitality contained within the stone are all evident to the observer.*"
In Vasari's words the admiration for Donatello's ability to infuse a stone statue with life is evident, even a century later. The *St George* (1416-1417) was the first completely successful representation of the heroic ideals of the Renaissance and was a direct ancestor of Michelangelo's *David*, sculpted almost 100 years later. The *St George* statue was made to stand in the niche that the Art of the armorers had dedicated to its patron saint on the façade of Orsanmichele. The platform with the scene of *St George slaying the dragon* presented important innovations of technique and composition. It was the first bas-relief to be composed using the new rules of perspective and the first example of Donatello's particularly flat reliefs that made use of minimal depths to create the effects of light and shadow and spatial depth. Today the original statue with its base is conserved in the National Museum in the Bargello Palace, and has been substituted by a copy in the niche at Orsanmichele.

Cantoria

Marble, 11.42×18.7×3.2 ft
1433-1439
Museo dell'Opera
del Duomo, Florence

Although universally referred to as *cantorie* (choirs or singing galleries), Donatello's work and its sister piece by Luca della Robbia were originally conceived as balconies for housing the organs of Florence Cathedral, each one installed at a considerable height over the doorways to the south and north sacristies respectively. Donatello was in Rome in 1432 when the project for the twin balconies was first suggested, so it fell to the younger but already promising Luca della Robbia to begin work on what would be his first major public sculpture. Luca's "pulpit" (as it was described in contemporary sources) was to house a brand new organ which had been ordered that very same year. Donatello received his commission for the companion piece as soon as he returned to Florence in 1433; he was assigned the less important of the two balustrades, since it was destined for the old organ. Although Donatello's frieze of wild dancing cherubs was not perfectly chased and polished (in contrast to the exquisitely finished panels of Luca's piece), Vasari observed that this apparent "imperfection" was in fact justified by the work's final location, high above the viewer, whose eyes would be drawn more to the effects of *chiaroscuro* (light and shade) and the interplay of forms than to intricately described details. The glass mosaic tiles which cover the background of the frieze and the small columns are characteristic of Donatello's penchant for vivid color and contrasting

materials, and serve to heighten the chaotic jubilation of the scene. Some of the cherubs are garlanded, while others appear seminude or wrapped in classically-inspired drapery, and their frenzied activity has rightly been compared with the Bacchic scenes found on Roman sarcophagi. The entire *cantoria* was in fact conceived by Donatello as an answer to the art of antiquity, from the grandiose supporting corbels to the *putti* in the two reliefs beneath the main frieze, who play instruments and take fruit from a vase.

147

MASACCIO

TOMMASO DI SER GIOVANNI DI MONE CASSAI
(SAN GIOVANNI VALDARNO, AREZZO, TUSCANY 1401 - ROME 1428)

Born in a small Tuscan village which was politically affiliated to Florence, Masaccio left home at an early age to continue his artistic education in the provincial capital (where he was already documented as a painter in 1417). In 1422 he was asked to join the Arte dei Medici e Speziali, a prestigious guild of merchants which also welcomed and supported artists, and the *San Giovenale Triptych* (or *Cascia Altarpiece*) for the church of San Giovenale a Cascia (in Arezzo) also dates to the same year. Recognized as one of the young master's earliest works, the painting reveals his close adherence to the artistic principles of the Renaissance. The *Madonna and Child with St Anne* was executed around 1424 along with the older artist Masolino, and the two painters also worked together on the *Polyptych of the Miracle of the Snow* of 1425 for the church of Santa Maria Maggiore in Rome. The following year, Masaccio alone was commissioned to paint a polyptych for the church of the Carmine in Pisa. The painting's central panel, representing the *Madonna and Child* (now in the National Gallery, London), displays the artist's complete mastery of the principles of perspective elaborated in Florence by Filippo Brunelleschi and Do-

natello, felt here particularly in the robust physical form of the Madonna and the architectural articulation of her throne. Around the same time (although the actual dating is still disputed), Masaccio and Masolino painted the monumental fresco cycle representing *Scenes from the Life of St Peter* in the Brancacci Chapel (church of the Carmine, Florence). Masaccio's powerful new narrative style contrasts with the late Gothic manner of the older painter to create a work of startling modernity, which would become a model for future generations of admiring artists. Immediately after the completion of the Brancacci Chapel frescoes, Masaccio painted the *Holy Trinity with the Virgin, St John and Donors* in the church of Santa Maria Novella in Florence: this work marked the apex of the artist's investigations into the representation of space and perspective, with the figures occupying a fictitious chapel comparable in every detail with contemporary Florentine architecture. Masaccio and Masolino were both documented in Rome in 1428, where they were involved in the fresco decoration of the chapel of Cardinal Branda Castiglione in the church of St Clement; the young master died suddenly in the same year, at the age of 27.

Madonna and Child with St Anne
Tempera on wood,
68.90×40.5 in
1424-1425
Uffizi, Florence

This painting was originally located in the church of St Ambrosius in Florence, where it was first documented by Vasari in 1568 as being a work of Masaccio. It was only in 1940 that the art historian Roberto Longhi distinguished the hands of

two separate artists in the picture: Masaccio was credited with the group of the Madonna and child, along with the angel in green on the right hand side holding back the curtain, while the figure of St Anne and the other angels were assigned to Masolino. The panel thus marked the beginning of the successful collaboration between the young Masaccio and the older Masolino, in a professional partnership which would lead them to paint the celebrated fresco cycle in the Brancacci Chapel. The traditional iconography of the subject required that the figure of St Anne be given precedence over the group of the Madonna and child: as the mother of Mary and progenitor of Jesus, Anne is indeed the unifying figure in the composition, occupying a dominant position with one hand on Mary's shoulder and the other held over the child in a protective gesture. The halo around her head is also bigger than the Madonna's, emphasizing her primary role. This established iconography is openly undermined by Masaccio's contribution to the picture, however: the powerful sculptural forms of his Madonna and child vie with the figure of St Anne to become the real focal point of the composition. According to a recent hypothesis, the choice of theme may be attributed to Nofri d'Agnolo Buonamici, a cloth weaver who is thought to have commissioned the panel for his family altar which was dedicated to St Anne. The saint was especially popular in Florence because of her link with an event of huge importance in the history of the city: the expulsion of the Duke of Athens on 26 July 1343, the feast day of St Anne.

The Holy Trinity with the Virgin, St John and Donors

Fresco, 21.88×10.40 ft
1426-1427
Santa Maria Novella, Florence

This fresco is one of the last works executed by Masaccio before his journey to Rome in 1428, where he died the same year. The iconography of the Trinity, with the Father holding Christ's cross and the dove of the Holy Spirit in the center, is not in itself unusual: what is striking is the location of the group inside a Renaissance work of architecture represented in perfect perspective. It is a mortuary chapel, and God the Father is standing on the tomb located immediately behind the cross. At either side of the cross, next to the columns, stand the mourners, Mary and St John the Evangelist, while the donors (who have yet to be identified with certainty) are depicted in the foreground. Lying right at the bottom of the fresco is a skeleton on a sarcophagus bearing the inscription: *IO FV G[i]A QVEL CHE VOI SETE / AND QVEL CHE SON VOI A[n]CO SARETE* ("I was what you are / and what I am you too shall be"). This portion of the picture must have been situated underneath the altar that was set in front of it: so it was not a simple *memento mori*, but a theologically more pertinent reference to the death and resurrection of Christ, repeated at every celebration of communion on the altar, above which loomed the representation of the Trinity. Giorgio Vasari, describing the work, commented that it is "made to recede so skilfully that the surface looks as if it is indented." In fact the foreshortening must have been a sort of cultural "shock" for his contemporaries, and constitutes one of the first systematic applications, verging on the virtuoso, of the principles of the mathematical perspective devised by Filippo Brunelleschi: indeed it has been suggested that the illusory space was designed and perhaps even drawn in outline by the great architect. In reality it is quite possible that Masaccio, while following the suggestions of his older friend, was capable of carrying out an exercise in perspective of this kind independently, and that he had the depth of understanding of Classical architecture that is presupposed by the representation of the coffered tunnel vault, modeled on the Pantheon in Rome.

ROGIER VAN DER WEYDEN

(TOURNAI, WALLOON REGION C. 1400 - BRUSSELS 1464)

The painter can probably be identified as Rogelet de la Pasture, documented as a pupil of Robert Campin in 1427. Rogier's association with the master of Tournai is also apparent in the stylistic elements of his earliest works, such as the *Deposition* (Prado, Madrid). Following his apprenticeship he moved to Brussels, where he was recorded in 1435 as being the town's official painter. Rogier's knowledge of the work of Jan van Eyck also informed his own style: in particular, the *Last Judgement* or *Beaune Altarpiece* (Hôtel-Dieu, Beaune) echoes van Eyck's *Polyptych of the Adoration of the Lamb*. In 1450 the painter traveled to Rome for the Jubilee, a trip which allowed him to see the art of important Italian cities such as Ferrara (where he also worked for Leonello d'Este), Florence and Milan. The Italian influence on Rogier translated into a reduced sense of drama, and an increased interest in the realistic representation of space in the paintings he produced during these years: the *Entombment of Christ* (Uffizi, Florence), for example, recalls the work of Fra Angelico and Masaccio. Paintings such as the *Triptych of the Seven Sacraments* (Musées Royaux des Beaux-Arts, Antwerp) and the *St Columba Altarpiece* with the *Adoration of the Magi* (Alte Pinakothek, Munich) are ascribed to his late period: here the artist focuses on the human element of the compositions, the monumental figures from the biblical tales. Rogier was also an exceptional portrait painter: the *Portrait of a Young Woman* (Staatliche Museen, Berlin) and the *Portrait of Francesco d'Este* (Metropolitan Museum, New York) reprise the naturalism of van Eyck, with an added psychological intensity. Rogier was in turn to exert a wide-ranging influence on the rest of Europe, and is considered one of the cornerstones of the great 15th century school of Flemish painting.

Adoration of the Magi (St Columba Altarpiece)

Oil on wood, 4.53×5 ft
c. 1455
Alte Pinakothek, Munich

This painting, one of Rogier's masterpieces, constitutes the central panel of a triptych probably from the church of St Columba in Cologne. The side panels represent the *Annunciation* (to the left) and the *Presentation of Jesus in the Temple* (to the right); when open, the triptych thus recounts three episodes from the life of Christ in chronological order. The work was an immediate success in Cologne, and by the 1470s it had been widely reproduced in painted copies, prints and glass decorations. It was executed following the painter's trip to Italy, and while it still displays a typically Flemish preoccupation with fine detail, it also betrays the influence of Italian painting, particularly in the monumentality of the figures and the natural, confident way they inhabit the pictorial space. The open arches of the crumbling stall allowed the painter to depict a wide, luminous background landscape, featuring tiny figures interspersed here and there, and a detailed view of a city (which some critics have identified as Cologne).

The roads winding through the valley and surrounding hills probably allude not only to the journey of the Magi in the foreground of the painting, but to the role of Cologne at that time as a popular destination for famous pilgrimages. Other contemporary references have been found in the Magi themselves, which may have been portraits of important figures of the period: Charles the Bald and Philip the Good of Burgundy, and Louis XI of France. However much the subject of the Adoration of the Magi might lend itself to the portrayal of contemporary aristocrats in the faces of the oriental kings, it is not certain that this is what Rogier intended in this painting; and perhaps only the exquisitely elegant king standing on the far right of the scene, almost as if to emphasize his detachment from the event, is actually an homage to a real noble.

Entombment of Christ

Oil on wood, 43.3×38 in
1463-1464
Uffizi, Florence

This panel was inspired by a
similar painting by Fra
Angelico (Alte Pinakothek,
Munich) which formed part
of the great altarpiece for the
church of San Marco in
Florence. Rogier seems to
have shared the spirituality of
Angelico's work, which was
intended to encourage prayer
and meditation through the
display of Christ's body to the
faithful in the same way that
the host does during the
consecration. But he
introduces a greater wealth of
detail and variety of
expressions that attenuate the
abstraction of the Tuscan
artist's composition. It should
also be noted that the subject
was foreign to the Flemish
tradition, which tended to
prefer the theme of the
Deposition from the Cross to
that of the Lamentation over
the Dead Christ so common
in Italian art. This does not
necessarily imply that the
picture was painted during his
visit to Italy. On the contrary,
it is believed to date from at
least ten years later, between
1463 and 1464. The link
with Italy appears to lie
instead in its commission by
the Medici family, the *de facto*
rulers of Florence at the time:
some scholars believe the face
of Nicodemus to be a portrait
of the family's influential
patriarch, Cosimo the Elder,
who was also responsible for
the reconstruction of the
church and monastery of San
Marco.

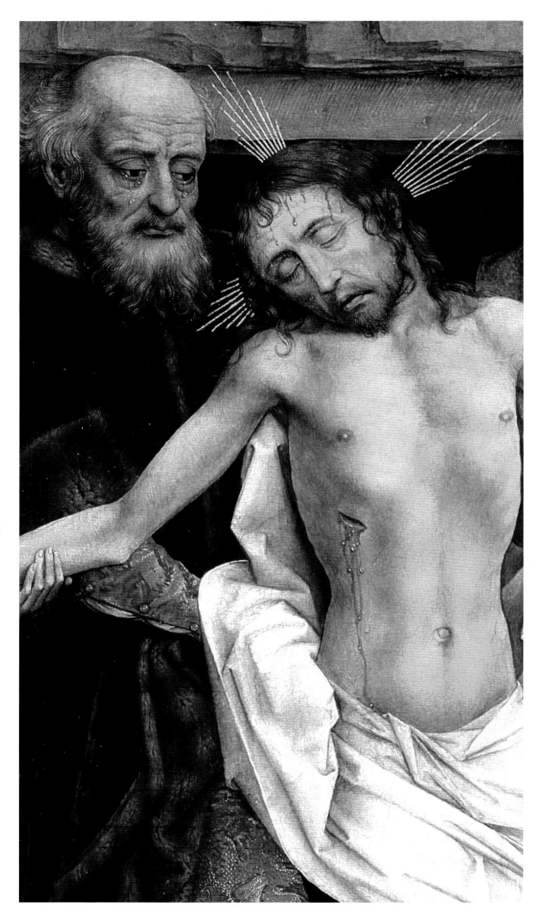

PIERO DELLA FRANCESCA

(BORGO SAN SEPOLCRO, AREZZO, TUSCANY C. 1420-1492)

Piero della Francesca's first major works already demonstrated a thorough knowledge of early 15th century Tuscan art. He is recorded as having been in Florence in 1439, when he collaborated with Domenico Veneziano on a fresco cycle in the church of Sant'Egidio (now lost). The young artist was particularly impressed by the frescoes of Masaccio and the clean spatial structuring and use of color of the work of Fra Angelico; he also concentrated his studies on the rules of perspective, as outlined by Leon Battista Alberti and Filippo Brunelleschi. Fresh from his Florentine experiences, the painter executed the *Baptism of Christ* around 1440-1445, whose intense energy is created by the strong contrasts of light and shade. In 1451 Piero painted a votive fresco for Sigismondo Pandolfo Malatesta, the Prince of Rimini (*Sigismondo Malatesta before St Sigismund*, Malatesta Temple, Rimini), a composition characterized by an atmosphere of abstract formal stillness. The next year, following the death of the incumbent Florentine painter Bicci di Lorenzo, Piero took over the decoration of the church of St Francis in Arezzo, producing his epic fresco cycle depicting the *Legend of the True Cross*. Three more masterpieces were completed around this time: the *Flagellation of Christ* (Galleria Nazionale delle Marche, Urbino), the *Madonna del Parto* in Monterchi and the *Resurrection* in his home town of San Sepolcro, in which the triumph of the risen Christ seems to be echoed by the awakening nature in the background landscape. From the 1460s Piero intensified his relationship with the Court of Urbino, whose reputation as an artistic and intellectual powerhouse was founded on its promotion of mathematical and rationalist debate. Here he painted the double portrait of *Federico da Montefeltro and Battista Sforza* (Uffizi, Florence) and the *Montefeltro Altarpiece* (Pinacoteca di Brera, Milan), which reveal an awareness of Flemish art and a new sensibility in the richness of the chromatic relationships. Piero also went on to formalize his enquiries into the theory of painting in his treatise *De prospectiva pingendi* (On Perspective in Painting): his scientific exposition of the harmonious connection between forms and space found its visual expression in the art he produced.

Baptism of Christ

Tempera on wood, 5.48×3.8 ft
1440-1445
National Gallery, London

In his *Life* of Piero della Francesca, the historiographer Giorgio Vasari wrote that the artist was "*a most diligent student of his art and frequently practised drawing in perspective; he possessed a remarkable knowledge of Euclid*". Piero was in fact renowned among his contemporaries for his intellectual, rationalist approach to art: painting was an integral part of his mathematical investigations, and vice versa, an idea he was to illustrate in his *De prospectiva pingendi*.
This panel, executed for the Chapel of St John the Baptist in the Cathedral of Sansepolcro, is one of the highest expressions of Piero's expository clarity. The geometric plan makes no distinction between figures and objects, subjugating everything to a purely rational order. The elements seem frozen in time: even the River Jordan is transformed by Piero into a pond whose mirror-like surface reflects the sky. The rigorous perspective is accompanied by an otherworldly light which falls uniformly on the entire scene, thus avoiding the traditional creation of hierarchies between elements in the light and elements in the shade. Piero's painting, the result of impassioned research, reads like an open book: monumental, simple and silent, a testament to an artist who until a century ago was marginalized because of his apparent lack of expression, but who now is one of the undisputed pioneers of 15th century painting.

**The Legend
of the True Cross:
The Battle of Heraclius
and Khosrau**
Fresco, 10.8×24.5 ft
c. 1452-1458
San Francesco, Arezzo

This is a very crowded and cruel battle scene, quite different from that between Constantine and Maxentius. The rules of perspective have been modified to accommodate the expressive requirements, so all of the available space is filled with overlapping figures, in a sort of horror vacui that effectively represents the violence of war. In this battle Piero mixed men wearing contemporary armor, with others dressed like Romans, and still others who were not dressed as warriors at all. It seems

clear that the former are the princes of Europe who came to assist the Christian emperor to defeat the pagan army dressed, as might be expected, like Romans. The significance of the men wearing civil garments has not yet been discovered and will require profound studies. This battle too reveals the appeal for an agreement among the Western sovereigns for a Crusade against the Turks.

The last scene of this episode is depicted on the far right, under a large canopy: the Persian king Khosrau kneels before Heraclius, who carries the baton of command, and other men among whom there are other portraits of Bacci family members. Most scholars believe that this was the last panel of the fresco cycle to be completed.

Montefeltro Altarpiece (Madonna and Child with Saints)

Oil on wood, 8.25×5.64 ft
c. 1472-1474
Pinacoteca di Brera, Milan

In spite of numerous studies, exhibitions and publications on the *Montefeltro Altarpiece*, the painting still elicits a wide difference of opinion among art historians. To this day, the date, original location and the occasion for which it was commissioned remains the subject of discussion and conjecture. The work, one of Piero's most celebrated masterpieces, was executed by Piero in the city of Urbino for Duke Federico da Montefeltro, who kneels devoutly in the foreground with hands joined in prayer. His portrayal in a full suit of gleaming armor has led to the theory proposed by some scholars that the altarpiece should be interpreted as a military *ex voto*; others, however, believe that the armor alludes to a joust of 1459, in which the Duke was seriously wounded and almost died. A third hypothesis sees the painting as a thanksgiving for a victory Federico won in Volterra on June 18 1472, obtained through the protection of the Virgin. The significance of the sleeping Christ child, object of veneration of both the Virgin and the Duke and focal point of the entire composition, is also open to debate. Tradition has it that Battista Sforza, the beloved wife of Federico, died in 1472 giving birth to their long-awaited heir to the throne, Guidobaldo. The altarpiece is hence seen by some as a moving tribute by the grieving Duke to his dead wife, whose beauty is recorded for posterity in the perfect face of the Virgin, just as the Christ child is presumed to be a likeness of the baby Guidobaldo. Romantic and persuasive though this reading might be, it seems to be contradicted by historical fact: Battista Sforza apparently died of an illness, possibly pneumonia caught during a hunting party.

ANDREA MANTEGNA

(ISOLA DI CARTURO, PADUA, VENETO 1431 - MANTUA, LOMBARDY 1506)

Andrea Mantegna is first documented as an apprentice in the studio of the Paduan artist Francesco Squarcione, who taught numerous pupils the rudimentary techniques of painting while at the same time instilling in them a deep interest in Classical art. In 1448 Andrea freed himself from his strict contractual obligations to the master, and for the first time took on an independent commission, albeit shared with Nicolò Pizolo: the fresco decoration of the Ovetari family chapel in the church of the Eremitani in Padua. Pizolo subsequently died, leaving Andrea to finish most of the chapel alone, which featured *Scenes from the Life of St James*, with the *Assumption of the Virgin* on the far wall, partly destroyed by bombing in 1944. While continuing his work on the chapel, he also executed other paintings, including the *St Luke Polyptych* (Pinacoteca di Brera, Milan). In 1453 Andrea married Nicolosia, daughter of Jacopo and sister of Giovanni Bellini, thus forging a close link with

the leading artists' studio in Venice of the time. The same period saw him paint the *Altarpiece of St Zeno* for the basilica of the same name in Verona, a composition with a visionary perspectival structure.

Following repeated demands from Duke Ludovico Gonzaga, Andrea transferred to Mantua in 1459 to assume the prestigious role of official court painter. It was here that the versatile master was to execute some of his seminal paintings: as well as the *Death of the Virgin* (Prado, Madrid) and the panels now in the Uffizi (which may originally have been destined for the Duke's chapel in the castle), he worked on the magnificent frescoes of the *Camera degli Sposi* (Bridal Chamber) in the Mantuan Ducal Palace. During his years in Mantua, Andrea also made trips to Florence and Rome, where in 1489 he painted a chapel for Pope Innocent III, now lost; and he further elaborated his Classically inspired pictorial language, as testified by the series of canvases of the *Triumphs of Cae-*

sar (now in Hampton Court Palace, England), which even during their long period of execution were hailed as the most important masterpieces in the collection of the Mantuan court. Andrea retained his position at court with the new Duke and Duchess, Francesco Gonzaga and his wife Isabella d'Este, for whom he painted the *Madonna of Victory* (Louvre, Paris) in 1496; and the *Parnassus: Mars and Venus* (1497) and *Minerva Chasing the Vices from the Garden of Virtue* (1502), both originally for the Duchess's *studiolo* (private apartment), and both now in the Louvre. By this time, Andrea was facing competition from a whole new generation of Italian painters; yet he maintained his authority as elder statesman and old master, and would always be celebrated as the man who articulated the canon of art through the prism of Classical antiquity.

St Luke Polyptych
Tempera on wood,
5.83×7.44 ft
1453-1454
Pinacoteca di Brera, Milan

If it was in Mantua and the court of the Gonzaga that Andrea Mantegna found his fame and glory, it was in Padua that he gained a thorough artistic training and first came into contact with the city university's lively intellectual community. He was commissioned to execute the *St Luke Polyptych* when staying in Padua in 1453, by the Benedictine monks of the Abbey of St

Justina: the work was intended for the altar of St Luke within the saint's chapel, where his remains were kept. In order to guarantee the work's quality, the monks drew up a contract with the painter which is still preserved in the city's Public Archives, stipulating that the young Andrea was to draw all the figures himself, buy the colors for the work (at his own expense), and paint a part of the original frame (now lost) in a vivid blue.

Uffizi Triptych with the Adoration of the Magi, Circumcision and Ascension

Tempera on wood,
central panel: 30.31×29.52 in;
side panels: 33,85×16.6 in
c. 1459-1462
Uffizi, Firenze

Although this work is now presented in the form of a triptych, it was not originally conceived as such: the three panels were only arbitrarily put together in their current neo-Renaissance style frame in 1827. They were first documented separately in the inventory of paintings belonging to Don Antonio de' Medici, son of the Grand Dukes Francis I and Bianca Cappello (1587). Nothing is known of their origin, nor of when they came into the collection of the young Medici; but it is possible that they are the "scenes with some rather small but very beautiful figures" which, according to Vasari (1568), decorated the chapel of the St George Castle in Mantua. If so, this would make these the first works carried out by Andrea for Ludovico Gonzaga after the artist's move to Mantua on the insistence of the Duke. Andrea was to remain in Mantua for the rest of his life, inspired by the flourishing artistic atmosphere both in the city and at court, which was in part a result of its role as seat of the convocation of the council assembled by Pope Pius II Piccolomini in 1459 to check the Turkish advance in the East after the fall of Constantinople. The architectural design of the castle had been drawn up by the Florentine Luca Fancelli, a collaborator of Leon Battista Alberti who sensitively executed the works Alberti planned for the city. Andrea was summoned to paint the interior decorations by virtue of his exceptional talent for evoking Classical antiquity in his work, a quality which would have been particularly appreciated by the court of Gonzaga, an environment steeped in the humanist culture of the ancients. The *Circumcision* in the right hand panel is set within a lavish Classical interior featuring polychrome marble, Classical reliefs and sculptural elements; while the dazzling use of color in the *Adoration of the Magi* and the *Ascension* are a perfect complement to the compositions' dramatic staging.

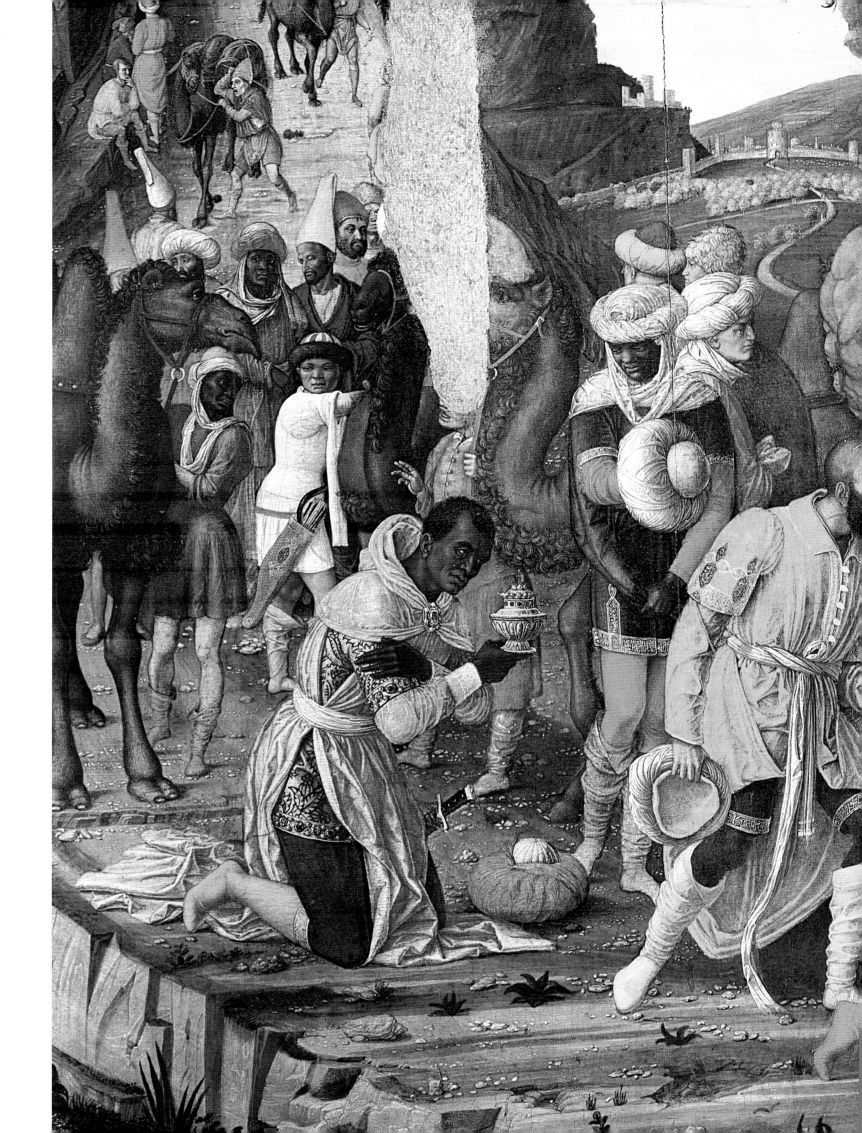

Dead Christ

Tempera on canvas,
26×31.9 in
c. 1470-1480
Pinacoteca di Brera, Milan

For over forty years, Andrea Mantegna was the undisputed master of the artistic scene in Mantua, his prodigious talent winning him the support of three generations of Gonzaga. The *Dead Christ* was one of many masterpieces executed during his Mantuan period. There is little other information on the work, its date or for whom it was painted: but it is evident that Andrea was particularly attached to it, and it is recorded as having been one of the works he bequeathed to his son Ludovico. The canvas's subsequent history is also checkered: at one point it was sent from Mantua to Ferrara, and from here made its way to Rome at the start of the 17th century, where it was documented in the collection of the Aldobrandini family until the early 19th century, when it finally entered the Pinacoteca di Brera in Milan in 1824. The painting is considered to be one of the finest expressions of Andrea's artistic genius: the virtuoso use of perspective in the dramatically foreshortened figure of the dead Christ creates a startling, almost violent effect, adding to the deeply moving atmosphere of the picture.

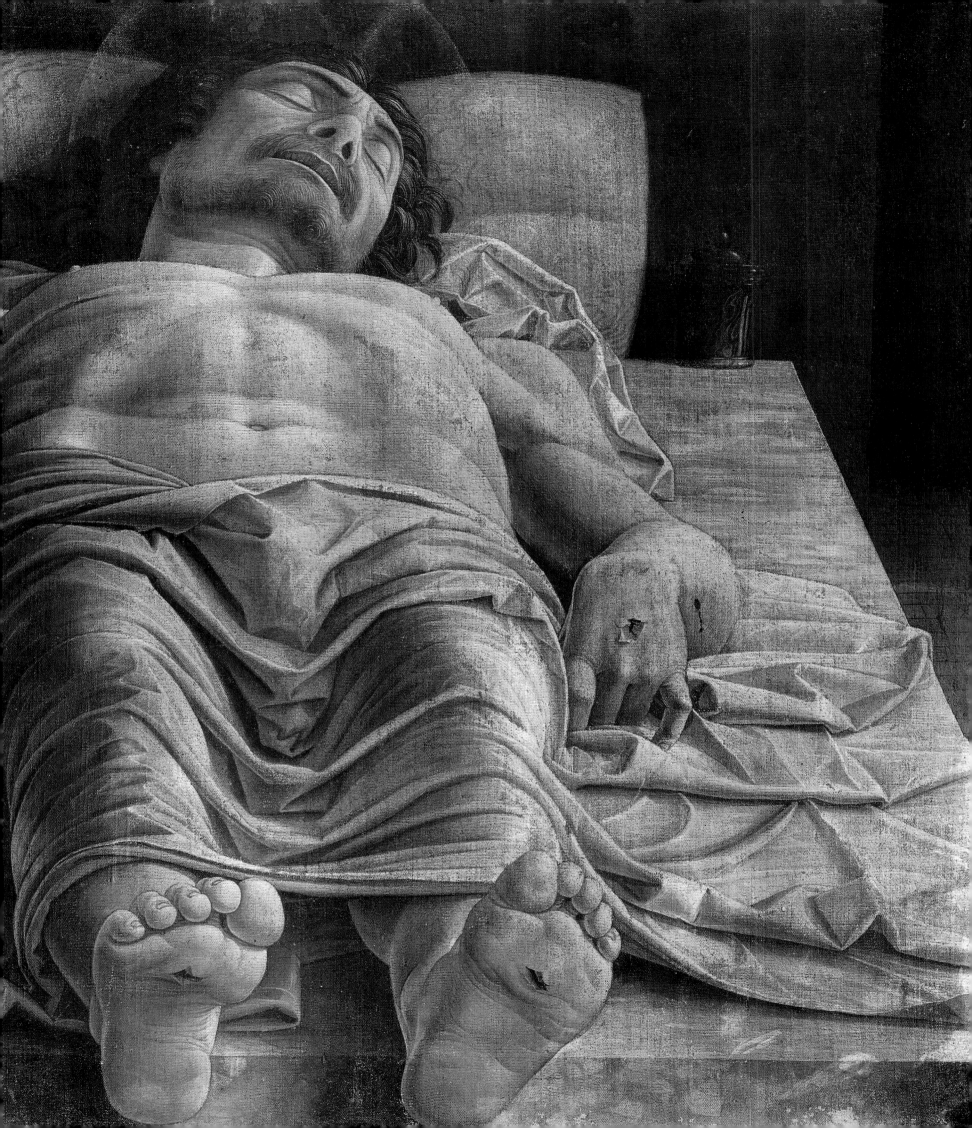

HANS MEMLING

(SELIGENSTADT, HESSE, C. 1435 - BRUGES 1494)

Hans Memling is first documented in Bruges in 1465, where he enjoyed a long career and worked for a number of agents of Italian banking families who were conducting their business in the Flemish city. Among these was the Florentine Tommaso Portinari, an associate of the Medici bank's branch in Bruges, for whom Memling painted a double portrait (*Tommaso Portinari and his Wife*, Metropolitan Museum, New York), and a panel featuring *Scenes from the Passion of Christ* now in the Galleria Sabauda, Turin. Another Florentine, Angelo Tani, who like Portinari worked for the Medici bank, commissioned the *Last Judgement Triptych* (Muzeum Narodowe, Gdansk), which was directly inspired by the painting of the same subject by Rogier van der Weyden, generally considered to be the younger artist's master. Memling was without doubt resoundingly successful: in 1474 he was admitted to Bruges's most prestigious guild, and by the end of his career he was one of the city's richest burghers. His style was brilliant yet measured, characterized by a radiant chromatic palette and the confident use of pictorial space, especially striking in mature works such as the *Mystic Marriage of St Catherine*, the *Triptych of Adriaan Reins* and the *St Christopher* (or *Moreel Triptych*) of 1484, all in the Memlingmuseum, Bruges. As a portrait artist in particular, Memling proved himself the heir to the previous generation's extraordinary Flemish masters, Rogier van der Weyden and Jan van Eyck, who exerted the most obvious influence on the younger painter: this is evident in works such as the *Diptych of Maarten Nieuwenhove* of 1487 (Memlingmuseum, Bruges), a portrait of exceptional sophistication. The work Memling undertook for his Florentine patrons helped spread his fame to Italy, where his portraiture was compared with that of the generation which had produced Sandro Botticelli and Antonello da Messina. Meanwhile, his devotional art reached its pinnacle in works such as the *Lamentation* (Galleria Doria Pamphilj, Rome) and the lively, engaging narratives exemplified by the *St Ursula Shrine* (Memlingmuseum, Bruges).

The Last Judgement Triptych
Oil on wood, 87×24 in
1467-1471
Muzeum Narodowe, Gdansk

In the central panel Christ the Judge is seated on a rainbow, surrounded by the twelve Apostles and by Mary and St John the Baptist, intercessors on behalf of humanity. Angels in flight display the instruments of the Passion and sound the trumpets of the Apocalypse. Alongside Christ, who is showing his wounds (to be saved it was necessary to have embraced the Christian faith, which was made manifest in the marks of the

Passion), the lily of innocence is set above his gesture of benediction, while the sword of justice corresponds to the gesture of his left hand, turned downwards. The rainbow separates the two worlds; on the plane of the Earth the Archangel Michael, at the boundary between the green meadow and the bare ground, weighs the souls. The damned are herded by black demons toward Hell, represented on the right wing of the triptych, while the souls of the blessed are welcomed by St Peter into Heaven, on the left wing. In stylistic terms, the figure of Christ is an almost exact copy of the Christ in a polyptych by Rogier van der Weyden (this is the only time in Memling's career that he would reproduce another artist's work so faithfully). The painter has taken great care in rendering the perspective, the light, and the reflections (especially on the globe and on the archangel's armor). Many of the blessed have realistic features, suggesting that some donors had requested that their portraits be inserted into the painting. The colorful history of the triptych, painted around 1467-1471, began with its commission by Angelo Tani, director of the branch of the bank owned by the Florentine family of the Medici in Bruges, probably on the occasion of his marriage to Caterina Tanagli, as the representation of the clients on the outer shutters of the wings suggests. It must have been intended for the Tani Chapel dedicated to St Michael in the Badia of Fiesole near Florence, a church that the Medici had built to celebrate the glory of their family and the

power of the bank: in fact all the chapels in the south aisle were set aside for its agents. Tani was not reappointed, however, and in 1465 his place was taken by Tommaso Portinari, who provided the Burgundian court with large sums of money and was in exchange authorized to levy duties on the import of wool into the Low Countries. Portinari is the man portrayed on the balance on the side of the blessed: his head has been painted over the one that was there before, suggesting that he may have contributed to the financing of the picture. Portinari also acquired three unused galleys from the duke of Burgundy and converted them into merchant ships flying the Burgundian flag but crewed by Italians. In 1473 Memling's *Last Judgement* was loaded on board the galley San Matteo, destined for England with a cargo of merchandise from Italy: alum, gold brocade, satin, damask and gold thread. But the vessel was attacked by a warship of the Hanseatic League commanded by the privateer Paul Benecke, who took part of the booty to Gdansk. Among the spoils was the triptych, which was donated to the city's cathedral. The adventures of the altarpiece were not over yet: in 1806 it was requisitioned by Napoleon's troops, taken to Paris and hung in the Louvre, then called the Musée Napoléon. Attributed at that time to Jan van Eyck, it was much admired by visitors.

Seven Joys of Mary

Oil on wood, 31.9×74.4 in
1480
Alte Pinakothek, Munich

In spite of its traditional title, the painting does not only illustrate the "Seven Joys of the Virgin" (or the principle episodes of her life, from the Annunciation to the Assumption), but also scenes pertaining to the life of Christ. The scenes might more accurately be described as "vignettes" without diminishing the importance of Memling's monumental work, one of the most ambitious and compelling masterpieces of 15ᵗʰ century Flemish art. The painting reprises the narrative, miniaturist style of his *Scenes from the Passion of Christ* of ten years earlier, now in Turin. It was commissioned by a married couple named Bultync, represented at the far left and right hand side of the panel, who donated it to the Guild of Tanners of Bruges in 1480 (as originally recorded in the frame which is now lost). The panel remained in the guild's chapel in the Church of our Lady until around 1780, and its location

behind the main altar of a church dedicated to the Virgin explains the choice of iconography. The high line of the horizon allowed Memling to unfold the episodes in the main body of his composition without interruption. These are arranged in a "u-shaped" sequence, which begins in the top left of the picture with the *Annunciation of the Virgin* and winds down to the *Nativity* at the bottom before reaching the center and focal point of the painting with the *Adoration of the Magi*; the narrative then curves upwards to the *Journey of the Magi* and finally culminates in the *Death of the Virgin*, whose position mirrors the painting's physical departure point. The recurring blue of the Virgin's garments and the carefully chosen palette limited to a few bright colors creates a stylistic link between the episodes which aids the clarity and legibility of the work as a whole, as do the figures' natural poses and movements, devoid of any artificiality. The different elements combine to create an extraordinarily considered work, whose many different scenes are unified in the warm afternoon light.

SANDRO BOTTICELLI
SANDRO FILIPEPI
(FLORENCE, 1445-1510)

Botticelli's earliest paintings are linked to the prestigious studio of Filippo Lippi, although by 1467 he was attached to Andrea Verrocchio's workshop, where some of the most influential painters of the Florentine Renaissance trained (including Leonardo da Vinci). The artist's most durable bond, however, which lasted throughout his long career, was with the powerful Medici family. The standard he painted for Giuliano de' Medici for the joust of 1475 was lauded by the poet Agnolo Poliziano; but he derived his inspiration above all from the refined humanist circle of Lorenzo the Magnificent. Under Lorenzo's patronage, Botticelli painted his exquisite series of portraits (including *Giuliano de' Medici* in the National Gallery of Art, Washington, and the *Young Man with a Medal* in the Uffizi, Florence), as well as the *Adoration of the Magi* (Uffizi, Florence) which included portraits of the leading Medici males. The family also commissioned the famous *Primavera* or *Spring* from him in 1478, whose sophisticated iconography reflected the learned cultural environment of the Florentine court.

Botticelli was summoned to Rome in 1481 to paint a number of *Scenes from the Life of Moses* in the Sistine Chapel, together with one *Scene from the Life of Christ* (the *Temptation of Christ*) and some papal portraits. These frescoes exemplify Botticelli's art at its most classical, in which he achieved a perfect balance between naturalism and formal abstraction. This same balance is evident in works after 1480, like the *Adoration of the Magi* in the National Gallery of Art, Washington, and the *Madonna of the Book* (Museo Poldi Pezzoli, Milan). The *Birth of Venus* (Uffizi, Florence) on the other hand, is informed by a different internal dynamic, and the search for a new mode of expression to reflect the profound religious tension Botticelli was experiencing at the time: his growing dissatisfaction with humanism is also apparent in the *Altarpiece of St Mark* of *c.* 1490, and the *Calumny of Apelles* (both in the Uffizi, Florence). The disjointed rhythm and complex symbolism of the *Calumny* echoes the sense of alienation from contemporary culture that Botticelli experienced towards the end of his life.

Madonna of the Magnificat

Tempera on wood,
diameter 46.45 in
1480-1481
Uffizi, Florence

With the words *Magnificat anima mea dominum* ("My soul magnifies the Lord"), the Virgin begins her song of thanks and praise to God when she goes to visit her cousin Elizabeth, who is pregnant with St John the Baptist. In Botticelli's magnificent *tondo*, Mary is writing this same prayer (as told in the Gospel of St Luke) in a book held open by angels, and for this reason the painting is known as the *Madonna of the Magnificat*. The left hand page of the book also contains a reference to the biblical episode of the Visitation: here some words can be made out of the prophetic canticle of Zachariah, the husband of Elizabeth, concerning the birth of their son John the Baptist. The various references to the Baptist, Florence's venerated patron saint, suggest that it was commissioned by a Florentine patron; while the circular shape, typical of panels found in antechambers or bedrooms, may indicate that it was meant for private devotion. These are only hypotheses, however, since the painting is not documented until 1784, when Ottavio Magherini sold it to the Uffizi. Botticelli's adaptation of the religious subject to the *tondo* form is unusual and attractive: the figures are masterfully reflected as if in a convex mirror. The Virgin's smooth contours are perfectly molded to the picture's circular shape, and the Christ child follows his mother's curves by arching himself into her lap. The Madonna and child's hands meet elegantly on the open book, which marks both the physical and spiritual center of the composition, reminding us of the future fulfillment of the prophecy of the Baptist; while the pomegranate they both hold in their left hands prefigures the Passion of Christ. At either side of the Virgin, two angels crown her as Queen of Heaven, while beyond the round window a serene landscape with a river unfolds into the distance. The superbly executed painting was reproduced several times by Botticelli's studio: there are at least five existing works with the same theme by his pupils.

Primavera

Tempera on canvas,
80×123.6 in
c. 1478-1482
Uffizi, Florence

Botticelli did not accept perspective as the key to the comprehension and representation of the world, and skeptically distorted it in his works. He preferred the symbolic language of myth and serene contemplation of ideal beauty. Botticelli's work exalted the Florentine tradition of drawing, based on the supple and elegant contours that sought to recreate the purity of antique vase painting, but denied the depth of space theorized by the early humanists, and preferred to positioned figures freely against a background animated by an intense though subdued sense of musicality. The subjects, drawn from the ancient texts of Lucretius, Ovid and Horace, were treated with modern sensibility, similar to the poetry of Agnolo Poliziano, another important protagonist at the scholarly court of Lorenzo, and depicted as figures drawn from ancient Greek mythology. Zefiro, the green breeze of Spring, blows into the little stand of orange trees from the right and embraces the fertile figure of Flora, who is transformed into Springtime and strews flowers on the ground. Venus, silent and sweet, watches as the three Graces, the goddesses of beauty and harmony, join hands to dance. In the meantime Mercury dissipates the last clouds of winter. A blindfolded Eros shoots his arrow of love from above. Commissioned by Lorenzo for a cousin between 1478 and 1482, this work was originally intended for the Medici palace on Via Larga in Florence. Later it was taken to the villa at Castello where Vasari documented its presence.

Birth of Venus

Tempera on canvas,
68.11×110 in
c. 1484
Uffizi, Florence

The goddess Venus stands before us on her shell, graceful and remote as an ancient statue and resplendent in her nudity, as the winds gently blow her across the foamy white waves to the shore. This luminous picture is one of the most celebrated in the history of art, and yet nothing is known of its creation. It was first recorded by Giorgio Vasari in the mid 16th century as being located in the Medici villa of Castello, along with the equally famous *Primavera* (*Spring*). The villa then belonged to Cosimo I, who may have bought the painting himself or else inherited it from his ancestors, members of a side branch of the Medici family. Among these was Lorenzo di Pierfrancesco, a refined collector and one-time owner of the *Primavera*, who may also have commissioned the *Birth of Venus* from Botticelli for his country villa. The painting closely follows a famous passage from the *Stanze* of Agnolo Poliziano, the favorite poet of Lorenzo the Magnificent: it does not illustrate the birth of the goddess from the sea (as the misleading 19th century title suggests), but her landing on the island of Cyprus. The painting's seascape background is rendered with extreme simplicity, and none of the rich detail found in the *Primavera*. All the attention is concentrated on the dazzling beauty of Venus, goddess of love, who is propelled to the shore by the passionate breath of the intertwined lovers to her left, the winds Zephyrus and Aura. The girl who receives her is one of the Horae, chaste maids of Venus. She holds up an exquisite pink cloak embroidered with spring flowers, which complements her own fine dress embroidered with roses and myrtle, flowers sacred to the goddess. In the Neoplatonic culture of 15th century Florence, which Botticelli and Poliziano both reflected in their work, nudity was not meant as a pagan, carnal exaltation of feminine beauty, but rather as the ideal of *humanitas*, or spiritual beauty composed of purity, simplicity and nobility of spirit.

HIERONYMUS BOSCH

JEROEN ANTHONISZOON VAN AEKEN
('s-HERTOGENBOSCH, NORTH BRABANT c. 1450-1516)

The son and grandson of painters, Hieronymus Bosch trained in the family studio and spent his entire career in his native town of Bois-le-Duc, a relative backwater compared with the major artistic cities of the Netherlands. Although there is little biographical information on the painter, he was known to have maintained close contact with the leading cultural and artistic centers of his time. Works such as the *Seven Deadly Sins* (Prado, Madrid), the *Marriage Feast at Cana* (Museum Boijmans Van Beuningen, Rotterdam) and the *Crucifixion* (Musées Royaux des Beaux-Arts, Brussels) are believed to belong to his early period; and while the themes are traditional, the paintings are distinctive for their unusually lively handling of color, and the almost sculptural quality of the drapery. Bosch took his inspiration from a wide variety of iconographic sources, figurative and literary, didactic and popular; and from his earliest works, his predilection for mysterious and disquieting subjects was obvious, an interest which would continue into his mature period in works like the *Ship of Fools* (Louvre, Paris) and the *Garden of Earthly Delights* (Prado, Madrid). Bosch reached the pinnacle of his expressive powers in these paintings, introducing a complex and ambiguous system of symbols through which he sought to denounce the folly of a world hurtling towards physical ruin and spiritual damnation. The artist's dream world is populated by visions, diabolical images and monstrous metamorphoses. His late works treated more traditional religious themes, such as the *Epiphany* in the center of the Madrid triptych, but they still displayed the Flemish artist's fervent imagination. Bosch's paintings were highly prized by contemporary collectors, and in the 19ᵗʰ century were subject to psychoanalytical interpretations.

Christ Carrying the Cross
Oil on wood, 22.44×12.6 in
c. 1490-1500
Kunsthistorisches Museum, Vienna

This visionary panel painting is one of Hieronymus Bosch's finest masterpieces, and a seminal work in the history of early 16ᵗʰ century Flemish art. Christ's ascent to Calvary is depicted in a startlingly original way: the simple, stark background contrasts with the chaotic, crowded foreground, which is divided into two separate areas one on top of the other. In the upper section Christ carries his heavy cross accompanied by a vicious throng of grotesque figures who gesticulate violently. To increase his suffering, pieces of wood have been nailed to Christ's calves, a common punishment in Flemish representations of the ascent to Calvary. The lower section depicts two thieves, in a scene not mentioned in the Gospel: the bad thief on the left hand side is tightly bound, while his counterpart on the right, the good thief, is shown kneeling in front of a monk to whom he confesses his sins. By including the monk in his picture, Bosch updates the biblical episode to his own era, the early 16ᵗʰ century, thus underlining its eternal and immutable message. At the same time, he reinforces the Church's position as the heir to Christ's authority: through its ministers (the monk) and sacraments (the good thief's confession), the Church has the power to forgive or punish men, just as Jesus forgave and punished the two thieves from the cross. The panel, which was badly damaged by being cut at several points, is all that remains of the left section of a lost altarpiece which featured a crucifixion scene in the center. During its 1923 restoration, a number of details were revealed which had previously been hidden by layers of paint added subsequently: on the back of the picture, the figure of a nude boy emerged whose meaning is still open to interpretation; and in the main scene, the background landscape and the tree which the good thief is tied to were uncovered.

Triptych of the Garden of Earthly Delights

Oil on wood, 86.61×76.77 in
1503-1504
Prado, Madrid

The oldest source which mentions this painting, the Spanish *History of the Order of St Jerome* of 1605, refers to its title as *Of the vain glory and ephemeral taste of the strawberry or strawberry-tree*. The fruit in fact appears in the central panel, but modern scholars prefer to use the more generic title of the *Garden of Earthly Delights*. Whatever its name, no single interpretation has yet been able to clarify every detail of its complex symbolism. This said, the picture is highly likely to be of religious significance, rather than the simple product of the painter's over-active imagination, as has been suggested without taking into account the culture and mentality of the period. The *History* quoted above also mentions that Bosch's works were highly regarded by the devoutly Catholic Philip II of Spain, in that they illustrated *"a painted satire on the sins and frenzied urges of men"*. In spite of the difficulty of interpreting the picture, it is evident that the different parts of the triptych are intimately connected. The exterior and interior of the panel complete each other: the two side shutters, when closed, depict the creation of the world, and function as an introduction to the next scene (the first one the viewer sees when the shutters are opened), that is the *Earthly Paradise*. The landscape extends from this first side panel to the central panel, creating a coherent continuum of pictorial space and content. The final image is unanimously recognized as Hell. In the theological context of the time, the only possible relationship between Earthly Paradise (first scene) and Hell (third scene) must have been sin: the mysterious figures in the central panel can therefore be taken to represent sin in general, and lust in particular.

The Haywain Triptych

Oil on wood, 53.14×39.37 in
1503-1512
Prado, Madrid

One of Bosch's greatest admirers was Philip II of Spain. Although he loved gravity and decorum, solemnity and order, he was nonetheless enchanted by the imaginative compositions of the Flemish painter, understanding that (as written in his biography) Bosch should be considered as "*a devout orthodox who portrayed our vices, painting men not as they appear, but as they really are*". The king acquired the *Triptych of the Haywain* from Felipe de Guevara in around 1570. It was probably inspired by an old Flemish proverb which goes, "The world is a haywain from which everyone takes what they can". The central panel depicts a frenzied crowd of figures greedily trying to reach the hay, emblematic of worldly riches and pleasures: though transitory, the people stop at nothing, including violence and bullying, to get to them. As with the *Garden of Earthly Delights*, there is a tight unity of space and content linking the three

scenes of the open panels. The left hand panel contains well-known biblical episodes: the fall of the rebel angels, the creation of Eve, original sin and the expulsion of Adam and Eve from Earthly Paradise. The scheme continues logically, following on from original sin to the central panel where men and women are depicted in their morbid craving for material

goods, leading lives of pleasure that will inevitably end in their damnation: a group of demons and monsters drag the haywain towards the right, where the eternal torment of Hell awaits (right hand panel). Because of his damning indictment of worldly vices, Bosch has often been seen as the forerunner of a number of ideas central to the

Protestant Reformation, so it is interesting to note how much he was admired by the arch Catholic Philip II, who of all the European sovereigns was the greatest supporter of the Counter Reformation.

LEONARDO DA VINCI

(VINCI, FLORENCE 1452 - CHÂTEAU DE CLOUX, AMBOISE, CENTRE 1519)

The son of notary Piero da Vinci, Leonardo was educated at his paternal grandfather's house until 1469, when he followed his father to Florence and joined the workshop of Andrea del Verrocchio. In 1472 he was admitted to the Florentine artists' Guild of St Luke, while remaining attached to Verrocchio's studio: this period saw him rapidly master a range of artistic techniques, collaborating closely with his teacher on works such as the *Baptism of Christ* (Uffizi, Florence). As an independent artist, he became a leading figure in the contemporary Florentine school which included Antonio Pollaiolo and the young Sandro Botticelli, executing early masterpieces such as the *Annunciation* in the Uffizi and the *Portrait of Ginevra Benci* (National Gallery, Washington). In 1481, the monks of San Donato in Scopeto commissioned him to paint the celebrated *Adoration of the Magi* (Uffizi, Florence): although the work remained unfinished after Leonardo left for Milan, its original and highly complex compositional structure bears witness to the young artist's visionary style, which marked a radical departure from the more traditional exponents of Tuscan painting. Leonardo arrived in Milan in the summer of 1482, having been summoned to the court of Ludovico il Moro, in whose service he would remain for almost twenty years. His first Milanese commission was for other clients, however: the Confraternity of the Immaculate Conception, for whom he executed the *Virgin of the Rocks*, the central panel of a polyptych. One of his major tasks for Ludovico il Moro was to design and execute an equestrian monument to commemorate Francesco Sforza, an ongoing project which Leonardo never completed; at the same time, he was occupied with a variety of other jobs for the Milanese court, spanning the diverse fields of military engineering, hydraulics and urban planning, as well as inventing machines for celebrations, jousts and shows. Throughout the 1490s Leonardo was also involved in the lengthy painting of the *Last Supper* in the refectory of the convent of Santa Maria delle Grazie in Milan, a work which was to have an extraordinary impact on Renaissance art for the solemn monumentality of its composition and for its imaginative reworking of a traditional religious subject. The cultural environment of the Milanese court fostered Leonardo's restless experimental genius, which was directed towards a myriad of different artistic and scientific endeavors. Following the fall of Ludovico il Moro, Leonardo fled from Milan and was briefly engaged as a military engineer by Cesare Borgia, before returning to Florence in 1503. Here, in the same year, he began the portrait of a lady known as the *Mona Lisa*, and was also commissioned to paint the now lost *Battle of Anghiari* in the Salone dei Cinquecento in Florence's Palazzo della Signoria, a work which started to deteriorate even before it was finished, but which was to become the model for an entire generation of Florentine artists, along with its companion piece, also lost, by his younger rival Michelangelo (the *Battle of Cascina*). Leonardo was in Milan a second time from 1506, until he transferred to Rome in 1513; here, however, he distanced himself from the magnificent Papal Court, which was dominated at that time by Raphael and Michelangelo. The aging artist then accepted an invitation from King Francis I of France, who installed him in the Château de Cloux at Amboise, and lavished honors on him until his death in 1519.

Lady with Ermine,
1485-1490.
Czartoryski Muzeum,
Kraków.

198

Virgin of the Rocks

Oil on wood, 78.35×48.03 in
1486-1490
Louvre, Paris

Leonardo started work on the first version of the painting in 1483, when the Confraternity of the Immaculate Conception commissioned an altarpiece for their chapel in the Milanese church of San Francesco Grande. The master was to paint the central part of the altarpiece with an image of the Virgin, while the execution of the side panels was entrusted to the De Predis brothers, who painted two *Angels Playing Musical Instruments*. However, the dating of Leonardo's painting is still uncertain, and oscillates between 1486 and 1490. It also seems that the picture was never delivered to the clients but remained instead in the studio of Leonardo, who in 1493 received an offer for it from a French collector and agreed to sell it at a higher price than the one initially established in the contract with the confraternity. The circumstances by which the painting arrived in the collections of the King of France and was subsequently hung in the Louvre are still a mystery. The altar of the Milanese church was adorned with a second version of the painting, probably begun after Leonardo had sold the original one and finished by 1499, during his first stay in Milan, or perhaps during his second visit to the city, in 1508. The panel was later sold to the Scottish painter Gavin Hamilton and after a few years was finally brought to the National Gallery of London (1880). Instead of the subject that had been commissioned from him (the Virgin between angels and

two prophets), Leonardo painted the Virgin with the infant John the Baptist adoring the Christ child and accompanied by an angel. This theme does not appear in the bible, but echoes the preaching of a well-known Florentine friar of the 14th century, Domenico Cavalca: on their return from the flight into Egypt, the Holy Family encounters the infant John the Baptist in the desert; John pays homage to Jesus, who blesses him and prophesies his baptism, something to which the water in the foreground of the Louvre version seems to allude. The meeting between the two children provided Leonardo with the cue for a composition based on a refined exchange of glances, denoting a level of

psychological insight highly unusual for the time. This is one of the very few paintings of the period in which the Christ child and the infant St John appear together. The iconographic theme was to return in other Florentine works by Leonardo and would later be taken up by both Michelangelo and Raphael. There are several differences between the versions in the Louvre and the National Gallery: in the English painting the angel does not point to John, unlike the French version; the haloes and John's cross are missing from the French version, and may not in fact be Leonardo's work but 18th-century additions. In general, in the National Gallery version the centrality of the Virgin and child is reasserted

while the role of the Baptist is diminished, as requested by the members of the confraternity. The painting is known as the *Virgin of the Rocks* because of the natural setting that forms its backdrop: this was perfect for the chapel in which it was to be located, as it had been erected on top of the Christian catacombs.

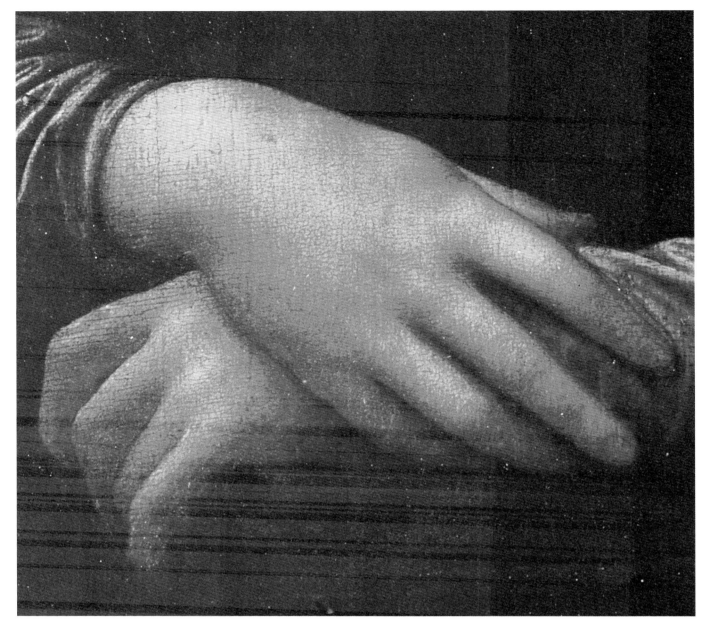

Mona Lisa

Oil on wood, 30.31×20.86 in
1503-1504 and 1510-1515
Louvre, Paris

Perhaps the most celebrated painting of all time, the *Mona Lisa* was brought to France by Leonardo himself. On seeing it, the French King Francis I immediately resolved to have it at any cost, and finally bought it for four thousand ducats. The painting remained in the private collections of the French monarchy until Napoleon had it removed to the Louvre in Paris. It was from here that Vincenzo Perugia, an Italian decorator employed by the museum, stole the picture in August 1911 and carried it back with him to Italy. Having reached Florence, he tried to sell it to an antique dealer, but was immediately caught out: the dealer informed the regional arts Bureau and Perugia ended up in prison. Once recovered, the *Mona Lisa* was exhibited for a short period in Florence, Rome and Milan, before being returned to France. The sensation caused by the theft only added to the painting's fame and mystique, which has remained undiminished ever since. The *Mona Lisa* is universally considered to be the ideal portrait painting, an exquisite blend of outward harmony and composure balanced with inner psychological depth; yet the woman's serene smile belies the deeper concerns of the passionate artist who created her. Leonardo kept the painting close to him all his life, and in a certain sense it came to represent his intense internal dialogue on painting and the world around him. The master's incessant quest for perfection, and his constant need to give his ideas substance, led him to retouch the portrait continually, and it remained a "work in progress" practically until the end of his life. All of Leonardo's innovative ideas and theoretical beliefs converged in this one picture, which became the prime vehicle for affirming the central idea of his philosophy: that the face was a mirror to the soul, and the portrait was its most direct artistic reflection. The face of the *Mona Lisa* attracted attention from the very first. Giorgio Vasari wrote of how Leonardo used every trick to tease out his model's smile (whom he identified as monna Lisa, the wife of the Florentine Francesco del Giocondo), amusing her with music and jokes while he painted, until he finally managed to obtain "*a smile so pleasing that it seems more divine than human*".

ART OF THE BENIN KINGDOM

(NIGERIA, 16ᵀᴴ CENTURY)

The famous bronze plaques of Benin (of which over nine hundred have been found) would at one time have decorated the pillars of the palace. Their rectangular shape, and the presence of different related figures which sometimes interconnect to form whole scenes, recall the illustrations in European books; and the plaques may indeed have been influenced by the kingdom's contact with Europe, although they do not appear to have a narrative content. The figures represented are mostly kings, leaders and attendants in ritual poses. The cosmological references to Olokun, god of the sea, may also be linked to the Portuguese presence in the 16th century, and can be seen in the geometric motifs engraved in the background: quatrefoils, crosses within circles, and rosettes, which refer to the four cardinal points, the four days of the Edo people's week, and the journey of the sun across the sky, associated with Olokun because it sets in the sea. The birth of the Benin Kingdom in the 13th-14th centuries predates the arrival of the Europeans, and Benin art also carries evidence of the people's trans-Saharan cultural exchanges, for example in the archeological findings of cowry shells (from the Indian Ocean) and glass beads, as well as the copper used in the bronze work.

As with the Ife art that preceded it, the bronze heads made for royal altars were of central symbolic importance as representations of power. Originally thought to have been commemorative, a more recent hypothesis has suggested that the heads functioned as war trophies, modeled after the defunct heads of their most dangerous enemies; these would then be displayed on war altars, or sent to the successors of their defeated adversaries as an intimidating deterrent. As with the bronze plaques and the heads of the queen mothers, these bronzes heads date back to the 15th and 16th centuries, a period of great expansion for the Benin Kingdom coinciding with the arrival of the Portuguese. Their stylistic diversity has been interpreted chronologically as a passage from the early preoccupation with naturalism (perhaps influenced by Ife art), to a progressive stylization, characterized by the stiffening of facial features, the elongation of the neck, and the increase in decorative and symbolic elements.

Figure of a Messenger
Bronze, h. 25.60 in
Second half of the
16th century
National Museum, Lagos

The objects worn and carried by this figure identify him as a representative of authority and highlight the close link between the power of the Benin Kingdom and the profitable trade relationship it enjoyed with the Portuguese. One of the motifs on the skirt is in fact that of a Portuguese head, and the cross on his chest also probably relates to the Portuguese. There may be a number of different symbolic associations attached to the cross, since it already belonged to the cosmology of the local peoples. The scarifications resembling "cat's whiskers", which start at the mouth and rise towards the ears, have been interpreted as the marks of a secret society, although they may instead relate to the Benin Kingdom's contact with their neighbor Kingdom of Nupe to the north, where these scarifications have been documented. In his left hand, the figure carries a ritual tool, a kind of hammer, which may act as an amulet placing the holder under the protection of Ogun, the god of iron and war.

This type of figure has traditionally been regarded as a messenger of the *oni* of Ife, sent to Benin to pay tribute to the accession of the new *oba*. The facial features, with large almond-shaped eyes, full mouth and flared nostrils, are typical of the Benin style.

Head of a Queen Mother
Brass, h. 21 in
16th century
National Museum, Lagos

The city Kingdom of Benin was ruled by a deified king, whose dynasty had foreign origins: it is thought that the first monarch came from Ife, sent by the elders who had grown tired of the misrule of the preceding dynasty. The king's "foreignness" contributed to the sanctity of his power in the eyes of the Benin people. According to a number of oral traditions, the first king also brought with him the technique of bronze smelting from Ife. In reality the relationship between Benin, Ife and Igbo-Ukwu has yet to be completely established. The powers of the *oba* were far-reaching and included the legislative, executive and judiciary speres. He had the authority to decree state executions, and he also owned all the land in the Kingdom, as well as having a monopoly over foreign trade. The mother of the sovereign was given the official title of "Queen Mother", and allowed to govern a district just outside of the city, with the power to confer titles and offices in her own court. Commemorative bronze heads would be placed on the altar dedicated to her, featuring a characteristic elongated headdress, made from coral beads, which would be wound around the beak-like hairstyle worn only by the queen mother. In the power structure of the Kingdom of Benin, an important distinction was made between the head of the palace and the head of the city. The latter represented the interests of the people outside of the dynastic line. This potential conflict was expressed symbolically through different animals: the formidable leopard for the authority of the king, and the scaly anteater for the head of the city; while the anteater was a docile creature, its scales could resist a leopard's assault.

ALBRECHT DÜRER

(NUREMBERG, BAVARIA 1471-1528)

The son of a goldsmith, Albrecht Dürer was first apprenticed to his father's workshop, where he learnt the technique of engraving with the burin. From 1486-1490 he moved to the studio of Michael Wolgemut and Wilhelm Pleydenwurff, specialists in woodcut engraving. A first trip to Venice in 1494-1495 enabled Dürer to broaden his knowledge of Classical and Italian Renaissance art, particularly that of Andrea Mantegna and Giovanni Bellini, whose influence can be felt in the Italianate *Dresden Altarpiece* (Gemäldegalerie, Dresden) and the *Seven Sorrows of the Virgin* (now split between the Gemäldegalerie, Dresden and the Alte Pinakothek, Munich), both painted for Frederick the Wise, Elector of Saxony, and the *Madonna and Child* in the National Gallery of Art, Washington. In 1495 Dürer opened his own workshop in Nuremberg, and became justly famous for his woodcut series of the *Apocalypse* (1498) and the *Great Passion*, works which clearly revealed his debt to the great engraver Martin Schongauer. During this period Dürer also immortalized himself in a series of self-portraits which affirmed a self-conscious pride in his identity as artist: the *Self-Portrait at 22* of 1493 (Louvre, Paris), the *Self-Portrait at 26* (Prado, Madrid) and the haunting *Self-Portrait in a Fur-Collared Robe* of 1500 (Alte Pinakothek, Munich). His interest in the problems of spatial representation, which had matured during his visit to Italy, found its expression above all in religious paintings such as the *Paumgartner Altarpiece* (Alte Pinakothek, Munich) and the *Adoration of the Magi* (Uffizi, Florence), even though these were resolved in a typically northern European style. Between 1505 and 1506 the artist was again in Venice, where the city's German community commissioned him to paint the spectacular *Feast of the Rose Garlands* altarpiece for the church of St Bartholomew (now in the Narodni Gallery, Prague). Following his return to Nuremberg, Dürer executed another series of works which drew stylistically on his Italian experiences, particularly in the *sfumato* technique of

the background landscapes, such as the *Martyrdom of the Ten Thousand* and the *Adoration of the Trinity* (both in the Kunsthistorisches Museum, Vienna). Dürer's seminal allegorical engravings *Knight, Death and the Devil* and *Melencolia I* also belong to this period. From 1512 the artist was in the service of the Emperor Maximilian I, for whom he painted two portraits (in Vienna and Nuremberg). After the death of the sovereign, Dürer made an important journey to Holland to witness the coronation of Charles V and seek his patronage, and came into contact with contemporary northern artists,

of whom Lucas von Leyden left a particularly lasting impression. On Dürer's death, he bequeathed his monumental painting of the *Four Apostles* to his home town of Nuremberg (Alte Pinakothek, Munich), a work at the apex of his stylistic development and also a testament to his profound religious beliefs. Dürer's astonishing artistic genius achieved a perfect fusion between the virtuoso rendering of detail and imaginative flair of the northern European school, and the handling of color, form and spatial perspective characteristic of Italian painting.

Paumgartner Altarpiece: Nativity with St George and St Eustace

Oil on wood, 61.82×98.40 in
1498-1504
Alte Pinakothek, Munich

This altarpiece was commissioned by the brothers Stephan and Lukas Paumgartner to commemorate their father Martin Paumgartner, who had died in 1478. The two young clients are represented in the side panels of the triptych in the guise of St George (Stephan) and St Eustace (Lukas), while their father is painted in miniature at the bottom left of the central panel, together with his sons. Their mother, who had also recently died, and sisters are all depicted opposite, at the bottom right. This is one of the first works Dürer painted following his Italian trip of 1494-1495, and the techniques of perspective he learnt while in Italy are superbly elaborated in the alterpiece. The pictorial space is defined and delimited by the vanishing points of two groups of buildings in ruins, connected by a monumental brickwork arch, within which the central scene of the Nativity unfolds. The arch is a typical painterly device of Italian origin whose function was to lend depth to the composition: the viewer's gaze is drawn out towards the

distance, where an angel floating in an aura of light under the arch is announcing Christ's birth to some shepherds. Further in the foreground, and again framed by the arch, are two more shepherds, who are humbly approaching the Holy Family on bended knee. Two other men look out from the ruined building on the left; their role is not entirely clear, and perhaps they are also simple shepherds. The Virgin's arms are folded across her chest in a sign of devotion, while Joseph leans on the base of the wooden pillar supporting the roof, in a realistic gesture denoting his elderly age. The exquisitely observed plants growing from the Classicizing ruins allude to the birth of the Christian world (personified by the infant Jesus) from the ruins of the Pagan one. The work was removed from the church of St Catherine in Nuremberg and donated to Maximilian of Bavaria. It is in a good state of conservation, although the predella and one of the paintings on the reverse of the two side panels (the *Annunciating Angel*) was lost, while the *Virgin Annunciate* is still intact.

Self-Portrait in a Fur-Collared Robe

Oil on wood, 26.38×19.29 in
1500
Alte Pinakothek, Munich

According to Dürer's writings on art, a good artist had to possess *Kunst* (theoretical knowledge) and *Brauch* (practical ability) in equal measure. Dürer's firm belief in his elevated social status as artist was also implicit in this idea: he was no longer to be considered a mere artisan, like the artists of the Middle Ages and early Renaissance had been, but an intellectual. It was in Italy that the master had acquired this new sense of self, which suited his refined personality and insatiable curiosity. The environment in Nuremberg, however, was rather different: artists there were still associated with the traditional craftsman's workshop. Dürer's attitude was borne out in a letter written to his friend Willibald Pirckheimer just before leaving Venice in October 1506: "*Oh, how I shall freeze after this sun! Here I feel like a gentleman, at home only a parasite.*" In the course of his life Dürer expressed his sense of importance as both artist and intellectual through a series of self-portraits which also trace the fundamental stages of his stylistic development. It was quite exceptional for an artist of the time to affirm himself so insistently through the vehicle of self-portraiture, and Dürer painted more than any of his contemporaries. Significantly, he was also one of the first artists to sign his works consistently, and his famous, ubiquitous monogram functioned both as a mark of pride and a stamp of identity. Three of his portraits have survived, all diligently signed and dated, in which the painter portrayed himself as a man of increasing sophistication and maturity: the final one, the *Self-Portrait in a Fur-Collared Robe* painted at the age of 29, represents Dürer at the pinnacle of his career. The frontality and symmetry of the composition is more reminiscent of the iconography of Christ than of traditional portraiture. The root of this may lie in Dürer's interest in Neoplatonic philosophy, which he would have come into contact with through his Italian contemporaries: in Neoplatonic terms, the artist was considered to perform an almost sacred function through his ability to perceive and understand the very essence of things and reinterpret this truth in visual form.

1500

ADürer

Albertus Durerus Noricus
ipsum me proprijs sic effin
gebam coloribus aetatis
anno XXVIII

211

Adoration of the Magi

Oil on wood, 39×44.68 in
1504
Uffizi, Florence

The *Adoration of the Magi* is the most important painting executed by Dürer in the decade between his first and second trips to Italy. These journeys were almost pilgrimages for the artist, who went in discovery of an artistic universe entirely new to his northern sensibility; and the German artist would always have a passionate admiration for Italian art. Commissioned by Frederick the Wise of Saxony for his castle in Wittemberg, the sumptuous altarpiece was completed in 1504, as indicated by the date "inscribed" in the square stone in the foreground, along with the artist's characteristic monogram. By 1603 the painting was in the imperial collections of Vienna, and from there was given to the Uffizi in 1793, in exchange for a painting by Fra Bartolomeo. Dürer here echoed the Venetian style in his fine use of color, dominated by clear, cool blue tones. The main innovation, however, is in the way the monumental perspective (taken from Italian art) combines perfectly with a northern naturalism and attention to detail. As in the *Paumgartner Altarpiece*, Dürer's meticulous observation of nature is particularly evident in his treatment of the plants growing out of the ruins; his bravura was the result of a lifelong interest in the study of real plants, animals and other objects that characterized his whole artistic oeuvre. The insects resting on the stones in the foreground are depicted with the same scrupulous realism, although in this context they also have a precise symbolic meaning: the light colored butterfly on the left and the stag beetle on the right allude to the salvation of humanity through Christ's sacrifice. The architectural ruins in the background, which recall ancient Roman remains, are another clear homage to the art and culture of Italy.

AZTEC MOSAICS

(MEXICO, 14ᵀᴴ-16ᵀᴴ CENTURY)

The Aztecs and the peoples who belonged to their empire developed a sophisticated mosaic art which was used to decorate objects of increasing complexity. They continued to produce disks encrusted with turquoise which probably functioned as ceremonial shields used by the nobility. Other objects, however, were more elaborate than those of the past: in addition to the polished wooden disks, highly ornate masks and the handles of ritual knives also began to be decorated with mosaic work. There was a corresponding increase in the different primary materials used to make the tiles, and their polychromy afforded the artists greater freedom to create complex decorations which, like Aztec ceramics, are referred to as "codex-style". Turquoise was one of the most precious stones used by the Aztecs: it came from afar, probably the modern day United States, and must have been brought to Mexico along the far-reaching trade routes of the *pochtecas*, the merchants. Turquoise was therefore principally used for making highly valued objects with a ritual and ceremonial function, such as wooden masks, breastplates and shields. These masks, just as the earlier stone ones, were probably designed to represent the main gods of the Aztec pantheon, although beyond this their function is still not entirely clear: many scholars believe them to have been worn during ceremonies by high-ranking people impersonating the divinities, perhaps in the reenactment of creation myths or stories of legendary heroes. As with the stone versions, some of the masks' eyes and mouths are inlaid with shells, and it is likely that the mosaic technique was the same as that used during the *tolteca* period: Sahagún wrote that the tiles were applied on a base of wood, using natural glue.

Mask of Tezcatlipoca

Turquoise and lignite mosaic on human skull, h. 7,87 in 16ᵗʰ century
British Museum, London

Among the many Aztec masks decorated with mosaic work, this example is highly unusual: the tiles, of lignite and turquoise, have been applied not onto wood, but onto a support made from a human skull whose rear section has been cut away.
Two speres of pyrite are used for the eyes, encircled by surrounds made from shell. A particular type of shell, *Spondylus Princeps* (common to the Pacific) is also employed for the nasal section. All of the materials used in the mask were imported from afar, highlighting the importance of the god represented: Tezcatlipoca, or "Smoking Mirror". The two wide bands across the face (covering the eyes and the mouth) helped to identify the mask with the god, whose face was often depicted with alternating stripes of different colors. In Aztec mythology, Tezcatlipoca was one of the gods who created the four eras preceding the final one, that of the Fifth Sun. His era was known as "Four Jaguar", in which the men

whom the god had generated were transformed into jaguars: Tezcatlipoca was hence also linked to this animal. The god was represented in various ways, but was generally associated with night and war. When portrayed as a whole figure, he is recognizable by his missing foot, lost during a fight with the monster of the Earth; a serpent emerges in its place. Sometimes the foot comes out of a mirror, also associated with the god and an indication of his ability to control the hidden forces of creation and destruction: by extension, it symbolized human destiny. The rear part of the mask is lined with leather, and leather straps are also attached to the sides of the skull, which may have been used to tie the mask to the person or statue which was to impersonate the god, as suggested in the codices; it is equally possible that they were added subsequently, after the Spanish conquest.

Following pages:
Breastplate,
1440-1521.
British Museum,
London.

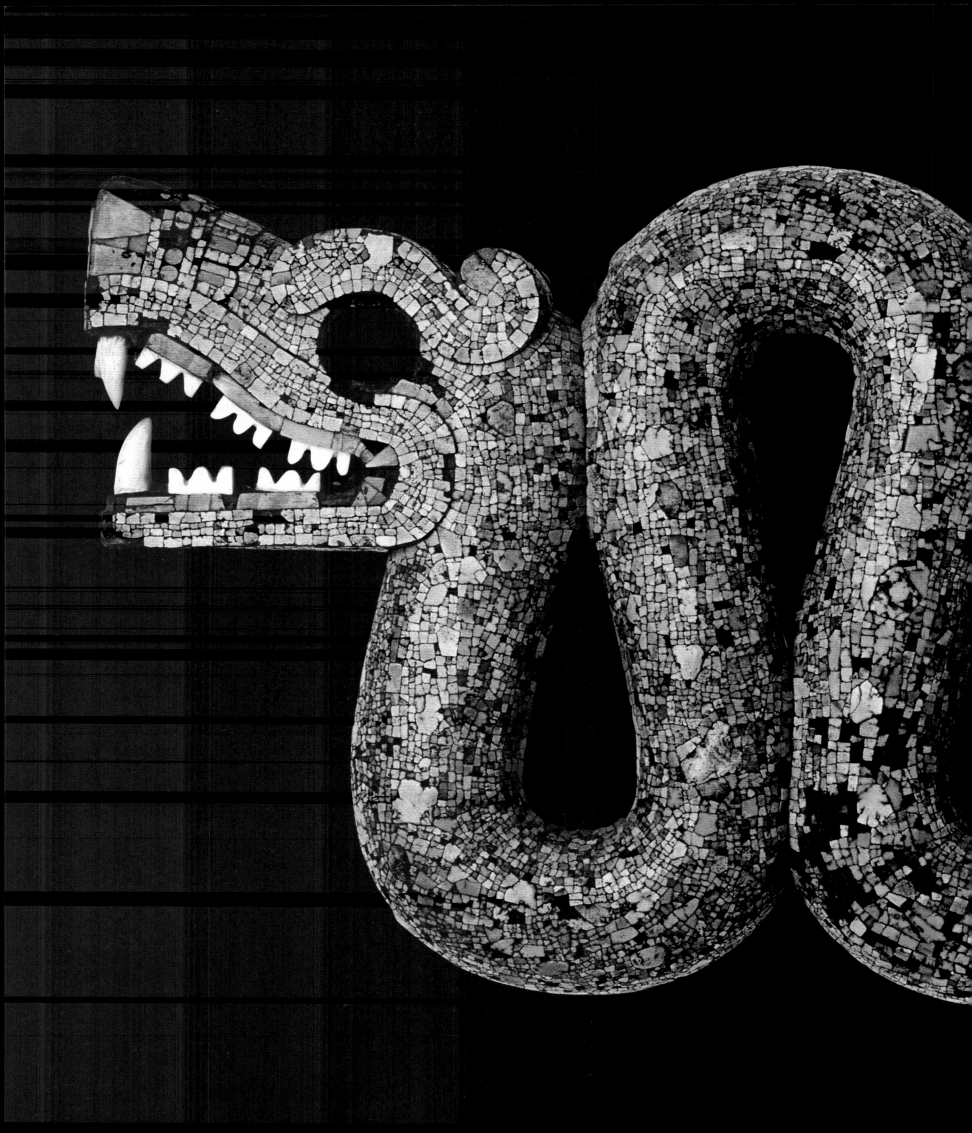

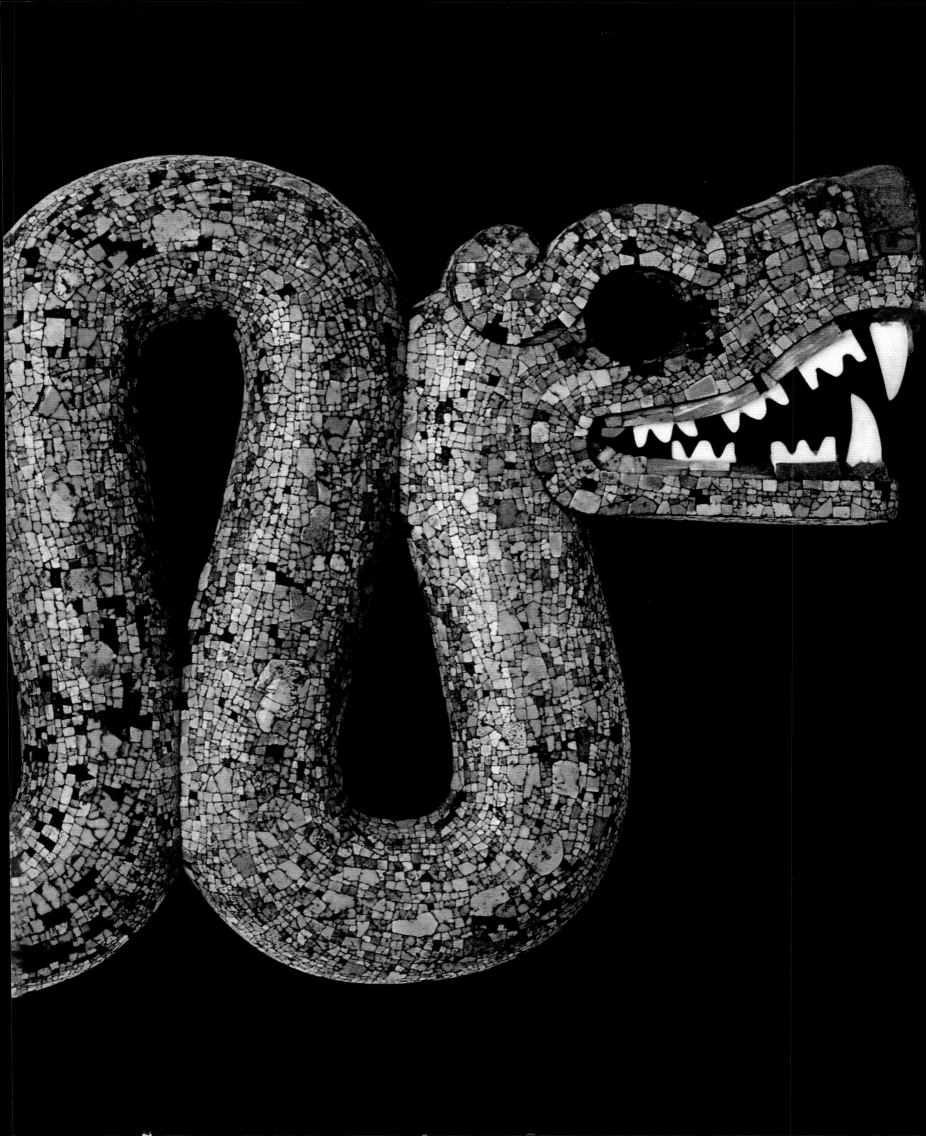

Funerary mask, from
Teotihuacán.
Pigorini Museum
of Prehistory and
Ethnography, Rome.

Mask (usually thought
to represent the god
Quetzalcoatl, although
it could be a
representation of
Tonatiuh the sun god).
British Museum,
London.

MICHELANGELO

MICHELANGELO BUONARROTI
(CAPRESE, AREZZO, TUSCANY 1475 - ROME 1564)

Michelangelo descended from an old Florentine family of the minor nobility, and at a young age was sent for a humanist education under Francesco da Urbino. It soon became apparent, however, that Michelangelo's prodigious talent was better suited to an artistic training, and against his father's wishes he joined the workshop of Domenico Ghirlandaio. In Florence he was quickly admitted to the rarefied intellectual circle of Lorenzo de' Medici where, among other things, he had the opportunity of studying the antique statues in the Medici family collection. His drawings after the work of Giotto and Masaccio, along with his first sculptural works (the *Madonna of the Stairs* and the *Battle of the Centaurs* in the Casa Buonarroti, Florence) reveal the artistic direction the young Michelangelo was taking. In 1494 the nineteen-year-old Michelangelo left Florence for Bologna, before moving to Rome in 1496; and during his first decade in Rome he affirmed himself as one of the leading artists of the era. Several of Michelangelo's youthful masterpieces in marble belong to this period, including the *Bacchus* (Bargello, Florence), the *Pietà* in St Peter's Basilica, the *Taddei Tondo* relief (Royal Academy, London), the Bruges *Madonna and Child* and the *David* in the Accademia, Florence. In 1505 the artist was commissioned by Pope Julius II to design and sculpt his grandiose tomb monument, an impossibly ambitious project which, after an extremely long and tortuous gestation period, was to remain unfinished. From the very first, Michelangelo clashed with the pope over the tomb, leading to the artist's desertion of Rome in 1506; Julius finally caught up with him in Bologna, where he was compelled to sculpt a bronze statue of the pontiff which was destroyed only a few years later. In 1508, the contract for the decoration of the Sistine Chapel ceiling was drawn up; and the extraordinary frescoes were completed by Michelangelo over four years of grueling work. The artist conceived and painted a monumental architectonic scheme within which he inserted the figures of the *Prophets* and *Sibyls*, with the epic *Scenes from Genesis* covering the entire main central section. After the death of Julius II in 1513, Michelangelo signed a second contract for the pope's tomb monument, for which he eventually sculpted his celebrated so-called *Slaves* or *Captives* (two of which are in the Louvre, Paris, and another four in the Accademia, Florence); and the imposing *Moses*, the only one of these works to be included in the final version of the tomb, located in the Roman church of San Pietro in Vincoli. During the 1520s, Michelangelo was also involved in several important projects for the Medici family church of San Lorenzo in Florence: as well as his designs for the façade, which were never executed, he was the architect of the New Sacristy (built as a "reply" to the existing Old Sacristy by Filippo Brunelleschi) and the Laurentian Library. The *Medici Tombs* carved by Michelangelo for the family chapel in the New Sacristy marked a pinnacle of formal composure, with the heroic depiction of brothers Giuliano and Lorenzo de' Medici and the four allegorical statues beneath representing a deep meditation on the dignity of man. After the sack of Rome in 1527 and the expulsion of the Medici from Florence, the artist assumed a central role within the government of the newly formed Florentine Republic; the Medici returned to power not long afterwards, however, and 1530, and Michelangelo was formally pardoned for his role in the Republic by the Medici Pope Clement VII, who summoned him back to Rome. From 1536 Michelangelo was once more employed in the Sistine Chapel, this time to work on the terrifying *Last Judgement*; he also took charge of the ongoing reconstruction of St Peter's Basilica, and was responsible for the cross-shaped floor plan and the immense dome. The sculptures of his late period, such as the *Rondanini Pietà* (Castello Sforzesco, Milan) can be understood as an intense reflection on the destiny of humanity: here Michelangelo abandoned his characteristic quest for formal beauty to express instead the existential anxiety of a man approaching his own death. The master's artistic evolution was precisely mirrored by his philosophical and poetic writings; and in wider terms, the huge arc of his career, informed by his passionate, multifaceted personality, embodied the cultural diversity of the Renaissance period he came to epitomize.

Pietà

Marble, h. 68.5 in
1499
Basilica of Saint Peter,
Vatican City

In 1498 Cardinal Bilhéres de Lagraulas, Abbot of San Dionigi and Ambassador of Charles VIII, gave Buonarroti the commission for the very famous sculptural group, which was to be placed in the Chapel of Santa Petronilla in the ancient Basilica of Saint Peter. The same patron asked the artist to follow a northern iconographic model of the Virgin holding the body of her son in arms after the deposition from the cross. As opposed to the composition of the German original, frozen in an unnatural scheme, Michelangelo, however, preferred to create an image of extreme naturalness, with soft, fluid lines. It is the only work signed by him, on the sash which crosses the Virgin's breast. The signature, according to Vasari, indicated the pride of the artist in his achievement. The lyrical intensity of the work, the refined smoothness of the marble and the plasticity of the forms all contribute to make it a work of perfect equilibrium. The absorbed expression on the face of Mary reveals her withheld grief; the body of Jesus, surrendered in exhaustion to the immense pain it has borne, brings the holy scene into the dimension of humanity; the fineness of the garments, the monumental composition and the perfection of the features and anatomy endow the scene with a divine aura and timelessness. Perhaps it was this "absolute" beauty which led to the famous episode so frequently mentioned since, when, on Whit Sunday May 21st 1972, a madman attacked the group with a hammer, entailing a lengthy period of restoration to repair the damage and fill the holes.

Holy Family (Doni Tondo)

Tempera on wood,
diameter 47.24 in
(not including frame)
c. 1507
Uffizi, Florence

Vasari recorded that, when Michelangelo was in Florence at the beginning of the 16th century, *"Agnolo Doni, a Florentine citizen and friend of Michelangelo… decided that he wanted something done by [the artist]"*, and the master was thus commissioned to paint a *tondo* for him with the Virgin raising the Christ child towards Joseph. When the picture was finished, Michelangelo demanded a fee of seventy ducats, but Agnolo *"thought it strange to pay so much for a painting"* and offered to pay only forty; the artist was so incensed that he raised his charge to a hundred ducats, and in the ensuing negotiation he ended by obtaining a hundred and forty, twice as much as he had originally asked for. Michelangelo knew the true quality and worth of his great painting, and time has proved him right: the *Doni Tondo* is now, of course, priceless, and occupies a unique position in the history of art, not just because it is the only movable painting which can be attributed with certainty to the artist, but because it ushered in the birth of Mannerism. Michelangelo's revolutionary idea was to arrange the Holy Family group in a sculptural composition at the center of the *tondo*, with the Virgin in the foreground depicted in a radical twisting "serpentine" motion which would inspire the typical *figure serpentinate* of the Mannerist style. According to one of the more persuasive interpretations of the picture, the three holy figures symbolize the world of the New Testament, which supercedes the Pagan age represented by the nudes in the background, who are undressing in preparation for their baptism. The low wall behind the Holy Family marks a clear division between the present and past with its allusions to original sin; the young figure of John the Baptist is the precursor to the salvation which awaits humanity in the new Christian era. The painting was thought to have been commissioned by Agnolo Doni in 1504 on the occasion his marriage to Maddalena Strozzi, but a recent theory suggests that, in the light of the baptism imagery, it was actually made to celebrate the birth of their daughter Maria, who was baptized on September 8 1507.

Ceiling of the Sistine Chapel

Fresco
1508-1512
Sistine Chapel, Vatican Museums, Vatican City

From 1980-1989 an ambitious restoration project was carried out to clean the frescoes of the Sistine Chapel ceiling, removing layers of dirt accumulated over the centuries and returning the extraordinary scenes to their original, colorful splendor. Michelangelo was first called to Rome in 1505 in his capacity as sculptor, when Pope Julius II assigned him the onerous task of executing his tomb monument, which was originally to have taken pride of place in the new St Peter's Basilica. The arguments and complications that ensued have been well documented: while the artist devised a grandiose and costly design for the tomb, the pope poured his attention and funds into the colossal project for the reconstruction of the Basilica. The volatile Michelangelo did not take kindly to being sidelined: one day, offended by Julius's refusal to grant him an audience, he suddenly abandoned Rome without taking official leave of the pope. Following a truce, the artist reluctantly accepted the pope's commission to paint the Sistine Chapel ceiling, in an attempt to mend their damaged relationship. Little is known about Michelangelo's training as painter, other than his period of apprenticeship with Domenico Ghirlandaio (which Michelangelo would subsequently downplay); and apart from the Sistine Chapel frescoes, the self-defined *scultore* produced few other paintings. It is not surprising, then, that the architect Donato Bramante was perplexed by Julius II's decision to entrust a commission of such magnitude to Michelangelo, an artist known predominantly for his sculpture. Michelangelo started to work on the ceiling in May 1508, building the scaffolding and removing the existing decoration (a star-studded sky dating back to Sixtus IV) to prepare for his own frescoes. He devised a highly complex decorative program: within an astonishing *trompe l'oeil* architectonic frame, his Old Testament scenes unfolded in relation to the existing New Testament episodes painted along the sides of the Chapel walls by Perugino, Botticelli and Luca Signorelli. On October 31, 1512, the scaffolding was finally dismantled to reveal the full magnificence of Michelangelo's masterpiece.

Creation of Adam
Fresco, 9.18×18.70 ft
1510-1511
Sistine Chapel, Vatican
Museums, Vatican City

Before work could get
underway on the Sistine
Chapel ceiling, Michelangelo
had to overcome two
problems: erecting the
scaffolding and assembling a
team of assistants. Under

Julius II, the Sistine Chapel
had become one of the prime
locations of the liturgical life
of the papacy, and it was
inconceivable to keep it
closed for years while the
ceiling was painted. It was

therefore necessary to invent
a scaffolding structure which
would not impede the
religious ceremonies that
regularly took place in the
Chapel. The first solution,
devised by the architect

Donato Bramante and involving a platform suspended from the ceiling by cables, did not meet with Michelangelo's approval. In particular, the artist asked how he could be expected to fill in and paint over the holes made for the cables once the scaffolding had been taken down. Bramante's vague response – "*We'll think of something later*" – led Michelangelo to build his own alternative, a platform supported by a number of beams jutting out of the Chapel's side walls. The structure was reasonably stable, and could also be fitted with steps, making it easier to decorate the side vaults and lunettes. The ceiling was to be painted using the challenging *buon fresco* technique, which required the color to be applied relatively quickly

229

onto the plaster while it was still damp. Michelangelo grouped together a team of specialized assistants from Florence for the job, but Giorgio Vasari recounted that they were immediately fired by the artist. The anecdote was instrumental in creating the myth of Michelangelo as an eccentric, heroic genius, capable of enduring years of solitary, back-breaking work at serious cost to his health. In reality, the artist did use assistants throughout the course of the project, although it is true that they played a very minor role in the execution of the finished work. As the years went by, their numbers dwindled, and in the end their tasks were limited to painting the decorative framework and relatively unimportant parts of the frescoes. Only Michelangelo was skilled enough to paint the enormous main figures in *buon fresco*, such as Adam in the Creation scene, who measures over two meters.

Last Judgement
Fresco, 44.95×40 ft
1536-1541
Sistine Chapel, Vatican Museums, Vatican City

As a believer, Michelangelo held the profound conviction that religious art should strengthen and inspire the faith of the viewer, and his own art was always directed to this end. As he wrote in a letter to a friend, he defined his talent as "*that art that God has given me*". In 1534 Michelangelo was recalled to Rome by Pope Clement VII to paint another monumental work in the Sistine Chapel, this time on the far wall of the building. The work began in 1536 with the removal of existing frescoes painted in the 15ᵗʰ century

by Perugino: a large *Assumption* and the first two episodes from the series of *Scenes from the Life of Moses* and *Christ*. Five years later, dogged by controversy and censure, Michelangelo's fresco was completed. Even before its official unveiling, the *Last Judgement* had already attracted some ferocious criticism on moral grounds. The nudity of the figures, intended by Michelangelo to express their spirituality, was considered scandalous, inappropriate to the subject, the location and, more generally, to the particular historical moment. Following the shock of the sack of Rome in 1527 and

the Reformation, the Church was involved in the battle against Protestantism, and had to defend itself from accusations of paganism, corruption and immorality: the *Last Judgement* was seen by many as promoting, rather than negating, these concepts. Michelangelo did not accept the criticisms with good grace, and he exacted his revenge on Biagio da Cesena, master of ceremonies of the pontificate who had forcefully condemned his scandalous nudes, by portraying him as the hideous Minos in the fresco. On January 21 1564, the Council of Trent ruled that the parts of the fresco

considered to be obscene must be covered up. This task, one of a series of censorships which would be performed on the work over the successive centuries, fell to Daniele da Volterra, who added loin-clothes or "breeches" to the offending nudes and in the process gained the unflattering nickname of "Bragettone" or "breeches-maker".

231

GIORGIONE

GIORGIO DA CASTELFRANCO
(CASTELFRANCO VENETO, TREVISO, VENETO 1477/1478 - VENICE 1510)

The scant documentary evidence on the life of Giorgione has fed the myth that now surrounds his work. He was probably a pupil of Giovanni Bellini, and studied the paintings of Antonello da Messina; Leonardo's trip to Venice in 1500 would also have played an important role on Giorgione's artistic development. His revolutionary style is immediately evident from the *Pala di Castelfranco* (*Castelfranco Altarpiece* or *Madonna and Child between St Francis and St Nicasius*), in the cathedral of his native Castelfranco, a painting revealing his early mastery of perspective, with solid architectural forms opening out onto a vast background landscape. In 1508 Giorgione worked on the frescoes of the Fondaco dei Tedeschi in Venice together with the young Titian, of which few fragments remain. The Venetian chronicler Marcantonio Michiel, writing in the 1520s-1530s, recorded a series of works by Giorgione in the houses of Venetian patricians. Among these were some of his most celebrated masterpieces, such as *The Tempest* (Gallerie dell'Accademia, Venice) and the *Three Philosophers* (Kunsthistorisches Museum, Vienna). These works, characterized by their enigmatic allegorical mood, are a reminder that the artist frequented Venice's major intellectual circles at the time. Giorgione's late period is beset by problems of attribution, with some of his works having also being ascribed to the younger Titian: the *Sleeping Venus* (Gemäldegalerie, Dresden), the *Concert champêtre* (*Pastoral Concert*, Louvre, Paris) and the *Madonna and Child with St Anthony and St Roch* (Prado, Madrid). Even during his own lifetime, Giorgione's contemporaries recognized his genius, and he was already being described as one of the greatest artists of his age; and his innovative technique that favored the use of *colore* (color suffused with light), over *disegno* (traditional draughtsmanship), gave him a deserved reputation as the pioneer of the Venetian colorists.

Three Philosophers
Oil on canvas, 48.8×56.88 in
1505
Kunsthistorisches Museum, Vienna

Giorgione usually painted relatively small-scale pictures, meant for the enjoyment of a few sophisticated patrons, which also explains their often impenetrable subjects. This is certainly true of the *Three Philosophers* which was painted for the Venetian nobleman Taddeo Contarini, whose circle of aristocrats was dedicated to literature, poetry and philosophical debate. There have been numerous hypotheses on the significance of the work, described by older sources as "three philosophers in a landscape", "three mathematicians" and "three Magi waiting for the comet". During the 19th and 20th centuries, the figures were variously seen as personifications of ancient philosophy (the old bearded man), Aristotelianism (the man wearing a turban, identified as the Arabian philosopher Averroes), and natural philosophy (the seated young man, interpreted as Copernicus). The mystery will perhaps never be solved: it is probable that the painting's cryptic meaning, if indeed there is one, was only known by the artist, the client, and his elite circle of friends. Nonetheless, it is reasonable to conclude that the earliest description of the work as "three philosophers in a landscape" (Marcantonio Michiel, 1525) is the most accurate: it may also indicate that the central subject of the painting is not just the three figures, but the way they relate to the surrounding environment, that is the deep-rooted bond between man and nature. Arguably for the first time in the history of art, Giorgione's landscapes in works like this and *The Tempest* assumed the same importance as the human figures, and were hence treated with the same attention to detail. In this, Giorgione probably revealed his debt to Leonardo and Antonello da Messina, both of whom seem to have influenced his style during the latter half of his career; a style which, as Giorgio Vasari also commented, became softer and more tonal, based on the fusion of light and color which was to characterize the distinctive Venetian school of painting.

The Tempest

Oil on canvas, 32.28×28.74 in
c. 1505
Gallerie dell'Accademia,
Venice

Writing in 1530, Marcantonio Michiel described this remarkable little painting, then in the Venetian "cabinet of curiosities" of Giorgione's patron and friend Gabriele Vendramin, as "*the little town on canvas with the tempest, the gypsy woman and the soldier, by Giorgio of Castelfranco*". As Michiel's reductive note suggests, the subject of the work must already have been incomprehensible to Giorgione's contemporaries, and none of the many subsequent interpretations have succeeded in solving its mysterious symbolism definitively. *The Tempest* is one of those paintings with an implicit iconographic code so complex that art historians have found it almost impossible to unlock: certain elements of the picture will always remain obscure, perhaps because it was made for one of the sophisticated Venetian humanist groups who enjoyed works with a hidden meaning, the key to which was only known to few initiates. Listed in the inventory of the Vendramin family during the 16ᵗʰ and 17ᵗʰ centuries, the painting then passed into the collection of the Manfrin until 1875, when the Museum of Berlin staked its claim on it; however, the Italian government declared that it must remain in Italy, so it went to the Giovannelli family before finally being acquired by the Gallerie dell'Accademia in Venice in 1932. Giorgione captured the precise meteorological moment of a storm about to break, heralded by the sudden flash of lightning that tears through the heavy rain clouds: the landscape and figures seem to be almost suspended in time as the dramatic forces of nature prepare to unleash. One relatively persuasive theory on the painting's allegorical subject was put forward by the scholar Salvatore Settis in 1978, who saw it as a meditation on the fate of humanity after Adam and Eve's expulsion from the Garden of Eden: the human figures would thus represent Adam and Eve with their baby Cain, with the lightning and coming storm symbolizing the wrath of God; while the broken columns in the background are a foreshadowing of the humans' mortality.

RAPHAEL

RAFFAELLO SANZIO
(URBINO, MARCHE 1483 - ROME 1520)

Raphael was the son of the painter Giovanni Santi, author of a celebrated rhymed *Chronicle* and head of a Florentine workshop where the young Raphael received his first artistic tutelage, before moving on to study with Perugino. By 1500, the seventeen-year-old was already recorded as a "master" working in Città di Castello, where he stayed until 1504, the year he executed the *Betrothal of the Virgin* (Pinacoteca di Brera, Milan); a work clearly informed by the style of Perugino, as well as the cultural and artistic environment of Urbino. In 1504 Raphael traveled to Florence "to learn", as he wrote in a letter; and the city was indeed to prove a great source of inspiration to him, especially through his contact with the work of Leonardo and Michelangelo. In particular, the *Deposition* (or *Baglioni Altarpiece*, Galleria Borghese, Rome) reveals the influence of Michelangelo, while the perceptive subtlety of Leonardo's atmospheric effects is recalled in Raphael's *Madonna of the Meadow* (Kunsthistorisches Museum, Vienna) and in the *Portrait of Maddalena Doni* (Palazzo Pitti, Florence). Towards the end of 1508 Raphael was called to Rome by Pope Julius II, to participate in the decoration of the new papal apartments along with an elite team of other artists gathered from all over Italy. Soon he was made responsible for the entire room known as the Stanza della Segnatura, in which he painted his fresco masterpieces the *Disputation on the Holy Sacrament* (or *Disputa*), the *School of Athens*, the *Parnassus* and the *Virtues*, following an iconographic program inspired by an abstract doctrinal scheme. After this success, Raphael (now the master of his own well-organized workshop) devised the decoration for the second room, known as the *Stanza d'Eliodoro*, which narrates episodes relating to the papacy and the Church: the *Expulsion of Heliodorus from the Temple*, the *Deliverance of St Peter from Prison*, *Pope Leo the Great and Attila* and the *Mass at Bolsena*. These years also saw Raphael paint some of his most important portraits, such as that of *Julius II* (National Gallery, London) and *Baldassare Castiglione* (Louvre, Paris); and at the same time, he reached a pinnacle of technical excellence and poetic idealization in his religious pictures, as exemplified by the exquisite *Sistine Madonna* (Gemäldegalerie, Dresden) and the *St Cecilia* (Pinacoteca Nazionale, Bologna). In Rome, the artist's interests would turn to architecture and the study of Classical antiquity; and after the death of Donato Bramante, he assumed, among other official duties, the office of architect of the Fabbrica di San Pietro, the body in charge of the reconstruction work on St Peter's. In the latter part of his short career, Raphael was increasingly aided by his assistants; the famous *Portrait of Leo X with Cardinals Giulio de' Medici and Luigi de' Rossi* (Uffizi, Florence) and the *Transfiguration* (Vatican Picture Gallery, Rome) date to this period, works which represent the final elaboration of Raphael's pictorial style, an artistic evolution which would have a fundamental impact on entire generations of future artists.

Deposition
(Baglioni Altarpiece)
Oil on wood, 72.44×69.3 in
1507
Galleria Borghese, Rome

The *Deposition* altarpiece was commissioned in 1507 in Perugia by the noblewoman Atalanta Baglioni, who wanted to pay tribute to her dead son, Grifonetto.
Perugia was at the time being torn apart by rival family factions who were conducting a bloody war to gain control of power in the city.
Grifonetto had been caught up in the feuding: in 1500, having massacred a large number of his own family in cold blood, he sought refuge at his mother's country villa; but Atalanta was disgusted at her son's act and refused to help him.
Forced to return to Perugia, Grifonetto ran into a number of his relatives who had miraculously escaped the bloodbath, and was in turn slaughtered. According to contemporary accounts, Atalanta reached her dying son just in time to hear him utter his last words, and was finally seen leaving his dead body with her clothes and face spattered with blood.
The pain and torment at the loss of her son was movingly expressed by Raphael in the Virgin of the *Deposition*.

School of Athens

Fresco, base 22 ft
1509-1511
Stanza della Segnatura,
Vatican Museums,
Vatican City

Raphael started work on the *School of Athens* not long after Michelangelo had erected the scaffolding in the Sistine Chapel to prepare for his own vast fresco. The instigator of both of these exceptionally ambitious projects was Pope Julius II. Elected in 1503, the pope had vigorously seized the political reins of the Papal State, putting himself personally in charge of the army, reconquering cities such as Bologna which had rebelled against the previous pontificate, and reestablishing the Church's authority far and wide. Within the context of this political revolution, art was also used as propaganda to spread the image of a Church that was unified, rich and powerful. The grandiose artistic enterprise had begun in 1505 with the tearing down of the ancient St Peter's Basilica built under Constantine; the architect Donato Bramante had been given the task of designing a new, modern structure symbolic of the Church triumphant and worthy of the gigantic tomb monument to Julius which the pope had commissioned from Michelangelo in the same year. Julius also refused to live in the apartments of the previous pope, the detested Alexander VI Borgia, setting aside a different series of rooms; and in 1507 he assembled a talented team of artists to decorate the new living quarters, which would subsequently come to be known as the Vatican Stanze. Raphael, who arrived in Rome in 1508 at the pope's invitation, initially joined the group of artists already

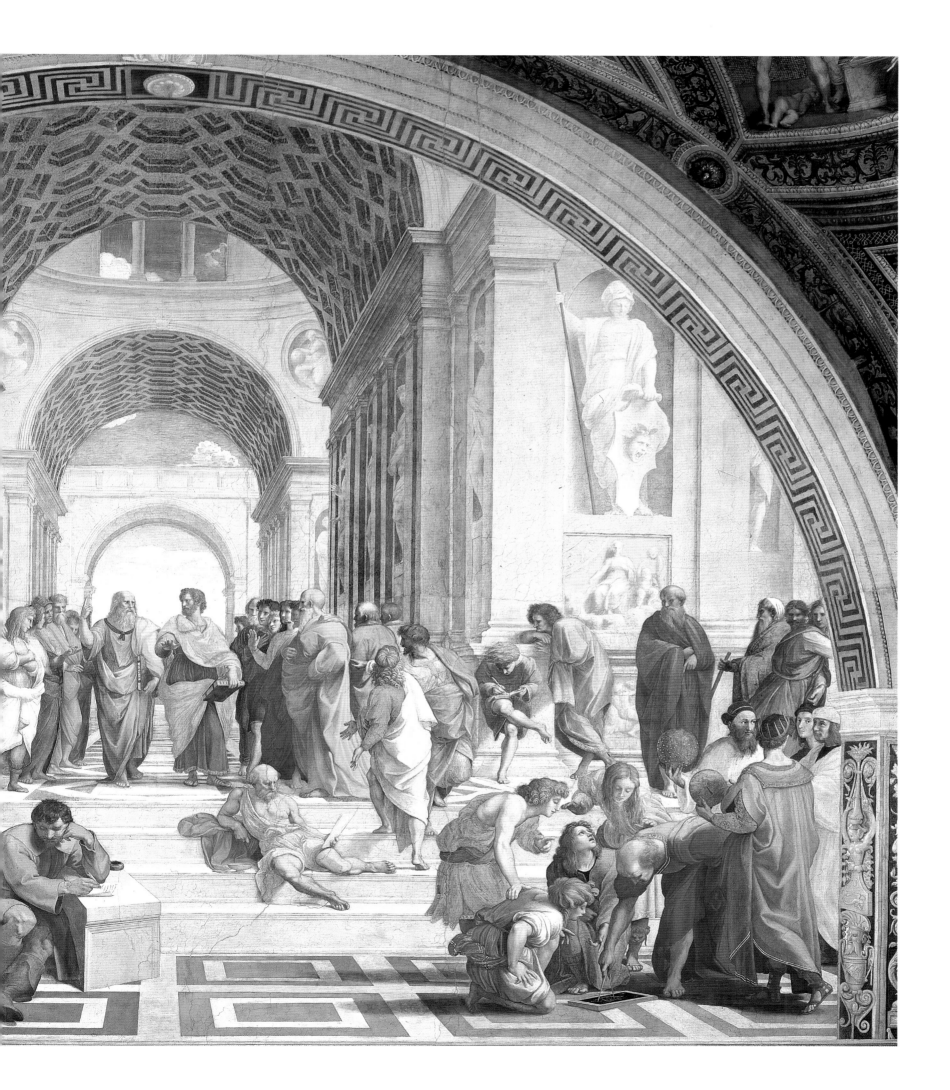

working in the Stanze, but having won the admiration of Julius, he quickly supplanted his colleagues. In spite of his lack of experience of painting *buon fresco* over such large surfaces, he was given sole responsibility for the whole project, which he dedicated himself to until his early death. Along with his team of assistants, Raphael decorated four Vatican Stanze, whose current names relate to the themes of the frescoes: the Stanza della Segnatura (where the *School of Athens* is located), the Stanza d'Eliodoro, the Stanza dell'Incendio, and the Stanza di Costantino.

Madonna of the Chair
Oil on wood, diam. 28 in
c. 1513-1514
Galleria Palatina, Palazzo Pitti, Florence

This is one of the most perfect, celebrated and copied of Raphael's works. The highly original iconography and composition, combined with the strikingly imaginative details of the Madonna's multi-colored shawl, striped head covering and the chair she is sitting on, have fascinated and delighted visitors to the Medici Collections over the centuries. The picture even inspired a 19th century German writer to suggest that it represented the young daughter of a wine producer with her two children, painted from life by Raphael on the cover of a wine barrel. A *tondo* answering to the description of Raphael's work was first mentioned in a source of 1589, citing it as being housed in the most prestigious part of the Medici Collections, the Tribune of the Uffizi, although it is not known when and how it came to be there. Others identify it as the *tondo* by Raphael which was in the chapel of the Ducal Palace of Urbino in 1609, and

subsequently sent to Florence with the della Rovere dowry in 1631. The work represents the culminating moment of *tondo* painting in Florence, which here achieves an ideal harmony of form in the way the figures are perfectly adapted to the round format. The Madonna is depicted from the side, sitting on a chair with her legs slightly raised (probably resting

on a footstool), and gently holding the infant Christ in her arms as the child St John the Baptist looks on them lovingly. The tender intimacy between mother and child is portrayed with a moving realism, both in their affectionate embrace and the sweetness of their gazes, directed towards the observer: the serious expression of the

baby Jesus, lively and uncombed just like a real child, is complemented by that of his mother, suffused with a sadness which presages the destiny of her son. Raphael's innate artistic confidence succeeded here in imbuing his divine subjects with an intensely human quality without compromising their dignity.

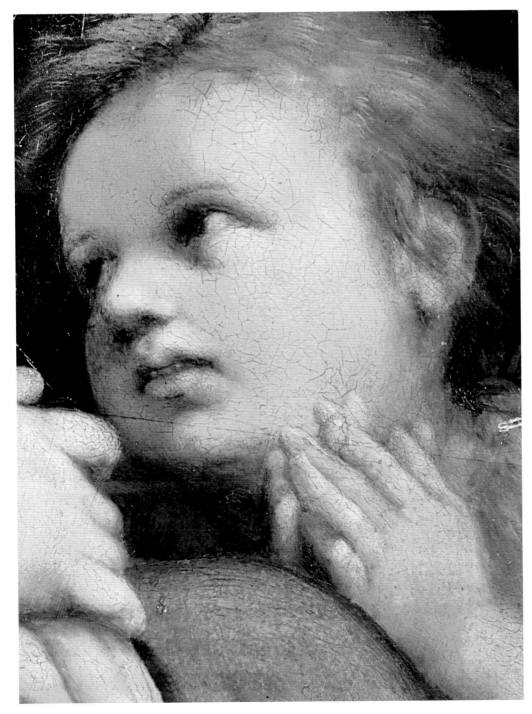

TITIAN

TIZIANO VECELLIO
(PIEVE DI CADORE, BELLUNO, VENETO *c.* 1490 - VENICE 1576)

Titian's artistic education began in Venice, in the studio of Giovanni Bellini, but at eighteen he joined the workshop of Giorgione, with whom he shared a lyrical style and virtuoso use of color. In 1508 the two painters collaborated on the decoration of the Fondaco dei Tedeschi in Venice: the frescoes were mostly destroyed, but a few surviving fragments (such as the *Justice* in the Gallerie dell'Accademia, Venice) reveal the young artist's precocious mastery of perspective. In 1511 Titian decorated the Scuola del Santo in Padua with a series of frescos depicting the *Miracles of St Anthony*, set within serene landscapes. In the succeeding years Titian painted a number of monumental canvases such as *Votive Picture of Jacopo Pesaro* (Musée des Beaux Arts, Antwerp), along with other works which demonstrated his enduring debt to Giorgione: the *Concert champêtre* (Louvre, Paris) was for a long time considered to be by Giorgione, although most critics now believe it to be one of Titian's youthful paintings. Titian quickly established himself as the leading artist of the Venetian Republic: his magnificent *Assumption* in the church of Santa Maria Gloriosa dei Frari, finished in 1518, is a triumph of monumentality and was to have an enormous impact on his contemporaries. The master's style progressively evolved to focus more on color, a predominant element in the first canvases of his series of *Bacchanalia* (1518-1519, Prado, Madrid), which also reveal the influence of Michelangelo, evident in the *Resurrection of Christ* (or *Averoldi Altarpiece*) of 1522 (Santi Nazzaro e Celso, Brescia). At the same time, Titian was also developing a highly individual style of portraiture focusing on the upper half of the body with the hands in full view, as exemplified by the *Man with a Glove* (Louvre, Paris). The intense psychological introspection of his portraits were synthesized into the solemn *Pesaro Altarpiece* (Santa Maria Gloriosa dei Frari, Venice), where the donors play a primary role within the religious scene. Titian went on to assume a role of pivotal importance in contemporary art, working for the courts of Mantua, Ferrara and Urbino and spreading his influence even further afield by taking on commissions for the kings of Spain and France. Around 1540, the arrival in Venice of the Mannerist style from Rome, Tuscany and Emilia marked a crucial turning point for the artist, which saw him move away from the expressive power of color towards a more sculptural rendering of forms achieved through draftsmanship, as exemplified by the *Christ Crowned with Thorns* in the Louvre, Paris. This change in direction was in turn to have a profound impact on younger Venetian masters such as Tintoretto, Veronese and Bassano. Titian's journey to Rome of 1545-1546 seems to have brought about a reevaluation of his interest in Mannerism, however: the portraits of *Pope Paul III with his Nephews* (Museo di Capodimonte, Naples) and *Charles V on Horseback* (Prado, Madrid) show a return to the free use of color. The master's late works are characterized by a palette lit up with sudden bright flashes; the brushwork is looser and more relaxed, and the forms almost seem to disintegrate into the shadows, as for example in the *Rape of Europa* (Isabella Stewart Gardner Museum, Boston) and the *Martyrdom of St Lawrence* (El Escorial, Madrid and Chiesa dei Gesuiti, Venice), among the artist's last and most dramatic achievements. Titian's long and illustrious career confirmed him as one of the most importance protagonists of 16th century painting, who continued to exercise an enormous influence on successive generations of artists.

Concert Champêtre (Pastoral Concert)

Oil on canvas, 43.30×54.33 in
1509-1510
Louvre, Paris

Titian painted this work shortly after the end of his apprenticeship with Giorgione, who had just died. The older master bequeathed his pupil a tremendous artistic legacy, and the *Concert champêtre* can almost be seen as Titian's tribute to the memory and teaching of Giorgione. The painting's naturalism and refined allegorical content are so distinctly Giorgionesque in character that it has been alternately attributed to both artists, although it is now generally considered to be the work of the younger artist. The canvas depicts two young men sitting in a field: the first, elaborately dressed in a red costume and beret, plays a lute, while the second listens to him attentively. In the foreground, a female nude sits with her back to the viewer facing the two men, and stops playing her flute to listen to the young man's melody. Another female figure stands on the left, nude apart from the light colored drape wrapped around her legs, and pours water into a well or fountain. The scene is illuminated by a cool, clear light, and you can almost hear the delicate tune filtering through the silence of the valley. Titian's subdued colors, applied with soft, broad brushstrokes, contribute to the atmosphere of calm which subtly envelops the entire scene, while the suffused light emphasizes the softness of the grass and the rounded forms of the nudes in the foreground. The painting was thought originally to have belonged to Isabella d'Este, Duchess of Mantua, before passing to Charles I of England in 1627; fifty years later it was bought by Louis XIV of France, and it is now a key work in the collection of the Louvre.

Venus of Urbino
Oil on canvas, 27.16×46 in
1538
Uffizi, Florence

In March 1538 the scion of the Duchy of Urbino, Guidubaldo della Rovere, made several demands on his agent in Venice to buy the "nude woman" from Titian, at the same time repeatedly asking his mother for the money to pay for it. The austere duchess steadfastly refused her son and did not part with a single ducat for the painting, which remained in the artist's studio while Guidubaldo continued to assure Titian that he would buy it, even at his own personal cost. Thanks to his persistence, the painting was finally brought to Urbino a few months later; and it quickly became so famous that Titian was subsequently commissioned to execute a number of similar works. In 1631 the canvas was taken to Florence as part of the dowry of Vittoria della Rovere, wife of the Grand Duke Ferdinand II, and it entered the Uffizi in 1694. The painter interpreted his theme with absolute modernity, subjugating its mythological content to the realistic depiction of a contemporary scene set in a noble Venetian palazzo. Venus is thus depicted as a splendid young nude woman lying languidly on a bed, probably waiting to be dressed by the maids in the background who are taking a sumptuous outfit out of the open chest. In her right hand she holds a small posy of roses, flowers sacred to the goddess Venus, like the myrtle plant standing on the windowsill behind her. A little lapdog sleeps at her feet, a traditional symbol of marital fidelity. The woman's pose is new and provocative, however, and her enticing gaze is directed straight at the viewer, as if to underline the sensuality of her nudity. Of the many interpretations that have been put forward, one of the more convincing reads the painting as an allegory of the erotic aspect of marital love.

Portrait of a Man (Young Englishman)
Oil on canvas, 43.7×38.11 in
1540-1545
Galleria Palatina, Florence

One hypothesis on the identity of the man is that he was Howard, Duke of Norfolk, hence the portrait's alternative title of the *Young Englishman*. This has not been proved with certainty, however, and other scholars prefer to refer to the work as the *Man with the Blue-Green Eyes*, in reference to the subject's magnetic gaze, slightly tinged with melancholy, yet at the same time self-assured and proudly directed towards the observer. This was one of Titian's most treasured portraits, whose apparent simplicity belies its true artistic and psychological complexity. The choice of monochrome tones enriches, rather than diminishes, the expressive power of the subject: his face stands out against the monotone background. Titian defied contemporary poets and writers who sustained that only poetry and literature could adequately reveal a person's innner emotions and character: his portraits, like those of Leonardo or Dürer, penetrated right to the soul of the sitter, displaying a psychological depth and intensity that paralleled the most perceptive writers of the time. It is thanks to the genius of artists such as Titian that the visual arts rose to their place alongside poetry and the liberal arts in the course of the 16ᵗʰ century.

AZTEC
FEATHERWORK

(MEXICO, 16TH CENTURY)

Featherwork was one of the most highly regarded arts in pre-Columbian Meso-America, and the craftsmen who dedicated themselves to it were held in great esteem by Aztec society. They were entrusted with creating valuable objects fit for nobles, governors and the elite soldiers: ceremonial headdresses, shields and fans, as well as the war dresses worn by the eagle warriors. Few examples of this art form have survived, however. Some, like the *Feather Headdress of Montezuma* (Museum of Ethnology, Vienna) are now in European museums, having been sent as gifts to Charles V of Spain either by the Aztecs themselves or by the Spanish conquistadors in Mexico. Feather objects were traditionally made by piecing together small sections of paper (made from agave or bark) on which the design would be traced, and then attaching the feathers using natural glue. The work was done from the outside in, starting with the background and ending in the central decoration. Feathers were also used to create pictorial representations, by cutting and carving the plumes of rare birds. The only surviving examples of this artistic technique are from the colonial era, since all the pre-Columbian pieces have been lost.

**Feather Headdress
of Montezuma**
Bird feathers
16th century
Museum of Ethnology,
Vienna

This is the only pre-Columbian headdress which has survived into the 21st century, and is one of the best preserved examples of Aztec featherwork art. Only the *tlatoani*, members of the nobility and warriors, were allowed to wear precious objects such as necklaces, bracelets and headdresses, which were mainly used in religious ceremonies. Some of the headdresses were so elaborate that they needed heavy wooden supports which would be strapped to the back to prevent them from falling off. They came in a wide variety of designs, as attested by their depiction in the codices of the years immediately following the Spanish conquest. The so-called headdress "of Montezuma" is semi-circular and made from hundreds of quetzal bird feathers, which must have demanded hours of painstaking work. The front has a circular decoration of hummingbird feathers, with gold leaf arranged in the forms of a half moon and turret.

The headdress, now in Vienna, has become the focus of a fierce battle to repatriate this and other Aztec works of art to Mexico.

In reality, whether this is actually the headdress Montezuma sent as a gift to the King of Spain, it is one of the few Mexican objects with a reasonably legitimate right to be in a European collection; unlike many other Aztec artworks which found their way into European or American museums after having been looted or stolen.

PIETER BRUEGEL THE ELDER

(BREDA ?, NOTHERN BRABANT 1528/1530 - BRUSSELS 1569)

Originally from Northern Brabant, Netherlands, Pieter Bruegel trained in Antwerp where in 1551 he joined the city's artistic association, the Guild of St Luke. The next year he made a trip to Italy, traveling as far south as Naples and Sicily; his stay in Rome of 1553 was documented in engravings after his own drawings. Engraving remained his main activity after his return to Antwerp in 1554, and there is no evidence of his paintings until the end of the 1559, when Bruegel executed his *Dutch Proverbs* (Staatliches Museum, Berlin) and the *Fight Between Carnival and Lent* (Kunsthistorisches Museum, Vienna). His later religious paintings, such as the *Tower of Babel* (two versions, in Vienna and Rotterdam) and the

Adoration of the Magi (National Gallery, London) display a stronger compositional structure, particularly in the representation of the landscapes. Bruegel's mature works reveal a startling freedom and originality, exemplified in *The Wedding Dance* (Institute of Arts, Detroit), *The Blind Leading the Blind* (Museo Nazionale di Capodimonte, Naples), *The Peasant Wedding* (Kunsthistorisches Museum, Vienna) and the *Land of Cockaigne (Land of Milk and Honey)* in the Alte Pinakothek, Munich: here the artist experimented with virtuoso stylistic effects featuring unusual viewpoints and perspective, which amplify the extraordinary, lively narratives, confirming Bruegel as one of the most visionary painters of the late Flemish Renaissance.

Tower of Babel

Oil on wood, 45×61 in
1563
Kunsthistorisches Museum,
Vienna

This gigantic, fantastical structure is Bruegel's radical vision of the biblical Tower of Babel, represented in twin paintings which the Flemish artists' biographer, Carel van Mander, recorded in the collection of Rudolph II in 1604. The first work is now in Vienna, while the smaller version is in the Boijmans Van Beuningen Museum in Rotterdam. Bruegel's picture is a clear exposition of the meaning of the Old Testament episode: an allegory illustrating human pride, and the disastrous consequences of ignoring God's will. The colossal tower, depicted from a novel bird's-eye viewpoint, appears at first sight to be solid and strong. Yet in reality, the construction is foundering: part of the front has already fallen away, and it appears to be sinking under its own colossal weight, threatening to collapse onto the surrounding city. The tower is, on closer inspection, absurd, and its design illogical and unsound. Significantly, the painter loosely based his tower on the architecture of the Colosseum, the scene of numerous Christian martyrdoms and thus a perfect symbol of the Romans' arrogant defiance of God. The upper levels all lead to an inner central structure whose precise function is unclear; the galleries seem to be at odds with the external walkways, a series of horizontal terraces constructed one on top of the other and supported by vertical buttresses: the horizontal-vertical design is out of sync with the internal galleries, so that the outer "shell" is structurally incompatible with the inner one. The tower momentarily impresses the viewer with its monstrous dimensions and apparent robustness, but is quickly revealed to be an impossibility. In the foreground to the left, Bruegel has depicted a group of tiny human figures, dwarfed by the tower: the king, his court and a number of stonemasons. As they look on in bewilderment, it is clear that they are powerless to save the doomed construction, the ultimate symbol of human folly.

The Peasant Dance

Oil on wood, 45×64.56 in
1568-1569
Kunsthistorisches Museum,
Vienna

This frenetic *kermesse* (or village festival) was recorded in the inventory of the Kunsthistorisches Museum at the start of the 17th century, but subsequently had a colorful history: in 1809, the painting was carried off to France as part of Napoleon's war booty, along with what is thought to be its companion piece, *The Peasant Wedding* (also now in Vienna). Both works were returned to Vienna soon afterwards, however, in 1815, when they were also restored. As with the *Wedding*, Bruegel's *Peasant Dance* is one of the finest depictions of a rustic life in Flemish art, and constitutes a precious historical document of 16th century customs: it was on the strength of works like this, where the artist represented the peasant classes in Flanders with remarkable energy and gusto, that he gained his nickname "Peasant Bruegel". An acute observer of contemporary life and the human comedy, Bruegel's characters can by turn appear engaging, grotesque, or even movingly poetic. Here, he has painted a local festival with a sharp, almost cruel sense of humor: the men and women are portrayed starkly, and appear coarse, verging on childish as they abandon themselves to their simple pleasures (drinking, dancing, playing music). Their physical and psychological defects are there for all to see, and viewers are left to draw their own conclusions on the moral of the painting. The numerous elements of everyday life – the clothes, earthenware, scraps of food on the table – are rendered with an incisive attention to detail, and transport the observer into the very heart of the peasants' world. Human weaknesses, brought to the fore in the festive atmosphere, are represented by the drunken figures on the left, and the kissing couple behind them. The larger figures in the foreground, "captured" by Bruegel from a low angle, help to draw the viewers into the scene, at the same time underlining the painting's monumentality; the "lowly" theme may be a world away from the refined, noble beauty which characterized Italian Mannerist art of the same period, but it has its own inimitable dignity.

PERSIAN MINIATURES

(IRAN, 16ᵀᴴ CENTURY)

Miniature painting of the Safavid Dynasty (1502-1722) follows a continuous stylistic line from the preceding Timurid era (1387-1502). One of the great artistic geniuses of the 15ᵗʰ century was Bihzad, active at the court of Husayn Bayqara and documented in Herat before moving to Tabriz in around 1522, where he became director of the Royal Library. During the first phase of the Safavid Dynasty, Tahmasp completed his masterpiece, a magnificent series of miniatures illustrating the *Shah nama* manuscript ("Book of Kings"), now generally known as the *Shah nama of Shah Tahmasp*; the work was probably finished around 1535, and in 1567 was donated by the king (who had lost interest in the arts) to the Ottoman Sultan Selim II when he succeeded his father Suleiman to the throne. The manuscript was subsequently dispersed across a number of public and private collections, although the miniatures were also published together in a major study on the text. Other great miniaturists of the period include Sultan Muhammad, Mir Musavvir and Aqa Mirak.

Important painting schools also flourished in the cities of Mashhad and Qazvin, which produced beautiful miniatures illustrating the *Garshasp nama* (for example Or. 12985 in the British Library, London) by artists including Muzaffar 'Ali and Sadiqi Beg. Although Shiraz and Herat became powerful political centers, they did not forget their artistic traditions. One of the preeminent masters of the 17ᵗʰ century was Riza 'Abbasi, whose name is not linked to any one particular manuscript, but who executed a series of individual paintings in a style which Aqa Mirak had already popularized from 1540. Riza's work is generally characterized by the meticulous observation of detail: his figures are real portraits, although sometimes in caricature, with slender, lightly rounded bodies, a model which was also copied in contemporary fabrics. The work of Muhammad Zaman should also be mentioned: active in the second half of the 17ᵗʰ century, Zaman deeply admired Italian art, and his miniatures are unusual and interesting fusions of widely differing pictorial traditions, which he attempted to reconcile.

Sultan Mohammad, Rustam Sleeps while Rakhsh Fights Off a Lion
From the *Shah nama*
Illuminated manuscript
c. 1515-1522
British Museum, London

The warrior Rustam and his faithful horse Rakhsh were on a long journey to rescue a king held captive by a demon in a distant country. They stopped to rest in a dangerous forest, not realizing that they had camped at a lion's lair. After Rustam had fallen asleep, the lion returned and attacked Rakhsh. The horse and the lion struggled fiercely together, until Rakhsh managed to trample his attacker to death. Many dangers lurk among the dense landscape of trees, rocks and streams – such as the marauding snake raiding a nest of birds. An assortment of strange faces loom out of the rock formations, including the faces of a lion and a horse, echoing Rakhsh and his adversary.

**Sultan Mohammad,
Hushand Celebrates
the Discovery of Fire**
From the *Shah nama
of Shah Tahmasp*
Illuminated manuscript
c. 1520-1522.
Metropolitan Museum,
New York

The painting illustrates a
scene from the Persian epic,
the *Shah nama* (*The Book
of Kings*). According to the
text, in the reign of Hushang,
grandson of Gayumars, the
world came to understand
the usefulness of minerals and
the art of smithery, as well
as agriculture and irrigation.
One day Hushang spied
a horrible dragon lurking
behind the rocks. He hurled
a stone at it, which missed
the monster but hit a larger
rock causing sparks to fly up.
Realizing the significance of
this phenomenon, Hushang
built a large fire and held a
feast to celebrate its discovery.
The witty yet profound
characterizations of people
and animals are characteristic
of the liveliest of Sultan
Muhammad' s creations. No
Persian artist has excelled
in presenting a world so
overflowing with life and so
rich in exuberant detail as
Sultan Muhammad, to whom
this painting is attributed.
Using color, he created a
somewhat otherworldly
atmosphere suitable to
the remote, early phase of
civilization depicted in this
miniature celebrating the
discovery of fire.

Bayazidi Brought Before Timur

From the *Zafar Nameh*
Illuminated manuscript
Late 16th century
British Library, London

In this scene from the *Zafar Nameh* (*Book of Victory*), Timur sits enthroned under a canopy with attendants by his side and receives Bayazidi. On the right there are soldiers from Timur's victorious army, while on the left Bayazidi's defeated men are brought in roped together. After defeating Bayazidi legend says the beaten ruler was carried everywhere in a cage at the order of Timur, the Mongol conqueror who waged many wars against the Persians.

CARAVAGGIO

MICHELANGELO MERISI
(MILAN 1571 - PORTO ERCOLE, GROSSETO, TUSCANY 1610)

Following his apprenticeship in Milan with the painter Simone Peterzano, Caravaggio transferred to Rome around 1592-93. Here he began to work in the studio of Cavalier d'Arpino, where he painted still lifes of flowers and fruit, and a number of novel genre scenes with adolescent boys such as the *Boy with a Basket of Fruit* (1593, Galleria Borghese, Rome) and the *Boy Bitten by a Lizard* (two versions: National Gallery, London and Roberto Longhi Foundation, Florence). The next year he went into the service of his first highly influential Roman patron, Cardinal Francesco Maria del Monte, who commissioned him to decorate the private study in his own house (Casino Ludovisi), from 1594-1599, along with a number of individual paintings, including the *Musicians* (or *Concert*, Metropolitan Museum, New York), the *Fortune Teller* (two versions: Pinacoteca Capitolina, Rome and Louvre, Paris), the *Lute Player* (Hermitage, St Petersburg), the *Medusa* (Uffizi, Florence) and probably also the *Bacchus* (Uffizi, Florence) and the *Basket of Fruit* (Pinacoteca Ambrosiana, Milan). Through his benefactor, Caravaggio came into contact with some of the most prestigious and powerful Roman families who commissioned several more important private works from him, such as the *Cupid* (or *Love Victorious*, Staatliche Museen, Berlin) and the *Supper at Emmaus* (National Gallery, London and Brera, Milan). Between 1599 and 1601, Caravaggio also painted his first major public works in Rome: the three seminal canvases relating to the life of St Matthew for the Contarelli Chapel in San Luigi dei Francesi (1599-1601), and the revolutionary *Conversion of St*

Paul and *Crucifixion of St Peter* for the Cerasi Chapel in Santa Maria del Popolo (1600-1601). In these mature works, Caravaggio achieved an exceptionally lucid representation of reality articulated in monumental scenes captured with dramatic perspectival effects. Other masterpieces produced during his Roman period include the *Rest on the Flight into Egypt* (Galleria Doria Pamphilij, Rome), which reveals the influence of the Lombard-Veneto culture of his formative years, the *Entombment* (*c.* 1603, Vatican Picture Gallery, Vatican City), the *Madonna dei Palafrenieri* (Galleria Borghese, Rome), the *St Jerome* (Palazzo Pitti, Florence) and the *Death of the Virgin* (*c.* 1605, Louvre, Paris). After killing a man in a brawl, Caravaggio was forced to flee from Rome and arrived in Naples in 1607, where he executed several large-scale paintings, notably the *Seven Works of Mercy* (Church of Pio Monte della Misericordia, Naples) and the *Madonna of the Rosary* (Kunsthistorisches Museum, Vienna). In 1608 Caravaggio left Naples for Malta, where he painted his striking late works the *Beheading of St John the Baptist* for the Order of the Knights of Malta (Co-Cathedral of St John, Valletta), and the *Sleeping Cupid* (Palazzo Pitti, Florence). After another skirmish, the artist absconded back to Naples, but the emissaries of the Knights of Malta caught up with him and attacked him. Caravaggio was arrested and imprisoned for a couple of days before being released; then, intent on returning to Rome, where he hoped for assistance from the pope, he disembarked at Porto Ercole, where he finally died, delirious and raving, on July 18 1610.

Bacchus

Oil on canvas, 37.4×33.5 in
c. 1596-1597
Uffizi, Florence

This painting, now considered one of Caravaggio's finest masterpieces, was only rediscovered in the store rooms of the Uffizi as late as 1913. It was immediately attributed to the master by the art historian Roberto Longhi, and since then has taken its place among the most famous works in the Uffizi. There is no information, either from primary or secondary sources, on its execution, but it is known to be a youthful work from his early Roman period, probably produced at the start of his successful relationship with Cardinal Francesco Maria del Monte, his first major patron. As with the equally celebrated *Medusa*, it is presumed that the *Bacchus* was commissioned by the cardinal as a gift to his friend the Grand Duke Ferdinand I de' Medici, whom the powerful prelate represented at the Papal Court. As a highly cultivated man, the cardinal helped to broaden Caravaggio's own education, particularly with regard to mythological and allegorical themes from antiquity. The *Bacchus* clearly displays the artist's knowledge of Greco-Roman culture, yet there is something profoundly modern about the picture which transgresses its Classical roots. Caravaggio interprets the subject with an extraordinary freedom and realism, creating an image whose relationship to

antiquity appears complex and ambiguous: on the one hand, the figure's pose, leaning on a couch resembling a Roman triclinium and with a drape thrown over his shoulder like a toga, recalls Classical representations of banquets; but the extreme naturalism of the portrayal – the young god's dirty fingernails and flushed cheeks, the wine glass cheekily tipped towards the viewer, the bruised fruit in the basket underneath – belie the cultured theme and inject the painting with a sensual, immediate realism. It is likely that the painter used a mirror to achieve his radically realistic effects.

Entombment

Oil on canvas, 118.1×79.9 in
c. 1603
Vatican Picture Gallery,
Vatican City

This dramatic altarpiece was commissioned from Caravaggio by Girolamo Vittrice for his family funerary chapel in the Roman church of Santa Maria in Vallicella. Following his remarkable religious paintings in the churches of San Luigi dei Francesi and Santa Maria del Popolo, this is another example of the artist's revolutionary approach to sacred themes on a grand scale. By the beginning of the 17ᵗʰ century, Caravaggio had already developed a highly recognizable and innovative style based on an intense realism which some observers found shocking: taking his models directly off the streets of Rome, he painted them from life and heightened the naturalism of his scenes by using strong, theatrical lighting effects to render figures and objects with even greater plasticity.

When applied to genre scenes, Classical subjects and still lifes, the master's new pictorial language allowed him to represent nature with impeccable precision, be it a basket of fruit in various states of decay, the reflection of a window on a vase filled with water, a bunch of flowers or a gypsy fortune teller's sleight of hand. The breathtaking virtuosity of Caravaggio's naturalism had won him profound admiration among his Roman clients; when applied to religious subjects, however, the technique attracted censure as well as approbation, particularly in the case of the *Death of the Virgin* (discussed below), which was dogged by controversy.

The extraordinary realism of the *Entombment*, on the other hand, only served to magnify the pathos of the scene, its drama balanced by the tight composition; and it met with the complete approval of the client.

Death of the Virgin

Oil on canvas, 145.3×96.5 in
c. 1605
Louvre, Paris

This work instantly gained notoriety when the clients, the Barefooted Carmelites of Santa Maria della Scala in Rome, refused to accept it for its perceived irreverence. According to various biographers of Caravaggio, the friars accused the painter of having depicted the Virgin with an outrageous lack of respect, as a "*dirty whore*" and a "*bloated courtesan with bare legs*". Rumors abounded that Caravaggio had used the corpse of a drowned prostitute for his model. The infamous painting nonetheless captured the imagination of Pieter Paul Rubens, who was in Rome on behalf of the Duke of Mantua, and he quickly bought it for a few *scudi*. From Mantua the canvas went over to England, and was then obtained by Louis XIV of France for the Palace of Versailles before being transferred to the Louvre in 1793. This was probably Caravaggio's last painting in Rome before he had to escape from the city after being accused of murder. The very qualities which so offended the original clients are now justly regarded as evidence of the artist's genius: the simplicity of the composition and iconography, informed by his characteristic naturalism, created a masterpiece of profound humanity. The Virgin, peaceful in death, has a serene expression, in contrast with the mourning figures surrounding her. Their desperation is reflected and amplified by the poor, stark setting bathed in the half-light, but the encroaching gloom is dispersed by the vivid red of the Virgin's garment and the drape suspended above her. Light dramatically falls onto the scene from the top left, traveling diagonally across the bald heads of the apostles to illuminate the focal point of the Virgin's face; as well as giving substance to the forms, it lends the picture an extra dimension of spirituality, providing an outward symbol of the presence of God.

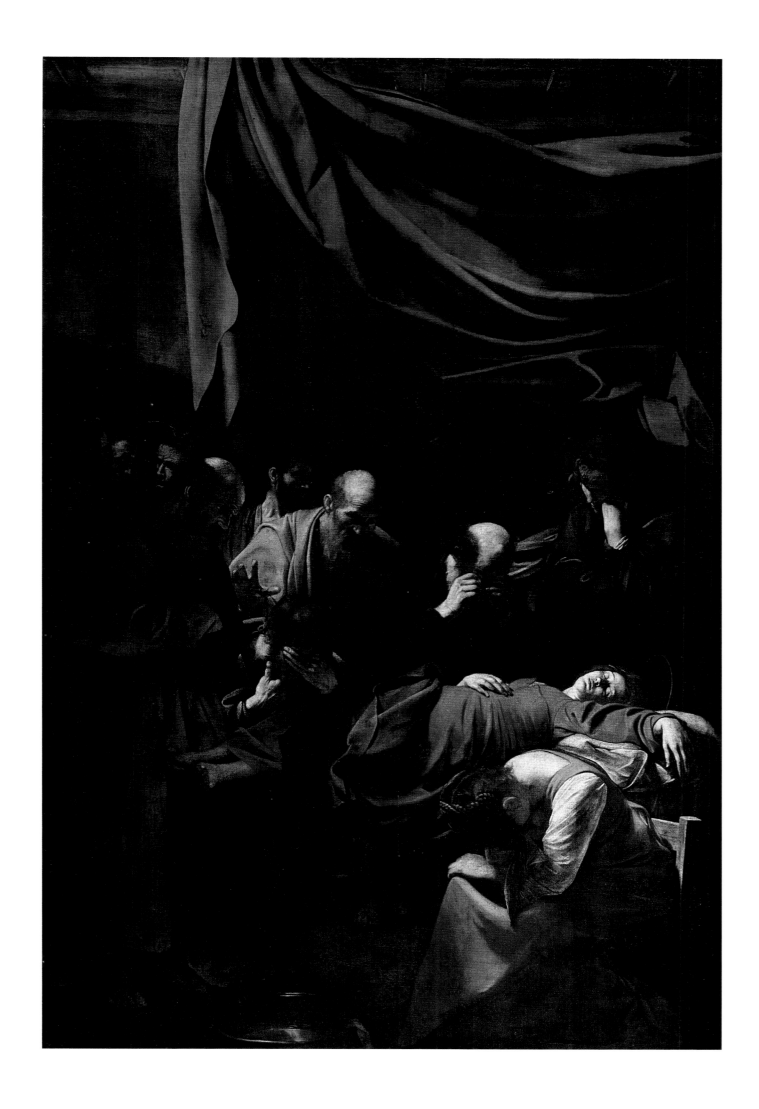

GEORGES DE LA TOUR

(VIC-SUR-SEILLE, LORRAINE 1593 - LUNÉVILLE, LORRAINE 1652)

Georges de La Tour was a baker's son born in Vic-sur-Seille in the French Duchy of Lorraine. His educational background remains unclear, but the Caravaggesque quality of his painting style with its highly dramatic lighting effects has led several scholars to believe that he must have traveled to Italy in his early years. After marrying the daughter of a minor local dignatory, La Tour moved to the village of Lunéville (Lorraine) in 1620, where he received prestigious commissions from Duke Henry II and his court which enabled him to achieve a certain level of affluence. Difficult times were to follow, however: the war between the empire and France, along with the plague and subsequent famine in Lorraine probably had a deep emotional impact on La Tour, reflected in the intense mood of introspection of paintings such as the *St Sebastian Tended by St Irene* and the *Penitent Magdalene* (both in the Louvre, Paris). In the light of the troubles besetting the region of Lorraine, La Tour left Lunéville somewhere between 1636 and 1643 and transferred to Paris, where he is recorded as having been "Painter to the King", Louis XIII. Shortly afterwards he returned to Lorraine, where he remained from 1644 to his death in 1652. His late period in Lorraine is characterized by an even greater sublimation of his already simple, spare style, displayed in celebrated works such as *Discovery of the Body of St Alexis* of 1648 (Musée des Beaux-Arts, Nancy), and the *Denial of St Peter* of 1650 (Musée des Beaux-Arts, Nantes), which may have been painted with the help of his son Étienne.

Penitent Magdalene
Oil on canvas, 50.4×37 in
1630-1635
Louvre, Paris

This magnificent canvas was rediscovered in 1944 in a salt mine in Bavaria, southern Germany. Three years earlier, an unscrupulous dealer had sold it to the Museum of Cologne against the will of the French owner, but just before the allied bombings it had been taken away from the city and hidden for its own protection. In 1949 the painting was reconsigned to the French authorities and entered the Louvre. La Tour returned to the subject a number of times, perhaps because the theme of reflection on mortality mirrored the artist's own distressed psychological state at the time: during this period, Lorraine had been devastated by plague and war, and his art increasingly became a conduit for his thoughts on the vanity of human life. Mary Magdalene is depicted as a woman who has renounced the world; in the solitude of a dark room, she meditates in silence, gazing at the flame of a candle (gazing at the flame of a candle) with a skull in her lap. The devices of the flame and skull serve to remind the viewer of the concept of passing time, and La Tour creates a relationship between the two elements through the continuity of the woman's gaze, focused on the flame, and her hand, which rests on the skull. The stark simplicity of her surroundings accentuates the intense mood of psychological introspection, while the Magdalene's calm composure expresses the inner contemplation of her soul. Overall, the spare pictorial style featuring simple geometric forms and pure, simple colors amplify the atmposphere of silent prayer. La Tour's extraordinary capacity for visual synthesis is accompanied by a technical brilliance displayed in the meticulous observation of objects and textures. As always in La Tour's work, the dominant element is the light, which unifies the composition and helps to give focus to the scene: the soft red tones confer a warm, suffused luminosity to the picture surface, adding to the enchanting quality of the scene.

269

St Joseph the Carpenter
Oil on canvas, 54×39.8 in
1635-1638
Louvre, Paris

Painted between 1635 and 1638, the picture shows the young Jesus assisting Joseph in his carpentry work. The theme, like that of the Virgin Mary learning to read, subject of a later work by La Tour, relates to the emphasis placed by the Church of the Counter Reformation on the education of children. The Jesuits were particularly committed to this activity, and Father Pierre Fourier had founded the Congrégation de Notre-Dame in Lorraine for the education of girls: the popularity of such compositions should be seen in relation to these pedagogical models. The representation of Joseph as a man of the people was a choice made by other "tenebrist" painters of the time, and in particular the Dutch Caravaggist Gerrit van Honthorst. The cult of Joseph had been encouraged in the 17ᵗʰ century, and in 1621 Pope Gregory XV had decided to make his feast day, March 19, an official religious holiday. From a stylistic viewpoint the composition is based, in a manner typical of La Tour, on the presence of a single source of artificial light, here the candle held by Jesus. The flame shines subtly through his fingers, a ploy used by the painter in other works as well. The play of light and shade on Joseph's wrinkled face, with its absorbed expression, and even the appearance of the man chosen to model the saint, are very Caravaggesque, especially when compared with the more summary rendering of Christ's face, the features almost canceled out by the bright light.

NICOLAS POUSSIN

(LES ANDELYS, NORMANDIE 1594 - ROME 1665)

Poussin acquired a broad knowledge of Italian painting during his formative years in Paris, from the works preserved in the royal collections, the Mannerist paintings of the school of Fontainebleau, and the engravings after Raphael and his pupil Giulio Romano. He then made the pivotal decision of traveling to Italy, which was to have a profound effect on his career: after stopping in Venice, he reached Rome in 1624, where he was to stay for most of his life. Poussin's early Italian activity reveals the influence of the Titian, especially the Venetian master's *Bacchanalia* which inspired a number of the French artist's mythological paintings, characterized by a bright, luminous chromatic palette: the *Triumph of Flora, Inspiration of the Poet, The Great Bacchanal with a Woman Playing a Lute (The Andrians)* (all in the Louvre,

Paris), and the *Death of Germanicus* (Institute of Arts, Minneapolis). The artist focused increasingly onto the ancient world, taking his historical and sacred subjects from the Greco-Roman repertoire which he depicted in compositions of great formal harmony (the *Rape of the Sabine Women*, Metropolitan Museum, New York and Louvre, Paris; and the first series of the *Sacraments* of 1636-1640). Another element central to Poussin's art was landscape. Following the example of Annibale Carracci, Poussin's vast bucolic scenes were the very ideal of Classical harmony and perfection, as exemplified by his *Landscape with the Funeral of Phocion* (Earl of Plymouth Collection, Oakly Park, Shropshire); and the sublime *Four Seasons* and *Landscape with Orpheus and Eurydice*, both in the Louvre.

Martyrdom of St Erasmus
Oil on canvas, 126×73 in
1628-1629
Vatican Picture Gallery,
Vatican City

Poussin's deep admiration for Rome, both ancient and modern, was well known. His biographer, Giovanni Pietro Bellori, told of how the French painter took a foreigner to see the Roman ruins one day. When the visitor expressed his desire to take something back to his own country as a memento of the city, Poussin picked up a handful of earth and declared, "*Here, sir, take this to your museum and say: this is ancient Rome*". Although the painter had spent his youth in Paris, where he had liberal access to the royal collections in the Louvre, his study of antiquity and the art

of the Italian Renaissance made him yearn to travel to Italy. His dream became a reality in 1624 when he arrived in Rome via Venice, and within a few years he rose to become one of the Italian capital's most celebrated artists; only the repeated threats of Louis XIII, who demanded the artist's presence in his French court, managed to coerce him back to his homeland in 1640, against his wishes. The *Martyrdom of St Erasmus* was the artist's first public commission in Rome, and he proudly signed it with the Latin version of his name, which reads *Nicolaus Pusin[us] fecit*. The altarpiece, originally painted for St Peter's Basilica, is a magisterial synthesis of the different cultural influences of the time. The subject is

absolutely in line with the precepts of the Catholic Reformation, which held it necessary to reevaluate the early Church's worship of martyred saints. Stylistically, however, Poussin was inspired by the works of Caravaggio, which he knew and admired. The saint's sacrifice is thus depicted not only as an extreme act of faith, but a cruel murder committed beneath the stern glare of a Pagan idol.

The Rape of the Sabine Women

Oil on canvas, 61.5×82.7 in
1637
Louvre, Paris

Poussin is regarded as one of France's greatest artists, in spite of his close connection with Rome, where he spent the better part of his life. It is clear from the artist's work why he "needed" the city: it provided him with an immense open-air iconographic repertoire, an inexhaustible historical font which fed his imagination and suggested his subject matter, predominantly taken from ancient history, mythology and biblical stories. *The Rape of the Sabine Women* is an archetypal Poussin theme: a legendary episode from the foundation of Rome. The imperious figure of Romulus stands out amid the chaos, raising his mantle as a signal to his troops: they were to capture the Sabine women *en masse* and carry them off to Rome

in order to populate their new city. The Sabine people had been lured to the spot on the pretext of attending a religious ceremony; they were therefore unarmed and impotent against the Roman soldiers. At the center of the composition, a young mother has been grabbed by mistake (the Romans had been told only to take single women), to the despair of her two children and the old wetnurse. Nothing in this painting is extraneous: every gesture has a meaning, every face expresses violence or fear, every movement describes a precise action. Everything, even the stylistic elements, contributes to the telling of the tale. This, above all, was Poussin's aim: to adapt his style to the individual subject he was representing. It is for this reason that there is often such stylistic disparity between works painted by Poussin during the same period, but whose subject matter is different.

GIAN LORENZO BERNINI

(NAPLES 1598 - ROME 1680)

Gian Lorenzo Bernini spent his formative years in the workshop of his father, a late Mannerist sculptor; here he dedicated himself to the passionate study of the great 16th century masters and the statuary of antiquity, particularly of the Hellenistic period, which would have a considerable impact on his own style. The young sculptor demonstrated his precocious talent in his early marble masterpieces, the four sculptures executed between 1619 and 1625 for Cardinal Scipione Borghese (all in the Borghese Gallery, Rome): *Aeneas, Anchises and Ascanius, Apollo and Daphne, David* and the *Rape of Proserpina*. The dynamic figures are captured in mid-motion at a climactic moment, as they interact with the surrounding space. Bernini developed a rich and complex Baroque language capable of achieving spectacularly dramatic effects which perfectly reflected the ideals of the Papal Court and the prevailing mood of the time. He rose to become the preeminent artist of his era in Rome, winning praise and favor from the nobility and most importantly from successive popes, who commissioned a long series of works from him for the new St Peter's Basilica over a period of more than forty years, from 1624-1667. The first of these works was the bronze *Baldacchino* or canopy over the tomb of St Peter, a colossal structure resting on elaborate spiral columns (which Francesco Borromini collaborated on), located directly over the center of the cross-shaped floor plan devised by Michelangelo; there followed the *Tomb of Urban VIII*, the *Equestrian Statue of Constantine*, the impressive *Scala Regia* (*Royal Staircase*), and the awe-inspiring *Cathedra Petri*, the throne of St Peter as Christ's vicar, a spectacularly grandiose work representing the Gloria as a crowd of exultant angels amid a blaze of golden rays falling on the sculptural group of the Four Fathers of the Church. The majestic *Colonnade* in St Peter's Square is a testament to Bernini's genius as architect, and he completed other major architectural projects such as the Palazzo di Montecitorio and the church of Sant'Andrea al Quirinale; he was also commissioned by Louis XIV to design plans for the Palace of the Louvre (which were never executed because they were thought to clash with the Classicist tastes of the French). Bernini was responsible for the famous Roman fountains of the *Four Rivers* in Piazza Navona, and the *Triton* in Piazza Barberini. In the course of his long career he also sculpted a series of portrait busts, including those of *Cardinal Scipione Borghese* (Galleria Borghese, Rome), *Costanza Buonarelli* (Bargello, Florence) and *Louis XIV* (Museum of Versailles), works noted both for their expressive realism and perceptive psychological acuity. The master's ability to interpret the spiritual sensibilities of the Baroque era is encapsulated by the celebrated mystical *Ecstasy of St Teresa* (1647-1652, Santa Maria della Vittoria, Rome) and the *Death of the Blessed Ludovica Albertoni* (1671-1674, San Francesco a Ripa, Rome).

Apollo and Daphne
White marble, h. 95.7 in
1622-1625
Galleria Borghese, Rome

The *Apollo and Daphne*, universally recognized as one of Bernini's masterpieces, is intimately linked to the *Aeneas, Anchises and Ascanius* which was originally located opposite, and the *Rape of Proserpina*. The mythological group, started in 1622, was part of an ambitious project devised by Cardinal Scipione Borghese, who wished to grace the rooms of his suburban villa with the stories and legends of Classical antiquity represented in sculptural form. As with the *Rape of Proserpina*, the literary source for the myth of Apollo and Daphne was Ovid's

Metamorphoses. In the Latin poet's tale, the god Apollo bragged of his mastery of the bow and arrow, inciting the rage of Cupid, who in revenge struck Apollo with one of his own fatal arrows and caused him instantly to fall in love with the beautiful Daphne.

To Apollo's misfortune, however, the nymph was devoted to Diana, goddess of the hunt, and had taken the solemn vow of chastity demanded by the goddess of all of her followers.

After several attempts to repel Apollo's persistent amorous advances, and realizing the impossibility of escaping the god's tireless pursuit, the nymph invoked the help of Diana, who rescued her from the lovesick suitor by transforming her into a laurel tree, which from then on was considered sacred to the goddess. Bernini depicts the visceral moment in which Daphne begins to metamorphose before the bewildered Apollo: her hands have already become laurel branches, the ends of her hair are turning into leaves, and her body is changing into a tree trunk. In spite of the nymph's nudity, the myth of Daphne was considered appropriate for the house of a cardinal: as early as the 15th century, it had been interpreted in moralizing Christian terms as an allegory of the incorruptibility of Virtue in her flight from temptation.

David

White marble, h. 27.5 in
1623-1624
Galleria Borghese, Rome

The *David* was originally commissioned for the villa of Cardinal Alessandro Montalto, grand-nephew of Pope Sixtus V and a refined connoisseur of the arts for whom Bernini had already executed other works. The statue had only just been rough-hewn when the cardinal died suddenly in 1623; it was then that Scipione Borghese acquired the block of marble, encouraging the artist to finish the piece quickly according to the scheme Montalto had devised for it, temporarily halting Bernini's work on the *Apollo and Daphne* which he had only begun in the previous year. It is said that the sculptor produced his vigorous depiction of the biblical hero

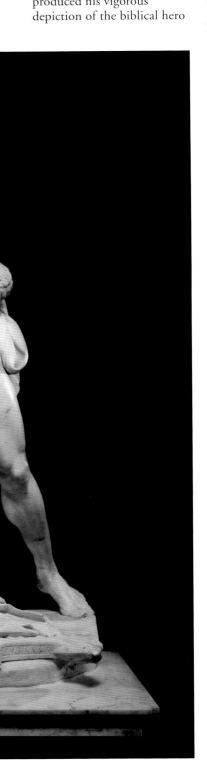

in only seven months, and according to an anecdote recounted by his son and biographer Domenico, he gave the figure his own features. The task of holding the mirror up to Bernini while he carved his likeness onto the face of David purportedly fell to none other than Cardinal Maffeo Barberini, the future Pope Urban VIII, who was himself subsequently immortalized by Bernini in a bust. David was the ancestor of Christ, and the most important king in the history of the Israelites. His feats are narrated in the Old Testament, but the accounts are disjointed and often contradictory: at times he is described as a handsome young man, at times as a brave warrior blessed with great cunning and physical strength. In the episode of his epic encounter with the giant Goliath, he first presents himself fully armed; but fearing that the armor will restrict his movements, he removes it all, confronting his enemy with nothing but his famous sling and calling on God to protect him. David's victory is symbolic of how faith can help the weak to triumph over the strong, and the humble over the arrogant. For the Church of the Counter Reformation, David was also the patron of sacred music and represented the relationship between culture and religion. It is therefore clear why Cardinal Scipione placed Bernini's masterpiece in the first room on the ground floor of his villa: it served as a reminder to visitors that they were entering the home not only of a devout Cardinal, but a cultured prince of the arts.

ANTHONY VAN DYCK

(ANTWERP 1599 - LONDON 1641)

Van Dyck was another precocious artistic talent: as early as 1615, at the age of just sixteen, he opened his own workshop in Antwerp, and only three years later the young master had joined the guild of painters and was collaborating with Pieter Paul Rubens. The works of this period, such as *St Martin Dividing his Cloak* (Royal Collection, Windsor Castle) reveal his debt to Rubens. From 1621-1627 Van Dyck was in Italy, spending most of his time in Genoa but also making trips to Rome, Florence, Bologna, Venice and Palermo. He was thus able to study the great works of the Italian Renaissance, which he copied in his sketch book now in the British Museum, London. The paintings he produced during his stay in Italy were particularly influenced by Titian, as seen in the soft color tones, use of *sfumato* and the elegance of the compositions. As well as numerous religious works such as the *Madonna of the Rosary* (Oratorio del Rosario, Palermo), Van Dyck executed a series of portraits of the Genoese aristocracy, mostly depicted full-figure like the *Portrait of Caterina Durazzo* (Palazzo Reale, Genoa), an outstanding example of his mature style. On his return to Holland he was appointed court painter to the Archduchess Isabella, and produced mainly portraits and altarpieces such as the *Ecstasy of St Augustine* (Church of St Augustine, Antwerp). Of his mythological paintings, the masterpiece *Rinaldo and Armida* (Louvre, Paris) is particularly striking for the light, deft touch which seems to anticipate the Rococo style. In 1632 Van Dyck moved to England, where he worked as official court painter to King Charles I, who even knighted him. The artist's portraits of the king are particularly famous (National Gallery, London; Louvre, Paris; Prado, Madrid). As well as portraying the monarch himself, Van Dyck painted numerous portraits of other members of the English aristocracy, depicted wearing sumptuous outfits against sweeping, luminous landscapes. An important record of the English nobility in the first half of the 17th century, the paintings would have a profound impact on the great English portrait painters of the 18th century, Gainsborough and Reynolds.

The Crowning with Thorns
Oil on canvas, 88×77 in
c. 1619-1620
Prado, Madrid

Having been sold by Van Dyck to Rubens in 1640, the canvas was subsequently bought by Philip IV of Spain, adding to the large series of paintings by the artist now in the Prado. Among his religious works, this undoubtedly represents one of the high points of his art. It depicts the Gospel episode in which Christ's jailers taunt him by placing a crown of thorns on his head, a stick in his hands, and mockingly call him the "King of the Jews". Van Dyck freezes the action to the moment in which Christ is about to be "crowned". The viewer's attention is drawn to Christ's naked white flesh, which emanates an almost other-wordly light symbolic of his divinity, and gives tone to the other colors. Christ's bare skin is practically flawless, and the traces of his recent flagellation are barely visible in the few drops of blood on his chest and arm. Transfigured by the light projecting from his own body, Christ stares downwards and appears mentally detached from his suffering. Even the assorted jailers and torturers seem to be affected by his calm endurance: their actions are slow, almost hesitant, and their faces are not diabolical or grotesque as tradition dictates, but simply somber and wretched, the faces of people forced to do an unpleasant job. The figures who look curiously through the barred window suggest a space outside the prison cell, reminding the viewers of their own role as witnesses. The painting's grand scale and large figures also help to draw the observers in, making them feel almost complicit: their emotional involvement heightens the sense of impotence and dismay at Christ's pain. Although the painting is intensely dramatic, it does not transmit violent emotions, but a contained suffering, immersed in a hushed silence which is only interrupted by the barking dog.

Portrait of Cardinal Bentivoglio

Oil on canvas, 76.8×57.9 in
1622
Galleria Palatina, Palazzo
Pitti, Florence

Significantly considered by Rubens as "*my best disciple*", Anthony van Dyck was not only a pupil of the older master, but his most important collaborator. The warm, florid impasto style of Rubens' mature Baroque period betrayed his enduring fascination with Venetian painting, acquired during his numerous journeys to Italy, although he was less interested in the vigorous, sculptural rendering of volumes than the depicting of silky, tactile textures. Van Dyck applied the lessons he learnt from Rubens to his portraiture, for which he was justly renowned by his contemporaries. His lively technique expertly reconciled the formal needs of the portrait, defined through the lavish outfits and jewelry, with an extraordinary psychological perspicacity, triggering a definitive change of direction in the art of portraiture away from the austerity of previous eras. Van Dyck's *Portrait of Cardinal Bentivoglio* was acclaimed as a true masterpiece: the Cardinal's physical presence and personality are depicted with astonishing immediacy, the studied pose and soft red tones creating a spectacularly compelling image which revealed Van Dyck as a worthy heir to the great Venetian masters such as Titian and Tintoretto.

VELÁZQUEZ

DIEGO RODRÍGUEZ DE SILVA Y VELÁZQUEZ
(SEVILLE, ANDALUSIA 1599 - MADRID 1660)

From his earliest works Diego Velázquez demonstrated a particular predilection for scenes involving everyday life and people, as seen in the portrait of *Mother Jerónima de la Fuente* of 1620 (Prado, Madrid). In stylistic terms, his youthful paintings betray the influence of Caravaggio in their intense realism combined with the plastic modeling of the figures and strong *chiaroscuro* effects. In 1623 Velázquez moved from his native Andalusia in southern Spain to the capital Madrid, having won the prestigious commission to paint King Philip IV's portrait. He quickly became the court's most esteemed painter, receiving numerous honors including the office of *apodentador mayor*, one of the court's highest positions, which gave him the right to live in a house attached to the Royal Palace. Velázquez made two trips to Italy, in 1629 and 1649, which were of fundamental importance to his artistic development. During his first trip he executed several famous works in Rome, including the *Forge of Vulcan* (Prado, Madrid), an original interpretation of the popular taste for Cara-

vaggism. His presence in Naples in 1630 would in turn have an impact on the local artists, particularly Jusepe de Ribera. Velázquez's second trip to Italy saw him take inspiration from the great Venetian painting tradition of the previous century, as revealed for example in the chromatic freedom of the celebrated *Rokeby Venus* (*Toilet of Venus*) in the National Gallery, London, painted shortly before 1650. The painter reestablished himself permanently in Madrid until the end of his life, and his mature phase is documented by grand masterpieces such as *Las meninas* (*The Maids of Honor*) and *Las hilanderas* (*The Spinners* or the *Fable of Arachne*). Here more than anywhere else, Velázquez displayed his remarkable ability to depict reality with a dispassionate, objective eye, making no concessions to what might be considered "pleasing" or "picturesque" for the sake of it. His realism was not extreme, however, but expressed through the masterful handling of color and light which marked him out as one of the most modern and avant-garde painters in Europe.

Los borrachos (The Topers or the Feast of Bacchus)
Oil on canvas, 65×74 in
c. 1628
Prado, Madrid

The subject of this canvas, executed by Velázquez in Madrid before his first trip to Italy, was apparently inspired by a story told to him by Pieter Paul Rubens about a party thrown in Brussels in 1612 by the Archdukes Albert and Isabella, which was suddenly intruded upon by a man dressed only in a linen sheet and crowned with vine leaves, together with eight companions. Velázquez's own painting echoed the Spanish literary tradition of treating classical and mythological themes with ridicule; and the canvas blends seriousness with irony in equal measure. As if to reflect this duality, the original grand title, cited in old inventories as the *Feast of Bacchus*, was quickly substituted with the rather more prosaic *Los borrachos*, "the topers" or "drunkards". Both titles are appropriate, and help to highlight the two contrasting components of the work, the pompous celebration of the mythological god (representing the ancient world), and the earthy depiction of tipsy modern folk (representing contemporary life). The composition can in fact be divided into two parts: the left section, presided over by the noble Bacchus, has the air of an academic, Classicizing work which corresponds perfectly to the original title, while the right section instantly undermines this by transposing the myth into an amusing, rather vulgar everyday scene whose protagonists are the *borrachos*. Bacchus remains the focal point of the canvas, however, his white, bare skin illuminated by a strong light. Sitting on a wine barrel against a Castilian landscape with a vine to the left of the picture, the god distractedly crowns one of his humble followers. The other figures who crowd around him are depicted in different poses and wearing different outfits, suggesting their contrasting social status. The soldier who is kneeling before Bacchus to receive the crown seems almost to be taking part in a religious ceremony, and along with the other two figures in the foreground, arranged to form a diagonal across the composition, he recalls one of the biblical Magi: another ironic allusion probably deliberately intended by Velázquez.

287

Las Hilanderas (The Spinners or the Fable of Arachne)

Oil on canvas, 65.7×99.2 in
c. 1655-1657
Prado, Madrid

The painting's original title was the *Fable of Arachne*, and it was listed as such in the 1664 inventory of the collection of the magistrate Don Pedro de Arce of Madrid. Later, however, its mythological origins were perhaps forgotten, and it came to be known simply as *Las hilanderas (The Spinners)*. The setting may have been inspired by the tapestry factory of Sant'Isabella in Madrid, which produced fine works for the royal court which Velázquez frequented. As with *Los borrachos* or the *Feast of Bacchus*, this painting's twin titles rather appropriately suggest the two different yet related subjects of the painting: in the foreground, and almost completely in the shadows, three women are busy spinning attended by two more at either side; while the illuminated scene in the raised area in the background depicts three more women, rather more lavishly dressed, who are looking at a tapestry which illustrates a mythological episode. The contrasting settings and lighting suggests that the main narrative is taking place in the background, like a picture within a picture. The mythological theme is taken from Ovid's *Metamorphoses*: the young Arachne, a weaver of beautiful fabrics, boasted one day that her art surpassed even Minerva's; so as a punishment, the goddess transformed her into a spider forced to spin for all eternity. In the tapestry, the painter has represented the moment when Arachne proudly shows a richly embellished swathe of cloth to the intimidating figure of Minerva, who is armed with a lance and shield. The subject may be read as a metaphor for the supreme creative genius of the artist prepared to challenge even the gods, and thus a celebration of art and painting, in spite of Arachne's unfortunate fate. It has also been posited that the three women spinning in the foreground could represent the Parcae, the mythical sisters who spun, measured and cut the thread of human life, suggesting a second theme, that of the passage of time: the spinners' actions seem to have been caught in the exact instance in which Minerva raises her right hand to condemn Arachne, perhaps alluding to the ability of painting to "stop" time, and capture life's fleeting moments for posterity.

Las Meninas (The Maids of Honor or the Family of Philip IV)

Oil on canvas, 125×108.7 in
1656
Prado, Madrid

In 1734 a terrible fire engulfed the Alcazar of Madrid (the old royal palace), almost completely destroying it. One of the few paintings to be saved from the blaze was *Las Meninas*, Velázquez's most famous masterpiece. The king, in fact, loved the picture so much that he had hung it in his own private apartments on the ground floor of the palace, which was the last to succumb to the flames. The highly original way Velázquez conceived of portraying the various subjects of the painting captivated his contemporaries from the outset, and ensured the painting's immediate success: indeed, the painter, who already enjoyed the respect and admiration of the royal court, achieved his pinnacle of fame with this work. Set in one of the rooms of the Alcazar, the picture is a "snapshot" in time: at the left stands Velázquez himself, in front of a large canvas on which he is painting the portraits of the king and queen, Philip IV and Marianne of Austria. The viewer only sees the back of the canvas, but the figures of the sovereigns are ingeniously revealed in the distant reflection of the mirror hanging at the far end of the room. In a complex interplay of appearance and reality, the king and queen become the observers of the "real" scene, which they are witnessing from the very same position as the "true" viewers of the painting, ourselves. Consequently, the "real" subjects of the portrait are not the king and queen but the young royals and their attendants, and perhaps most importantly Velázquez himself, whose elegant self-portrait captures the painter at the absolute peak of his career. It is a superb conceit, an intimate window onto the everyday domesticity of the royal household, and a proud statement by Velázquez on his own genius. At the center of the tableau is the Infanta Margherita, standing between the two maids of honor, doña Maria Agustina de Sarmento (who is kneeling to help her), and doña Isabel de Velasco (who is curtseying in deference to the king and queen); and it is these two *meninas*, a term of Portuguese origin, who gave the painting its nickname, by which it is now universally known.

REMBRANDT

REMBRANDT HARMENSZOON VAN RIJN
(LEIDEN, SOUTH HOLLAND 1606 - AMSTERDAM 1669)

The son of a miller, Rembrandt began working as an independent painter in 1625. His early work was largely dedicated to religious themes, characterized by theatrical compositional schemes and violent lighting effects which betrayed the influence of Caravaggio (filtered through the Dutch Caravaggisti of Utrecht), such as *Christ and the Pilgrims at Emmaus* (Musée Jacquemart-André, Paris). At the same time, the artist started on his famous series of self-portraits which would trace his entire life. In 1631 he moved to Amsterdam where he established himself as an excellent portrait painter, and in 1634 he married Saskia, the cousin of a wealthy art dealer. The city's Guild of Surgeons commissioned him to paint the celebrated *Anatomy Lesson of Doctor Nicolaes Tulp* of 1632 (Mauritshuis, The Hague), whose action is dramatized by the strong *chiaroscuro*. Rembrandt's technical brilliance and capacity for acute psychological insight is evident from this group portrait, as in his individual portraits such as *Saskia Laughing* (Gemäldegalerie, Dresden), *Joannes Elison and Mary Bockemolle* (Museum of Fine Arts, Boston) and *Man in Oriental Costume*

(Rijksmuseum, Amsterdam). Rembrandt was also a fine graphic artist, and made numerous drawings and engravings throughout his career, of which the so-called *Hundred Guilder Plate (Christ Healing the Sick)* of 1642-1645 (National Gallery, London) is particularly noteworthy. With the *Night Watch*, one of his most famous masterpieces, the artist reached the peak of his artistic achievement. However, following the tragic loss of three children and his wife, he abandoned his official portrait painting activity, to concentrate increasingly on the exploration of the inner self, and the emotional and spiritual aspects of human life. In his late paintings, the draftsmanship is much freer (notably in the *Supper at Emmaus, Holy Family* and *Bathsheba at her Bath* in the Louvre; *Aristotle with a Bust of Homer* in the Metropolitan Museum, New York; the *Woman Bathing in a Stream* in the National Gallery, London; and the *Polish Rider* in the Frick Collection, New York). Rembrandt also continued to paint his strikingly intense self-portraits, which form a lucid autobiography of his life, emotional state, and changing fortunes.

Doctor Nicolaes Tulp's Demonstration of the Anatomy of the Arm
Oil on canvas, 66.6×85 in
1632
Mauritshuis, The Hague

The picture, usually known as the *Anatomy Lesson of Doctor Nicolaes Tulp*, was commissioned by the Surgeons' Guild of Amsterdam. It was the first large group portrait executed by Rembrandt at the beginning of his period in the Dutch city. Tulp had given his first public lesson of anatomy on January 31,

1631, and the picture was painted on the occasion of his second public lecture, in the January of the following year. The demonstrations were held annually in chapels of deconsecrated churches or in a *theatrum anatomicum*, and an entrance fee was charged. The real subject of the painting is not an anatomy lesson, but a group portrait that alludes to an engraving of Vesalius. Andreas Vesalius (Andries van Wesel) had attended the universities of Louvain and Paris, and in 1537 was the first university professor to

practise anatomy personally. His work *De humani corporis fabrica libri septem* (*The Seven Books on the Structure of the Human Body*) was published in Basel in 1543, and almost all its editions carry an illustration of the author dissecting a hand. Considering that Tulp's teacher, Pieter Paauw, had been his pupil at the University of Padua, the choice of having himself represented at work was a way of declaring himself a follower of Vesalius. This distinguishes the painting from other group

portraits with anatomists, of which the oldest example known to us is the one painted by Aert Pieters in 1603, representing Dr. Sebastian Egbertsz along with twenty-nine other people. Around 1656 Rembrandt painted the *Anatomy Lesson of Doctor Jan Deyman* (Rijksmuseum, Amsterdam): here too the operation illustrated, the opening of the cranium, refers to Vesalius's book, and constitutes another declaration in favor of the method promoted by the physician.

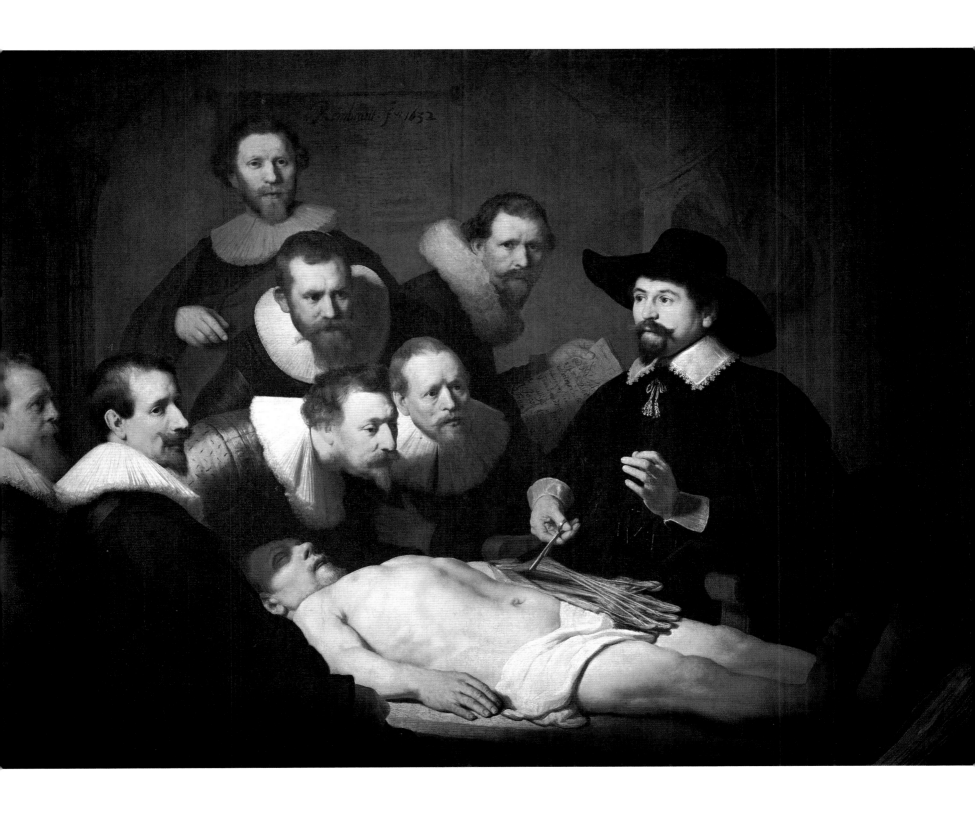

Descent from the Cross

Oil on wood, 35×25.5 in
1633
Alte Pinakothek, Munich

At the start of the 1630s, Prince Frederick Henry of Orange-Nassau, Statholder of the United Provinces, succeeded his father, and initiated an ambitious decorating project which was to encompass his various residences. At that time, Rembrandt was just starting his career in Leiden, and the prince developed a passion for his paintings, commissioning a number of works from him. The finest of these was a series of five panels on the theme of the Passion of Christ, which occupied Rembrandt for the whole decade, mainly because of his habitual reluctance to finish his works. The *Descent from the Cross* was one of the earliest of these paintings and must have been particularly admired by the prince, as it is thought to have influenced his decision to ask Rembrandt to execute the remaining paintings (probably destined for the Nooreinde Palace in The Hague). The artist referred to the works in one of the seven letters he wrote to Constantijn Huygens, the prince's Secretary who may have played an important role in helping him to obtain the prestigious commission: "*My Lord, my most gracious Lord Huygens, I hope that your Lordship will please tell his Excellency that I am hard at work on completing as quickly as possible the three paintings of the Passion that his Excellency himself has commissioned from me, that is a Deposition, a Resurrection and an Ascension of Christ to accompany the Raising of the Cross and the Descent of Christ from the Cross*". The intense pathos of the *Descent from the Cross* is heightened by the limp, almost pathetic body of Christ: Rembrandt has chosen to depict the dead god deprived of all power and majesty, as a human being rather than a divinity.

The Militia Company of Captain Frans Banning Cocq (The Night Watch)
Oil on canvas, 143×172 in
1642
Rijksmuseum, Amsterdam

The painting, finished in 1642, was commissioned by Captain Frans Banning Cocq, portrayed at the center dressed in black with a red sash, next to his lieutenant, Willem van Ruytenburgh. It is presumed that the captain bore the greater part of the expense, but we know that the other people portrayed also contributed to Rembrandt's fee: each of the sixteen civic guards represented here paid around a hundred guilders, depending on his position in the painting. The title *Night Watch* is deceptive, as it is refers not to the actual time of the day in which the scene is set but to the fact that in the 19ᵗʰ century the varnish which covered the paint had darkened considerably, creating the mistaken impression of the light of evening or night. It is not clear what situation is actually

represented, and the scene lends itself to multiple interpretations. The payments made by the people in the picture suggest that it was a straightforward group portrait, as this was the custom in the second half of the 17ᵗʰ century, at least where militia companies were concerned. It is also possible that it alludes to an important recent historical event, the siege of Amsterdam on January 15, 1641, but without any attempt to provide a realistic description of the place where the episode occurred, the gates of Amsterdam. The backdrop of the scene may also have been inspired by a theatrical set for the play Gijsbrecht van Aemstel by Joost van der Vondel. The work revolutionized the genre of group portrait painting, practised by several other great painters such as Frans Hals: Rembrandt broke up the group and succeeded in creating the impression that the militiamen were not posed, producing instead a scene that is filled with dynamism.

JAN VERMEER

(DELFT, SOUTH HOLLAND 1632-1675)

Jan Vermeer began his working life as an innkeeper and occasional art dealer, before joining the Guild of St Luke in 1653, the trade association for paint ers in Delft. His first paintings were influenced by the Caravaggists of Utrecht and by Rembrandt (*The Procuress*, Gemäldegalerie, Dresden; *Christ in the House of Martha and Mary*, National Gallery of Scotland, Edinburgh; *Diana and her Companions*, Mauritshuis, The Hague; and *Girl Asleep*, Metropolitan Museum, New York). Following these early works, Vermeer quickly evolved his own individual style, evident in famous paintings such as *Young Woman Reading a Letter* (Gemäldegalerie, Dresden), *Young Woman Interrupted at Music* (Frick Collection, New York), *The Kitchen Maid* (Rijksmuseum, Amsterdam), *Woman in Blue Reading a Letter* (Rijksmuseum, Amsterdam) and *The Lacemaker* (Louvre, Paris). Described as "the painter of the silent life of things", Vermeer developed a pictorial language that was exceptionally pure and clear, informed by the extraordinary observation of detail and lucid description of reality, both in his figures and objects. The master was essentially a painter of domestic interiors, with a few notable exceptions. For the most part, his canvases portrayed women absorbed in their work, or reading intently; the interiors are suffused with a soft, delicate light which alternately reflects, highlights, or creates shadows, evoking an almost magical atmosphere of suspended animation. This same atmosphere dominates his few excellent exterior views, such as the *Little Street* (Kunsthistorisches Museum, Vienna) and the *View of Delft* (Mauritshuis, The Hague). Stylistically, the works of his late period tended to be characterized by compositional schemes of greater complexity with strongly contrasting light and color; while thematically, they sometimes contained allegorical elements, exemplified by *The Allegory of Painting* (Kunsthistorisches Museum, Vienna), *The Geographer* (Kunstinstitut, Frankfurt) and *The Astronomer* (Louvre, Paris). Vermeer's work was largely forgotten until the mid 19th century, when it was reevaluated by the French realist school along with writers and critics such as Théophile Gautier, the Goncourt brothers and Marcel Proust.

View of Delft

Oil on canvas, 38.6×46 in
1660-1661
Mauritshuis, The Hague

Painted around 1660-1661, this is one of Vermeer's most celebrated works. The cityscape had been a fairly common genre in Dutch painting since the beginning of the century: in particular the layout of the composition, with the bank of the Schie River in the foreground and the city extending on the other side of the water, recalls the paintings of Esaias van de Velde or Pieter Bruegel the Elder. But what is lacking here is the eminently topographic interest displayed by the other painters of views of the period: Vermeer chose one part of the city, probably framed by a camera obscura on the upper floor of a house. The artist's main interest was the study of light, and a great deal of space was devoted to the depiction of the sky: storm clouds darken the buildings reflected in the river, while the bank in the foreground appears sunlit; the sky clears in the background, allowing rays of sunshine to fall on the tower of the Niewe Kerk, with a luministic effect that is probably also intended to be symbolic and political, given that William I of Orange had been buried in this church in 1622. Vermeer played with the harmony of colors with great skill, with the note of yellow on the houses in the background relieving the essential uniformity of the painting's tone. This brilliant touch was also to be praised by Proust, who recalled "*the patch of yellow wall painted with so much skill and refinement by the artist destined to be for ever unknown and barely identified under the name Vermeer.*"

The Astronomer

Oil on canvas, 19.7×17.8 in
1668
Louvre, Paris

The majority of Vermeer's masterpieces depicted women in discreet, intimate scenes of exquisite refinement. *The Astronomer*, a late work, is rare in that it represents a male figure: that of a scientist in his study, surrounded by astronomical instruments and completely engrossed in thought. Sitting at a table, he studies his globe intently, reaching out with his right hand to turn it. The signs on the globe are astrological, and there must have been similar examples in Holland at the time, as Vermeer never included an object in his paintings by chance: the painstaking recreation of reality in his fictitious world always required a concrete reference point. The astronomer appears perfectly real, yet the scene also has a magical quality which is altogether at odds with contemporary Dutch realism. Vermeer's genius was in the inimitable way he fused reality with dream in a delicate play of light and color: here, his subtle *pointillé* brushwork creates flashes of highlights over the astronomer's hair, face and hands, his green gown and the green cloth over the table, the globe and book. Although the painting appears to be lit from the window, everything in fact produces its own inner glow, and light blends into color as if all were covered in gold dust. The astronomer is depicted in profile, and his features are very gently blurred as in a soft focus photograph. The effect produces a figure at once realistic and idealized, almost as if to transform the astronomer into a symbol of what he represents: the admirable, thoughtful science of astronomy.

OGATA KENZAN

(KYOTO, KANSAI 1663 - EDO, KANSAI 1743)

A pupil of the great ceramist Ninsei, and the younger brother of the renowned painter Ogata Korin, Ogata Kenzan is recognized as one of Japan's finest ceramists. Living in the mid Edo period, Kenzan was the first of a series of artistically sophisticated merchant-craftsmen to open his own potter's studio, and also the pioneer of painted ceramics. Kenzan collaborated with his painter brother numerous times to produce their ceramic masterpieces. Kenzan was an excellent poet and calligrapher, and admired for his decorative work. His pottery was characterized by its smoky dark brown color, and the new style took his name: *Kenzan-yaki*. He also produced a particular type of vase known as *kakuzara*, whose form lent itself to elaborate multi-colored scenes with figures (sometimes taken from literature and similar to the traditional illustrations which accompanied the poetry of Fujiwara Teika in the 12ᵗʰ century), but also more modest images in shades of brown and copper which recall works from the Sung Dynasty. Kenzan primarily used the underglaze technique for his ceramics, while his porcelain was decorated with overglaze enameling. The master was probably not responsible for all the work ascribed to him, since at that time, craftsmen and artists who were specialized in different techniques often collaborated on a single object. There are numerous autograph pieces in Kenzan's characteristic lyrical, sophisticated style, however: the new habit of signing ceramic ware derived from the producers' desire to identify their own work, as well as the clients' need for unique, often valuable pieces to be guaranteed as genuine.

Bottom left, *Bowl with Chrisantemum Design,* early 18ᵗʰ century.

Bottom right, *Cake Tray with Bamboo Design,* early 18ᵗʰ century. Seattle Art Museum, Seattle.

Opposite, *Plate with Plum Branches Design, c.* 1720. Royal Ontario Museum, Toronto.

INDO-ISLAMIC ARCHITECTURE

(INDIA, 17ᵀᴴ CENTURY)

Indo-Islamic architecture has strikingly original characteristics, making it particularly interesting and rewarding to study. By the time Islam arrived in India, the Subcontinent already had an ancient artistic tradition, developed and refined over time by skilful artists and craftsmen and underpinned by strict rules which had remained essentially the same for centuries. These were based on the linear elements of the pillar and lintel, ignoring the dome and arch. The Islamic period saw the synthesis, sometimes difficult and not always successful, of two apparently irreconcilable archi-tectural styles. There are few surviving examples of the wooden architecture which must have been widespread across the Subcontinent at one time, but elements of certain stone monuments can sometimes give the impression of having been transposed from an earlier wooden model. Stone is by far the most common building material found in India; brick is very occasionally seen, and there are rare examples of tiles used to decorate interiors and exteriors. Although the artistic and cultural legacy of Islamic India is vast, it is still relatively undervalued.

Taj Mahal
1632-1643
Agra

The Taj Mahal is one of the world's most famous architectural monuments, and was built in memory of the favorite wife of Emperor Shah Jahan, Mumtaz Mahal, who is buried in the crypt beneath. The mausoleum is located at the end of a quadripartite *chahar bagh* on the banks of the River Jamuna, and was originally to have faced a twin mausoleum, in black marble, on the opposite shore, which was never built. The entire complex is organized and designed to emphasize the colossal white marble mausoleum, which rises imposingly from its high platform, with four beautifully proportioned minarets placed at each corner mounted by *chattri*. The Taj Mahal represents the summation of Asian architecture, an extraordinary and distinctive blend of Islamic, Persian and Indian styles which form a perfect whole. On first sight, the monument's enormous size and perfect symmetry are breathtaking. Naturally, every element is finished with astonishing attention to detail, including the delicate inscriptions and sinuous arabesques (in black) which decorate the arches; the lower panels, richly carved with flowers (recalling the most sumptuous contemporary carpets) are splendid, and exude a cool sensuality.

GIAMBATTISTA TIEPOLO
(VENICE 1696 - MADRID 1770)

Tiepolo's early work was directly influenced by his older contemporary Giovanni Battista Piazzetta, from whom he borrowed the diagonal compositional structure, vivid color scheme and dramatic *chiaroscuro* lighting seen in the youthful painting *Martyrdom of St Bartholomew* (Church of St Stae, Venice). During the 1720s the painter developed a more Rococo-style sensibility which culminated in the masterpiece of his early period, the huge frescoes executed for the Archbishop of Udine. These were Tiepolo's first attempts at creating grandiose illusionistic decorations over large surfaces, characterized by a lighter chromatic palette consisting of delicate pastel tones. Another reference point for the painter was the 16th century Venetian artist Paolo Veronese, admired for his majestic compositions and the subtle, precious treatment of light which perfectly harmonized the figures with their surroundings. Between 1730 and 1750 Tiepolo worked continuously, both on ambitious decorative fresco cycles and equally grand-scale canvas paintings, firstly in Bergamo, then in Vicenza,

Milan and Venice. To achieve the vast celestial backgrounds which provided the setting for his celebrated mythological, historical and religious scenes, Tiepolo often collaborated with the famous *trompe l'oeil* master Girolamo Mengozzi Colonna, as in the case of the *Story of Cleopatra* frescoes in Venice's Palazzo Labia (1747-1750). In 1750 the painter was summoned to Franconia in Germany to decorate a number of rooms in the prince-bishop's residence in Würzburg with historical frescoes celebrating the Franconian dynasty, a cycle representing the ultimate expression of Tiepolo's artistic achievement: his pictorial language was never so rich, sophisticated and triumphant, from the airy, expansive compositional arrangements to the exquisitely refined chromatic blending and expert handling of light. On his return to Italy, the artist continued his intense activity, moving towards a more intimate, lyrical style. In 1762 he left for Madrid, where he spent the last eight years of his life working on the prestigious commission to fresco the royal palace of Charles III.

Adoration of the Magi
Oil on canvas, 160×82 in
1753
Alte Pinakothek, Munich

This splendid and imposing altarpiece must have produced a striking effect in its original location on the altar of the Benedictine abbey church of Münsterschwarzach, where it remained until the start of the 19th century when the building was destroyed. The painting, signed and dated 1753, was commissioned while Tiepolo was in Germany working on his supreme masterpiece, the frescoes in the palace of the prince-bishop of Würzburg. This composition is organized along a sweeping diagonal which runs from the foot of the king standing at the far left of the scene up to the horizontal line of the structure, possibly an altar, behind the Virgin's shoulders. The area to the left of the diagonal is crowded with shadowy figures, some of whom can barely be seen, while the strongly illuminated area to the right is relatively empty, featuring only the youngest of the Magi (with his back to the viewer) and a few objects such as the necklace and crown lying on the steps, and

the broken wheel in the foreground. The arrangement thus creates a contrast between the two different sections at either side of the diagonal: the top left triangle is darker and busier, while the much brighter bottom right triangle contains just one figure and a number of apparently insignificant objects. It sets up a visual paradox, a favorite device of Tiepolo's which he used to create effects and moods that were intriguing and mysterious: details would be partially hidden, or their meanings obscured, encouraging viewers to look closer and fill in the "gaps"

with their own imaginations. The effect is amplified here by Tiepolo's rapid, summary brushstrokes which in places almost approximate to sketch work: the figures seem almost to quiver with an indefinable energy and movement, lending the image an ephemeral, dream-like quality which has the impression that it could vanish at any moment.

The Marriage of Barbarossa; The Investiture of Bishop Harold

Frescoes, 157.5×196.8 in
1750-1752
Residenz, Würzburg

In 1750 Tiepolo was invited to Würzburg to decorate the banquet hall known as the Kaisersaal in the Residenz of the new prince-bishop Karl Philipp von Greiffenklau. He may have been guided in the undertaking by the *Modest Opinions on the Painting of the Prince's Grand Dining Room* supplied by the court council. These had called for the representation of the scenes of the wedding of Emperor Barbarossa to Princess Beatrice of Burgundy, which had taken place at Würzburg in 1156, and the investiture of Bishop Herold of Würzburg as duke of Franconia by Barbarossa in 1168, two quite distant and different events that the painter was required to present as if they were linked by a relationship of cause and effect: in gratitude for the hospitality he had received on the occasion of the fruitful marriage, the emperor invested the bishop as a vassal of the Holy Roman Empire. The painter used the Rococo stuccoes of the room to frame the scenes in a theatrical setting on which the curtain is rising, with a markedly illusionistic effect. As was customary, in order to avoid damage to the walls, the decoration commenced from the ceiling, where Tiepolo painted *Apollo Leading Beatrice of Burgundy to the Genius of the German Nation*. It continued with the scenes at the sides, which were painted in such a way as to make them appear to be illuminated by the natural lighting of the room. *The Marriage of Barbarossa*

(1751-1753), set in a Palladian-style basilica and with figures dressed in 16th century clothing, is attended by papal nuncios and prince-electors, the grand marshal of the empire with his sword drawn, located under the imperial insignia as ceremony required, and the grand marshal of Franconia on the far right. On the left, kneeling and wearing an amaranth cloak, is the bride's father, while the officiating bishop has been given the features of the client. The dwarf and court jester, with his baton suspended in the void, connects the painted scene with the real space of the room. But attention is focused on the woman, in a scene that evokes Rubens's *Coronation of Marie de Médicis*. In the *Investiture* (1751-1753), Barbarossa offers the imperial scepter to the bishop to be touched in a sign of feudal submission, while the chancellor reads the parchment of investiture and two pages hold the pluvial and the crown, symbols of the two branches of power, the spiritual and the temporal. The imperial grand marshal with his sword unsheathed and the grand marshal of Franconia are present in this scene too. The page who is staring out of the painting and the dog in the foreground perform the same function as the dwarf in the *Marriage*. The decoration continued on the ceiling of the main staircase with the *Olympus and the Four Continents*, which features portraits not just of the client but also of Tiepolo and his son Giandomenico.

GIO. BTTA. TIEPOLO 1752.

CANALETTO

GIOVANNI ANTONIO CANAL
(VENICE 1697-1768)

Canaletto spent his early years training as a scenographer under his father, but soon decided to devote himself to painting. He began by creating imaginary views featuring Classical ruins, quickly progressing to real cityscapes (inspired by those of minor artists Carlevarijs and van Wittel), which immediately met with huge international success. Early views such as the *Rio dei Mendicanti: Looking South* (Ca' Rezzonico, Venice), *Santi Giovanni e Paolo and the Scuola di San Rocco* (Gemäldegalerie, Dresden) and *The Stonemason's Yard* (National Gallery, London) were characterized by strong *chiaroscuro* contrasts and the faultless rendering of perspective which revealed his background in theatrical scene painting. Canaletto increasingly concentrated on the study of natural light and atmospheric effects in ambitious canvases whose scenes were lit by an intense yet suffused luminosity, for example in the series of views of the Grand Canal, the Venetian squares and the towns and cities of the Venetian hinterlands or the Brenta Riviera. Canaletto's unrivalled reputation as a cityscape artist led Joseph Smith, the illustrious head of the British Consulate in Venice and an avid art collector, to commission him to paint six large views of St Mark's Square and the Piazzetta (1727-1728, Windsor Castle) and twelve smaller views of the Grand Canal (1729-1734, Windsor Castle), along with a series of thirty-one etchings of the Venetian lagoon, the Brenta Riviera and Padua, which the artist executed around 1740. From 1746, Canaletto moved to London where he produced several more cityscapes, particularly with the Thames (such as *The Thames and Whitehall from Richmond House*, Collection of the Duke of Richmond, Goodwood), as well as paintings of English country houses and castles (*Badminton House*, Collection of the Duke of Beaufort).

The Reception of the French Ambassador in Venice
Oil on canvas, 71.2×102 in
1726-1727
Hermitage, St Petersburg

Canaletto was truly a man of his time, the Age of Enlightenment: with the help of a *camera obscura*, a cutting-edge contemporary instrument which used refracting mirrors and convex

lenses to reflect an image, he patiently observed and copied the narrow alleys, squares, bridges and palazzi of his native Venice, producing his epic views and cityscapes. The *Reception of the French Ambassador in Venice* is perhaps the first painting of Canaletto's to illustrate a specific event, in this case the arrival of the French ambassador Jacques-Vincent Languet, Conte de Gergy, in Venice on November 4 1726. Every element is described with an acute attention to detail, from the fading, washed-out shades of pink and yellow of the Ducal Palace to the sumptuous clothes of the large crowd of dignitaries, the gondolas floating on the water, even the tiny oars which break the surface of the rippling water. Around the mid 1720s the artist abandoned the *chiaroscuro* effects which typified his earlier paintings to adopt a "clear style" which would inform the rest of his artistic production. On the back of some of his canvases, Canaletto left an inscription claiming to have represented the scene "*con ogni maggior attenzione*" ("*with the greatest care*"); yet the naturalism of his Venetian scenes was also infused by an enchanted atmosphere which appears to suspend the city in time, almost as if to halt the inevitable process of decline Venice was already succumbing to during Canaletto's lifetime.

317

Grand Canal
and Palazzo Bembo

Oil on canvas, 18.5×31.5 in
c. 1735
Duke of Bedford Collection,
Woburn Abbey

This is one of twenty-four views by Canaletto commissioned by Lord John Russell, the Duke of Bedford. Between 1729 and 1731 the duke made a Grand Tour of Europe, and in the last year of his journey stayed in Venice, where he met Joseph Smith and may have acquired some of Canaletto's works. He certainly bought others later on, since several of the canvases in his collection cannot have been painted before 1735. The pictures of the city's most celebrated views remained in his London home for about half a century, and when the building was demolished were moved to the "Canaletto Room" in Woburn Abbey, where they can still be seen today. Works like this demonstrate the artist's minute observation not only of every crack of the buildings, but also of the quivering reflections in the water. This analytical capacity suggested that he used a *camera obscura* and the scholar Decio Gioseffi recently demonstrated that the drawings in the *Quaderno Cagnola* (Gallerie dell'Accademia, Venice) were realized with the aid of this instrument. Canaletto made sketches and surveys on the spot, and also made notes in his sketchbook for subsequent elaboration. The paintings were executed in the artist's studio, but when transferring the sketches done outdoors onto canvas Canaletto maintained the individual points of view, thereby creating a multiple perspective that added to the fascinating quality of the scene and resulted in a more poetic

SACRED IMAGES OF OCEANIA

(OCEANIA, 18TH CENTURY)

In the Society Islands of French Polynesia, anthropomorphic effigies sculpted in wood and stone, and sometimes covered in coconut fibers woven and decorated with red feathers, typically represented the creators (*to'o*) or guardian spirits, mythical ancestors and minor deities (*ti'i*). A rare example of a wooden sculpture depicting an anthropomorphic being with two heads, whose precise meaning remains unclear, was found on Tahiti. One theory is that it relates to the world of magic and ritual and the dualism present in the religion of the Oceanic peoples; another is that the work actually represents the physical deformities of real individuals, who were considered supernatural because of their defects. A number of statuettes from the Cook Islands, which recall the anthropomorphic figures (*tiki*) of the Marquesas Islands and which were placed on the sterns of the pirogue boats, are generally attributed to the god of fishing. The examples from Rarotonga were made by specialized craftsmen and are characterized by disproportionately large heads with big eyes outlined by arches and excessively wide mouths, protruding stomachs and prominent navels and phalluses. In the Austral Islands, finely carved geometric and/or anthropomorphic motifs decorated different types of ceremonial objects: drums, ceremonial paddles and fly whisks with elaborate handles in ivory or wood, the most valuable of which also featured two human figures at the end. The stylistic uniformity and level of craftsmanship that distinguishes these objects have led to the hypothesis that they were made by a school of carvers using metal tools to speed up commercial production. Similar objects have been discovered in the Society Islands, probably the result of trade and cultural exchanges with the Austral Islands in the late prehistoric and protohistoric eras, although it is also possible that some pieces may have been used or even made in Tahiti or neighboring islands. Mangaia in the Cook Islands typically produced ceremonial axes with large quadrangular handles which were traded with Europeans in the 19th century. It has been suggested that the axes symbolized one of the aspects of Tane, the god of carpenters and wood sculptors. The wooden supports are decorated with refined engravings and fretwork designs which depict stylized geometric and anthropomorphic forms. One unique ceremonial object was found on the island of Mangareva: a wooden pole with four arms at the end, whose hands face upwards. On the basis of evidence collected by Meyer, the pole would originally have been placed on a temple platform next to images of gods to whom offerings were presented, possibly carved coconut shells and musical instruments made from bamboo, placed or hung from the hands of the sculpture.

Statue of a Divinity (A'a)
From Rurutu, Austral Islands
Wood, h. *c.* 47.2 in
Late 18th century
British Museum, London

In the realm of Polynesian art, the island of Rurutu in the Austral archipelago is noted for a type of wooden sculpture quite unique to this particular island, even if the works have certain stylistic qualities common to other parts of the region. The statue now in the British Museum was bought in 1821 by the London Missionary Society in Raiatea; and apart from the contemporary description of it made by the Reverend John Williams, there is no other written documentation on the work. The figure was sculpted from a single hard wood block: the large face has a circular profile, and the arms are held at the side of the body with the hands resting on the prominent stomach. The legs, proportionately much smaller than the face and the torso, have no feet, and are slightly flexed: a feature typical of traditional Polynesian sculpture. On the face, in place of the eyes, nose and mouth, and also on the torso, hips and limbs, are anthropomorphic figures in relief, portrayed in crouching positions or with their legs gently bent. The hollow back of the statue originally contained a large number of wooden figurines, at least twenty-four, which were destroyed in 1882. The wooden panel that closes the dorsal cavity features relief carvings of another five figurines, which according to Adrienne L. Kaeppler (1993) represented a genealogical metaphor associated with the spine and widely diffused in the Polynesian region. Some scholars have connected the Rurutu statue with one of the most important Polynesian divinities, Tangaroa, creator of men and of the pantheon of minor gods. Williams's own evidence identified the statue as A'a, the supreme god of Rurutu, the mythical deified ancestor from whom the entire population of Rurutu was believed to have originated. From its arrival in London, the sculpture immediately captivated the English, and later influenced 20th century artists such as Picasso and the sculptor Henry Moore, as well as inspiring a poem by William Empson.

*Wooden Sculpture
of a Fisherman's God*,
from Polynesian, late
18th - early 19th century.
British Museum,
London.

Opposite,
*Wooden Sculpture
of a Male Figure
with Two Heads*,
from Tahiti, Society
Islands, late 18th - early
19th century.
British Museum,
London.

THOMAS GAINSBOROUGH

(SUDBURY, SUFFOLK 1727 - LONDON 1788)

The young Gainsborough was largely self-taught until he moved to London at a very early age, where he started to attend Gravelot's drawing school and learn from the engravers for whom he found models. After his marriage he dedicated himself to painting full-time, initially in his native Suffolk, and then in Bath, becoming well known for his landscapes and refined portraits of the British upper middle classes such as *Mr and Mrs Andrews* in the National Gallery, London. In 1774 he returned to London, evolving an impeccably elegant and sophisticated style which characterized both his portraiture and landscape paintings: his slender portrait subjects with their fashionable clothes and hairstyles were exquisitely observed in every detail, yet their vibrant personalities also shone through the external trappings of wealth; and his landscapes,

though they presented an idealized vision of the English countryside, still managed to maintain their realistic identity. This virtuosity can be seen in examples such as the *Portrait of Mrs Siddons* and *The Morning Walk or Mr and Mrs William Hallett* (both in the National Gallery, London), and the various portraits of his daughters (National Gallery, London and Victoria and Albert Museum, London). Gainsborough was also famous for his imaginative bucolic paintings, the so-called "fancy pictures", charming scenes exemplified by *Two Shepherd Boys with Dogs Fighting* (Kenwood House, London) which very loosely recall the suggestive works of Murillo, Watteau and Greuze. He exhibited at the prestigious Royal Academy in London and painted for the king's family, developing a famous rivalry with his contemporary Joshua Reynolds.

The Morning Walk or Mr and Mrs William Hallett

Oil on canvas, 93×70 in
July 30 1785
National Gallery, London

Enveloped in an indefinable and highly evocative atmosphere, a young married couple walks slowly along a wooded pathway of their country estate. They seem to be taking their first tentative steps towards their future life together: their slightly anxious expressions suggest that the couple are still at a very early stage in their relationship and have yet to develop a comfortable intimacy with each other. They appear awkward, almost clouded by a faint air of sadness and uncertainty about what lies ahead of

them. William Hallett and Elizabeth Stephen married on July 30 1785, and they commissioned Thomas Gainsborough, the leading portrait painter of the time, to solemnize the occasion with this painting. It was a wise choice, since no other artist was capable of depicting his subjects with such expressiveness and sensitivity. Gainsborough's rival, Sir Joshua Reynolds, was the prime representative of the academic school of British painting which relied heavily on the models of Italian and French art of the 16th and 17th centuries, with their focus on mythological scenes and arcadian landscapes; Gainsborough, by contrast, preferred the tranquility of the English countryside, and never left

the British Isles, drawing inspiration from prints after the Dutch landscape artists and a few French contemporaries.
His work was the most eloquent visual expression of a renewed appreciation of nature within British culture and society, reflecting the growing trend of the British upper classes to escape from the increasingly chaotic cities to their splendid country residences, set in beautiful parkland which provided scenes of pure serenity to enchant the eye and soothe the soul. In spite of the insecurities of the young couple in the *Morning Walk*, the vision offered by Gainsborough is an ultimately reassuring one, of human beings in perfect harmony with nature.

Opposite,
*Conversation
in the Park*, 1746.
Louvre, Paris.

*Portrait of Lady
Alston*, c. 1760.
Louvre, Paris.

BENJAMIN WEST

(SPRINGFIELD, PENNSYLVANIA 1738 - LONDON 1820)

A self-taught artist in the American Neoclassical tradition, West began his career by painting a series of Neoclassical style portraits, executed between 1746 and 1759 in his native Pennsylvania, where he occasionally came into contact with John Wollaston, a famous British-born painter who had emigrated from London to the US. West also became a close friend of Benjamin Franklin, whose portrait he painted. In 1789 the artist embarked on a Grand Tour of Italy (by then considered to be an essential requirement for a rounded artistic education); there he was able to study the country's culture and classical art, as well as meet two great exponents of Neoclassical art, Mengs and Hamilton, who were in Italy at the same time. West copied paintings by Italian artists such as Titian and Raphael, whose influence is clearly felt, especially in his early work; he was also inspired by 17th century Roman Classicism, particularly the grand cycles of Annibale Carracci and his school (such as those in the Palazzo Farnese), reinterpreted with a major focus on figures over landscape and background setting. Indeed, from the outset, West placed the greatest emphasis on the study of forms, with anatomy and plasticity rendered in meticulous detail, so that his figures acquired the quality of idealized antique statues. In 1763 West decided to move to England, where he was commissioned by King George III to paint members of the royal family; the artist also painted two individual portraits of the king himself. Although at first the British painting fraternity barely tolerated West's presence and rising fame, he was subsequently appointed as official historical painter to the royal court. West also became friends with the famous English portrait painter Sir Joshua Reynolds, with whom he founded London's prestigious Royal Academy of the Arts in 1768. West was himself elected president of the Royal Academy from 1792-1805, and re-elected in 1806 until his death in 1820. As well as being a renowned portrait painter, West was deeply admired for his historical paintings, whose highly expressive handling of color and skilful compositional structure produced what the artist termed "epic representation", and captivated the public.

Omnia Vincit Amor, or The Power of Love in the Three Elements
Oil on canvas, 70.4×80 in
1809
Metropolitan Museum, New York

In a space resolved entirely in the foreground plane, the young god Love (Cupid) is depicted representing Virgil's poetic lines *Omnia Vincit Amor* ("Love Conquers All"), with both arms raised in a gesture of triumph. In his left hand, he lightly holds the reins of his exuberant horse Pegasus, while his right hand thrusts a shining torch up into the sky; next to him is a fearsome lion, whose powerful presence amplifies Love's own strength as victor over all.

Three feisty cherubs fly about, carefully arranged around the edge of the composition to increase the sense of dynamism and add flashes of brightness. The cherub at the top right rides a proud, fierce eagle, while the second, below him, helps to guide Pegasus; the third, at the far left of the picture, hangs precariously from Venus's waistband, and holds Love's quiver of arrows. All the elements of the picture reinforce Love's omnipotence: the demure figure of Venus appears behind him with an open-handed gesture as if to spur him on. West's ephemeral painterly style adds a new dimension to the traditional Classical subject: the evocative atmosphere is heightened by the impetuous light which falls across the painting, gleaming off the pallid white skin of Love and Venus. West's admiration of the great Renaissance Venetian colorists, along with the 17th century Flemish masters such as Rubens, reverberates in his painting. The figures gain a new sensuality, and their exaggerated gestures add drama to the scene, lending it an intense energy.

The painter's eclectic influences also included David and historical genre painting (following on from the German art historian Winckelmann's theories), particularly in the early part of his career as an aspiring Neoclassicist, together with his experiences of Roman painting gained during his Grand Tour, out of which he developed the rich, dynamic style loaded with emotive power which characterized this work.

GOYA

FRANCISCO GOYA Y LUCIENTES
(FUENDETODOS, SARAGOSSA, ARAGON 1746 - BORDEAUX, AQUITAINE 1828)

Francisco Goya y Lucientes trained in his home town of Saragossa under the painter José Luzán. In 1771, following a trip to Italy, he received his first important commission to paint the frescos of the church of Nuestra Señora del Pilar in Saragossa, executed in a style that was still influenced by the Baroque movement. Having established himself in Madrid in 1774, Goya was chosen to create cartoons for the royal tapestry workshop of Santa Barbara, and in the course of the next eighteen years he produced over sixty paintings, including *The Parasol* (Prado, Madrid). These works were greatly admired by the court, so much so that in 1789 the artist was nominated as official painter to King Charles IV. During the last two decades of the 18th century Goya worked intensively on a series of portraits of the Spanish high society, whom he represented with an almost unsettling psychological incisiveness and a precious color palette, as demonstrated in the *Family of the Infante Don Luis* (Magnani-Rocca Foundation, Parma), the *Family of the Duke of Osuna* (Prado, Madrid), *Ferdinand Guillemardet* (Louvre, Paris) and *La Tirana* (Accademia San Fernando, Madrid). After a serious illness in 1792 which left him deaf, Goya painted the extraordinary frescos in the shrine of San Antonio de la Florida in Madrid (1798); at the same time, and in private,

he frantically worked on a string of little pictures representing an array of madmen, fanatics and witches: the fantastical *Caprices (Los caprichos)* prints (1799) revealed his horror of superstition, evil and oppression of every kind. In complete contrast, Goya continued to produce grand-scale court paintings such as the celebrated *Family of Charles IV* (Prado, Madrid), along with several stunning female portraits: *Doña Isabel Cobos de Porcel* (National Gallery, London), the *Maja desnuda (Nude Maja)* and the *Maja vestida (Clothed Maja)* (Prado, Madrid). The *Disasters of War* print series and the canvas of the *Third of May 1808* (Prado, Madrid) dramatically evoked the country's struggle against the Napoleonic troops and the martyrdom of the Spanish people, as well as providing a more universal indictment against all acts of war and violence. In the years of the Spanish Restoration, the aging artist retreated to his country house near Manzanarre, the "*Quinta del sordo*" ("House of the deaf man"), where he obsessively painted the walls with profoundly disturbing "Black Paintings" (now in the Prado, Madrid), the visions of a deeply distressed mind. Towards the end of his life Goya seems to have found some peace, however: in 1824, he moved to Bordeaux in France, where he painted the delicate *Milkmaid of Bordeaux* (Prado, Madrid), one of his final works.

The Family of Charles IV
Oil on canvas, 110×132.2 in
1800-1801
Prado, Madrid

In 1799 Goya had achieved the highest accolade any painter could aspire to in Spain, that of "first painter of the king". Shortly afterwards, he received the extremely important commission of painting the entire extended royal family in a single portrait, and the resulting work would mark the pinnacle of the artist's success.

In the *Family of Charles IV*, Goya created one of the most psychologically intense group portraits of all time, and magisterially evoked the atmosphere of an entire era. Between March and June 1800, in the royal residence of Aranjuez, Goya began to make sketches and studies from life of his subjects, capturing the facial expressions, gestures and poses that revealed their very different personalities. When he started work on the painting proper (which took

him a year to complete, from July 1800-July 1801), he organized the scene using mannequins, which he then painted with the addition of the head studies made from life. Goya's final composition is surprisingly austere given the subject: there are no lavish decorations, elaborate architectural elements or sweeping landscapes to distract the eye from the main focus of the royal family, arranged in linear fashion against a muted background of two barely distinguishable

pictures. Goya's orderly composition probably followed court etiquette, but his outward deference to his subjects belies the biting irony with which he chose to expose the flaws and mediocrity of their characters. It is significant, for example, that the central figure in the painting is not the king, but the strong-willed Queen Maria Luisa: her proud, haughty expression contrasts sharply with the bland face of Charles, who in spite of his military regalia appears weak

and insipid. The young Don Francisco de Paula stands between them, and his bright red outfit and petulant expression, directed straight towards the viewer, seems to steal the attention from both king and queen. The young man standing to the left of the group is the future Ferdinand VII, accompanied by a woman (possibly his future wife) who is strangely depicted with her face turned away, so her features remain unseen. The woman at the right holding the baby is Princess Maria Luisa with her husband, the Prince of Parma.

Maja desnuda and Maja vestida (Nude Maja and Clothed Maja)

Oil on canvas, 38×74.8 in and 37.4×74.8 in
c. 1800
Prado, Madrid

Around the start of the 19th century Goya painted two portraits of a beautiful woman louchely reclining on a *chaise longue* bolstered by large, plump cushions. The first version depicted her in an elegant, clinging white dress nipped in at the waist by a broad pink sash which emphasized her physique. The second version was essentially the same, except for one major detail: the woman was completely nude. Although it has now been proved that the nude canvas would normally have been hidden behind the clothed one, the image of a naked female body without the pretext of an allegorical or mythological theme must have appeared extremely provocative at the time. Spanish art was in fact severely censored by the Inquisition during Goya's period, and nudity was largely prohibited, or at the very best extremely limited, even in mythological works. The *Maja desnuda* and *Maja vestida* have thus become some of the most renowned paintings in Spanish art, not only for their breathtaking quality, but above all for the curiosity aroused by the subject, the history, the identity of the woman and the two paintings' relationship to one another. What is known is that on January 1

1803, very shortly after their execution, both works were in the collection of the powerful minister Godoy, Count of la Paz, which has led to the suggestion that he also commissioned them. There have been various attempts to identify the young woman, which has excited bitter controversy. The most famous theory is that she was Maria Teresa Cayetana, Duchess of Alba, whom Goya painted in 1797 while staying at her house in Sanlúcar; this is not supported by the evidence, however, and nowadays the theory is generally dismissed. In 1868, Goya's grandson Mariano is said to have confided in the painter Luis de Madrazo that the model was a young woman in the care of one of Goya's friends; but there have been numerous other hypotheses (even proposing that Goya used two different models), none of which has been universally accepted. The two canvases were kept for a long time in the Accademia of San Fernando, where the nude version remained hidden, until 1901 when they were both exhibited at the Prado.

The Third of May 1808

Oil on canvas, 89×135.8 in
1814
Prado, Madrid

Not long after the defeat of Napoleon, the Regency Council of Spain summoned Goya to paint "the most noble and heroic actions or scenes of our glorious insurrection against the tyrant of Europe". The artist chose to paint two enormous canvases illustrating the rebellion of Madrid against the French on May 2 1808, which had been brutally put down the next day, when the insurgents and all those suspected of participating in the uprising had been shot dead. This canvas depicts the climactic point of the bloody historical episode, synthesizing three different moments in a single dramatic scene: a military firing squad prepares to shoot at the man on the left with his arms raised, while the bodies of the dead lie bleeding in the foreground, and others to the right of him prepare to meet their fate. Goya has purposefully not shown the faces of the firing squad: uniformly standing in formation, they are devoid of any individual identity and merely represent the inhuman arm of a superior power. The men facing execution, on the other hand, are highly individualized in their different expressions and reactions as they prepare for their fate. Other elements of the painting may possibly have religious connotations: in the background, the prominent church steeple could be a bitter reminder of the Church's inability to protect its people; the presence of a monk among the condemned men (recognizable by his tonsure) might also allude to the impotence of faith before the catastrophic events of history. The man about to be executed, on the other hand, appears almost apotheosized in the strong light falling on him which has no apparent natural source, and his outstretched arms recall Christ on the cross.

ANTONIO CANOVA

(POSSAGNO, TREVISO, VENETO 1757 - VENICE 1822)

Regarded as the finest exponent of Neoclassical sculpture, Antonio Canova trained in Venice, executing early works which recall the drama of Gian Lorenzo Bernini's Baroque works. The group of *Daedalus and Icarus*, however, (Museo Correr, Venice) displays a decisive move towards a new form of compositional structure. After moving to Rome (where Canova would produce most of his work), Canova was able to study antique statuary and came into contact with the group of Neoclassical artists who followed the doctrine set out by the German scholar Johann Joachim Winckelmann. The success of Canova's *Theseus and the Minotaur* (Victoria and Albert Museum, London), a group directly inspired by ancient models, won him the important official commissions to sculpt the tomb monuments of Clement XIV (Santi Apostoli, Rome) and Clement XIII (St Peter's Basilica, Vatican City). With the *Mausoleum of Maria Christina of Austria* (Augustinerkirche, Vienna) the sculptor redefined the traditional funerary monument, creating an innovative design featuring a solemn funeral cortege processing towards the dark door of the great pyramid. However, Canova received his highest praise for his mythological figures and groups, whose refined elegance were underpinned by an extreme formal rigor, as exemplified by *Cupid and Psyche (Reclining)* (Louvre, Paris), *Venus and Adonis* (Villa La Grange, Geneva), *Hebe* (Staatliche Museen, Berlin), *Italian Venus (Venus Italica)* (Palazzo Pitti, Florence) and *The Three Graces* (Hermitage, St Petersburg). The Napoleonic era coincided with the height of Canova's international fame, and he even portrayed the French dictator in the *Napoleon as Mars the Peacemaker* (Aspley House, London) and his sister *Pauline Borghese Bonaparte as Venus Victorious* (Galleria Borghese, Rome). In 1802 Pope Pius VII designated Canova as Inspector of the Ancient and Fine Arts and curator of the Vatican Museums, and in his new capacity as cultural ambassador he traveled to Paris in 1815 and succeeded in negotiating the return to Italy of a number of artworks handed over to France after the Treaty of Tolentino. That same year, he made a trip to London where he was able to see the magnificent Parthenon marbles; he was also commissioned by George IV to execute the group of *Venus and Mars* (Buckingham Palace, London). Canova's rare religious works are infused by a spirit of mournful pietism, such as the painting depicting the *Mourning of the Body of Christ* located on the altar of the Neoclassical temple of Possagno, which in 1830 became Canova's own mausoleum.

Cupid and Psyche (Reclining)
Marble, 53.9×67.7 in
1787-1793
Louvre, Paris

The legend illustrated in Canova's exquisitely graceful marble group is narrated by various ancient authors including Apuleius and Ovid. The young Psyche was so beautiful that Venus became jealous and sent Cupid to make her fall in love with the ugliest man on earth. However, as soon as Cupid set eyes on Psyche he too was struck by her staggering beauty, and was instantly besotted. The two became secret lovers, but could not meet in daylight since it was forbidden for a mortal to love a god. One day Psyche's curiosity got the better of her, and she dared to shine a lamp onto Cupid; the god was enraged and sent her away, and it was only after various trials and tribulations that she was finally reunited with her lover. Only someone of Canova's refined artistic sensibility was capable of breathing life into such a lofty, ethereal subject. From antiquity, the tale of Cupid and Psyche had been

interpreted in allegorical terms by writers and philosophers as representing the encounter between the human soul ("psyche" in Greek means "soul" or "spirit") and divine love. Canova captures Cupid and Psyche in their brief, stolen embrace, and for an instant, they appear as though they might melt into one another. The sinuous, soft lines of the figures create a balanced, fluid movement: the bodies, although on different planes, converge harmoniously, the arms forming a ring which frames their perfect faces. Yet this is ultimately an image of unfulfilled desire, subtly yet masterfully expressed by Canova: their arms intertwine lightly, and their fingers brush gently against each other's hair and flesh, but they do not hold each other close, and their lips are forever parted. Physically and metaphorically, Psyche is unable to abandon her body completely to her lover, since her human soul is destined to remain earth-bound.

Cupid and Psyche (Standing)

Marble, h. 59 in
1802
Hermitage, St Petersburg

This sculpture was so greatly admired by Canova's contemporaries that it soon came to be regarded as one of his most important works, and was repeatedly copied by numerous artists. The statue's history is particularly convoluted, however: originally commissioned by Colonel John Campbell, it was instead bought by Napoleon's brother-in-law Joachim Murat, along with its companion piece the *Cupid and Psyche (Reclining)*, for Murat's château of Villiers (both statues are now in the Louvre, Paris). In 1802 Canova sculpted a replica of the group for Campbell, but this time it was bought by Napoleon's own wife, Josephine Beauharnais, who had probably fallen in love with it when visiting Villiers. The entire Beauharnais collection was in turn bought by the Russian Tsar Alexander I, who first placed the *Cupid and Psyche (Standing)* in the Winter Palace, before having it transferred to the ground floor of the New Hermitage. Canova's second version of the mythological lovers is less dramatic than its companion piece, yet equally as enchanting: Cupid tenderly leans his head on Psyche's shoulder as she places a butterfly into his palm, a delightful act recounted in Apuleius's fable *The Golden Ass*. Although Canova was heavily influenced by Classical art, he was not a sterile imitator of it: while he aimed to achieve the ideal beauty embodied by Greco-Roman art, he was also able to imbue the cold marble with a warmth and humanity that was new and modern. Nowhere is this better exemplified than in this charming group of Cupid and Psyche, whose exquisite modeling led one of Canova's contemporaries to declare that he surpassed even the great Greek sculptor Praxiteles, observing how Canova had managed to render "*the very essence of their soft, plump flesh*".

AFRICAN HEADRESTS

(AFRICA, 19ᵀᴴ CENTURY)

African art is rarely an end unto itself: form is married to function, from both a practical and symbolic point of view. Art is therefore not exclusive to privileged areas such as religion and politics, but integrated into everyday life. Consequently, there is no real distinction between "high art" and "low art", and the categorization of artworks into "pure" (such as sculpture in the round) and "applied" (aesthetically elaborate yet functional objects) is merely expedient. In this context, 19th century African stools and headrests were more than simple items of furniture: they existed in strict relation to their owner, since they also carried a spiritual significance, and were as much an extension of the person's character as a useful object. Their forms were not neutral, but reflected aspects of the owner's personality, often reinforcing their sense of identity. Furthermore, their relatively small size, with seats very close to the ground, allowed them to have a dual purpose: by night, the stools became headrests for sleeping on, and by day they transformed back into seats. The versatility of the headrest-stool both as a functional and symbolic object explains their popularity throughout Africa. As well as ensuring a comfortable night's sleep (the minimal surface contact facilitated perspiration and kept the owner's head cool) their design meant that they did not ruin the owner's often elaborate hairstyle. Even more importantly, by promoting sleep, they were also associated with dreaming, an important way of communicating with ancestors and the spirit world. Among the Shona people of Zimbabwe for example, headrests were predominantly used by men as a means of visiting their ancestors at night time, who in turn would ensure the wellbeing and prosperity of the family. Significantly, the headrests were often buried with their owners, or else passed on to their kin. Sometimes they were also used by seers to make contact with the spirit world. Although the headrests' design might at first appear abstract, their geometric forms and motifs (both triangular and circular) actually appear to describe elements of the female body, in particular the legs, breasts and shoulders. By placing his head on the rest, the man would complete the figure. In many cases headrests were also synonymous with marriage and the higher social status it conferred, since married couples were permitted to have more elaborate hairstyles, which necessitated a headrest to preserve them.

Headrest
From Luba-Shankadi,
Congo (Democratic
Republic of Congo)
Wood, 7.1 in
Musée du quai Branly, Paris

This headrest featuring two anthropomorphic caryatids has been attributed (along with other stylistically similar objects) to a single workshop or possibly even just one artist active during the 19th century, traditionally referred to as the "Master of the Cascade Coiffure". The defining element is in fact the *mikanda* hairstyle (meaning "cascade" or "steps"), fashionable in the Luba region in the late 19th and early 20th centuries. It was a particularly complicated style, created with reeds held in place by small decorative hairpins which symbolically recalled the sacred anvil associated with the power of the Luba monarchy. The cascade coiffures took some fifty hours to create, and with care they would last for up to three months; so it was essential to use a headrest at night that would not spoil them. As well as serving an aesthetic purpose, these hairstyles also helped to distinguish the wearer's social position and profession. This headrest's two caryatid figures are represented in the act of embracing. The overall effect is one of great balance and harmony, achieved both through the figures' serene expressions and the formal symmetry of their position, which creates volume by framing the space around them. The seat and base of the headrest are connected by a succession of parallel and angled lines described by the legs, arms and the different planes of the hairstyles, giving the work an exquisite sense of unity.

KATSUSHIKA HOKUSAI

(EDO, KANSAI 1760-1849)

The artist known simply as Hokusai was a famous Japanese painter and color printmaker who exerted a profound influence on the Impressionists and European collectors of the late 19th and early 20th centuries, particularly for his celebrated woodblock print series of *Ukiyo-e*, or the *Thirty-six Views of Mount Fuji*, one of the masterpieces of world art. Hokusai was born in Edo in the ninth month of the tenth year of the Horeki period, to a family of artisans. At the age of eighteen, following his initial training as a wood carver, he entered the studio of Katsugawa Shunso, a color printmaker. However, the young Hokusai deeply opposed his master's artistic principles, which led to his expulsion from the school in 1785. For the best part of his life Hokusai led a simple, poor existence, proudly describing himself as a peasant. His outstanding *Ukiyo-e* series was created between 1826 and 1833; after his death, European collectors added a further ten prints to the original thirty-six, which treated the same theme (although they had originally been executed independently from the first series). The artist also left a written memoir (unfinished) which served as a kind of spiritual testament to his work, in which he declared, "*From the age of six, I had a mania for drawing the shapes of things. When I was fifty I had published a universe of designs. But all I have done before the the age of seventy is not worth bothering with. At seventy five I'll have learned something of the pattern of nature, of animals, of plants, of trees, birds, fish and insects. When I am eighty you will see real progress. At ninety I shall have cut my way deeply into the mystery of life itself. At a hundred I shall be a marvelous artist. At a hundred and ten everything I create; a dot, a line, will jump to life as never before. To all of you who are going to live as long as I do, I promise to keep my word. I am writing this in my old age. I used to call myself Hokusai, but today I sign myself 'The Old Man Mad About Drawing.'*" When Hokusai was suddenly taken ill and died, a *haiku* poem was found in his room which aptly represents his symbolic farewell to life: "*Even as a ghost/I'll gaily tread/The Summer Moors.*"

Boatmen crossing the Tamagawa River, from *Thirty-six Views of Mount Fuji, no. 39.* 1831. The Newark Museum, George T. Rockwell Collection, Newark.

**The Great Wave
of Kanagawa,
from the series Thirty-six
Views of Mount Fuji**
Color print, 9.8×14.2 in
1830
Private Collection

Hokusai's series of *Thirty-six Views of Mount Fuji* represents not only the artist's best-known work, but includes some of the most famous individual prints in the history of Japanese art. The first reproductions from the group of woodblocks are notable for their rich Prussian blue outline, subsequently replaced in later reprints by the more usual black ink, which was less prone to fading. The series displays a virtuoso use of color, and a lively rendering of exquisite detail. Hokusai's aim at the outset was a relatively simple one: to capture the beauty and power of nature across the seasons, in different weather conditions and from a variety of viewpoints. It was a form of visual travel journal which was to become increasingly popular following the relaxation (in around 1830) of the travel restrictions previously imposed by Japan's Shogun regime; but the series also allowed Hokusai to attract new clients and patrons, given that the strict Tokugawa censorship laws made it extremely difficult to depict the people of the ever-changing Japanese society. Another distinctive element of this particular work, as of the series in general, is the sympathetic bond the artist establishes between himself and the observer, joined in a common sense of awe inspired by the view of the imposing, perfect volcano, considered since time immemorial to be the realm of the gods. Hokusai masterfully represented the astonishment, fear, incredulity and anxiety which were all part of the everyday life experience of those who lived around Mount Fuji.

347

CASPAR DAVID FRIEDRICH

(GREIFSWALD, POMERANIA 1774 - DRESDEN, SAXONY 1840)

Caspar David Friedrich first studied under the architect Johann Friedrich Quistorp. In 1794 he enrolled in the academy at Copenhagen, and in 1798 moved to Dresden, where he spent the rest of his life. Here he came into contact with members of the German intellectual elite such as Goethe, Schlegel, Schelling and Novalis, and frequented the writers of the Phöbus group: Heinrich von Kleist, Theodor Körner and Amadeus G. Müllner. In 1808 Friedrich painted his first major work, *The Cross in the Mountain* (Gemäldegalerie, Dresden). His art was strongly influenced by the aesthetics of Schelling (particularly the *Discourse on the Figurative Arts and on Nature*, published in 1807) and the ideas of Schleiermacher, who saw the contemplation of nature as a means of spiritual elevation (Friedrich himself declared, "the only true wellspring of art is our heart"). The works of Philipp Otto Runge (*The Color-Sphere*, 1810) and Goethe (*Theory of Colors*, 1810) were also of great importance to the painter. From the second decade of the 19th century onwards the artist enjoyed a good reputation, and Frederick William III of Prussia himself bought two of his paintings at the Academic Exhibition in Berlin. Friedrich's success was further confirmed in 1817 when he became a member of the Dresden Academy, and the next year he married Caroline Bommer. During the following years he met and became friends with the Norwegian painter Johan Christian Clausen Dahl, with whom he went to live in 1820, and the German philosopher Karl Gustav Carus, the author of *Nine Letters on Landscape Painting*, who was his pupil. Together they formed the nucleus of what would come to be known as the "Dresden School".

In 1824 Friedrich fell ill, and developed an increasingly debilitating persecution complex which led to his progressive isolation and the almost complete interruption of his artistic activity up until 1827. Paralyzed in 1835 by a brain hemorrhage, Caspar David Friedrich died in Dresden in 1840.

The Cross in the Mountains (Tetschen Altarpiece)
Oil on canvas, 45×43 in
1807-1808
Gemäldegalerie, Dresden

This canvas was commissioned in 1807 by Count Franz Anton von Thun und Hohenstein for the private chapel of the castle of Tetschen in northern Bohemia, and finally completed by Friedrich in December 1808. The idea of making the landscape itself the "protagonist" of an altarpiece was radical in the extreme. The slender cross, although central to the picture, does not dominate it, and almost seems subordinate to the breathtaking power of the nature that surrounds it: the strong silhouetted fir trees, craggy mountain and extraordinary color and light effects of the sky are mesmerizing.

Unsurprisingly, the painting attracted fierce controversy, set off by the critic Friedrich Wilhelm Basilius von Ramdhor, who considered it bizarre. Friedrich's choice of landscape as an allegorical element in religious art can partly be traced back to the poet and theologian Gotthard Ludwig Theobul Kosegarten, who had commissioned a sacred work from Friedrich in 1806; however, it was also perfectly in keeping with the Romantic sensibility of the era which had found popularity among the younger generation of artists, writers and intellectuals.

The painter himself responded to von Ramdhor's criticisms, giving his own interpretation of the Tetschen Altarpiece in a letter to the Dresden-based writer Friedrich August Schulz published in the Journal des Luxus und der Moden: "*Jesus Christ, nailed to the tree, is turned here towards the sinking sun, the image of the eternal life-giving father. With Jesus's teaching an old world dies — that time when God the Father moved directly on the earth. This sun sank and the earth was not able to grasp the departing light any longer. There shines forth in the gold of the evening light the purest, noblest metal of the Savior's figure on the cross, which thus reflects on earth in a softened glow. The cross stands erected on a rock, unshakably firm like our faith in Jesus Christ. The firs stand around the cross, evergreen, enduring through all ages, like the hopes of man in Him, the crucified.*" The frame, which is an integral part of the work, was carved to Friedrich's own design by the sculptor Karl Gottlob Kühn.

The Sea of Ice (Arctic Shipwreck)

Oil on canvas, 38×50 in
1823-1824
Kunsthalle, Hamburg

The idea for this painting came from the polar expeditions of the ships Hecla and Griper, in 1819-1820 and 1824, which received extensive coverage in the press of the time and inspired the work of several landscape artists. The slabs of ice breaking and sliding one over the other had been studied by the artist in a series of oils painted in the winter of 1820-21 while observing the frozen River Elba. In Friedrich's work the representation of nature always had a religious significance. His statement *"the divine is everywhere, even in a grain of sand; once I depicted it in a canebrake"* is famous: a sort of Romantic pantheism that found its most fitting expression in the genre of the "sublime" landscape, with the depiction of endless spaces, of the sometimes terrible power of nature, capable of crushing human beings. The elements of the landscape take on a precise significance, in a sort of symbolic code that can be deduced from the artist's own writings and figurative works. The ice thus represents eternity, and the wrecked ship, the mortality of human life.

JEAN-AUGUSTE-DOMINIQUE INGRES

(MONTAUBAN, MIDI-PYRÉNÉES 1780 - PARIS 1867)

After his early artistic training at the Académie Royale de Peinture, Sculpture et Architecture in Toulouse, Jean-Auguste-Dominique Ingres transferred to Paris in 1797 where he studied under Jacques-Louis David. This period saw him paint a number of excellent portraits, including that of *Mademoiselle Rivière* (Louvre, Paris), and he also received several important official commissions (*Napoleon Bonaparte as First Consul*, Musée des Beaux-Arts, Liège). In 1806 Ingres left for Rome, where he lived until 1820, moving on to Florence for the next four years. During his stay in Italy he painted a series of portraits of high-ranking French expatriates, among them *François-Marius-Granet* (Musée Granet, Aix-en-Provence) and *Joseph-Antoine de Moltedo* (Metropolitan Museum, New York). On returning to Paris, he exhibited the *Vow of Louis XIII* (Cathedral of Nôtre Dame, Montauban) at the Salon of 1824, to great acclaim. Following his election to the Académie des Beaux-Arts in 1825, Ingres opened his own highly successful studio, becoming one of the dominant French artists of the era. His renowned portrait skills were much sought after by the upper classes, and paintings such as *La Comptesse de Haussonville* (Frick Collection, New York) and *Madame Moitessier* (National Gallery, London) are a spellbinding blend of formal composure and psychological intensity. In the public arena, Ingres continued to win prestigious commissions on grand themes such as the *Apotheosis of Homer* (Louvre, Paris). Although stylistically grouped with the French Neoclassicists, thematically Ingres' body of work is extremely eclectic. Alongside Classical subjects like *Oedipus and the Sphinx* (Louvre, Paris) and *Jupiter and Thetis* (Musée Granet, Aix-en-Provence), he was also inspired by Romanticism (*The Dream of Ossian*, Musée Ingres, Montauban; *Roger Freeing Angelica*, Louvre, Paris) and sentimental subjects from the troubadour tradition (*Paolo and Francesca* after Dante, Musée Condé, Chan-

tilly). The artist was also fascinated in the human form, and returned to one of his favorite subjects, the female nude, throughout his career: *The Valpinçon Bather* (1808), *La Grande odalisque* (1814) and *The Turkish Bath* (1863), all in the Louvre, are now considered to be among his finest masterpieces, even though their reception at the time was mixed. Ingres' genius manifested itself in the freedom with which he absorbed different currents such as Neoclassicism, archaic Greek art, Hellenism, Byzantine and Gothic art, Raphael, Orientalism, the Primitives and the Mannerists.

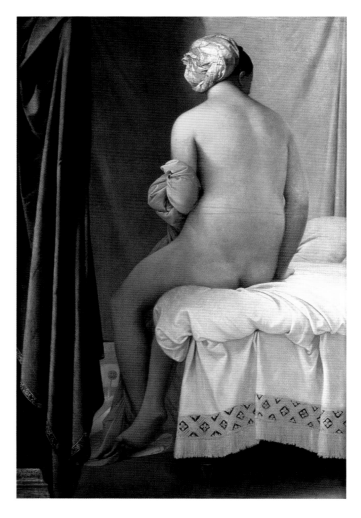

The Valpinçon Bather,
1808.
Louvre, Paris.

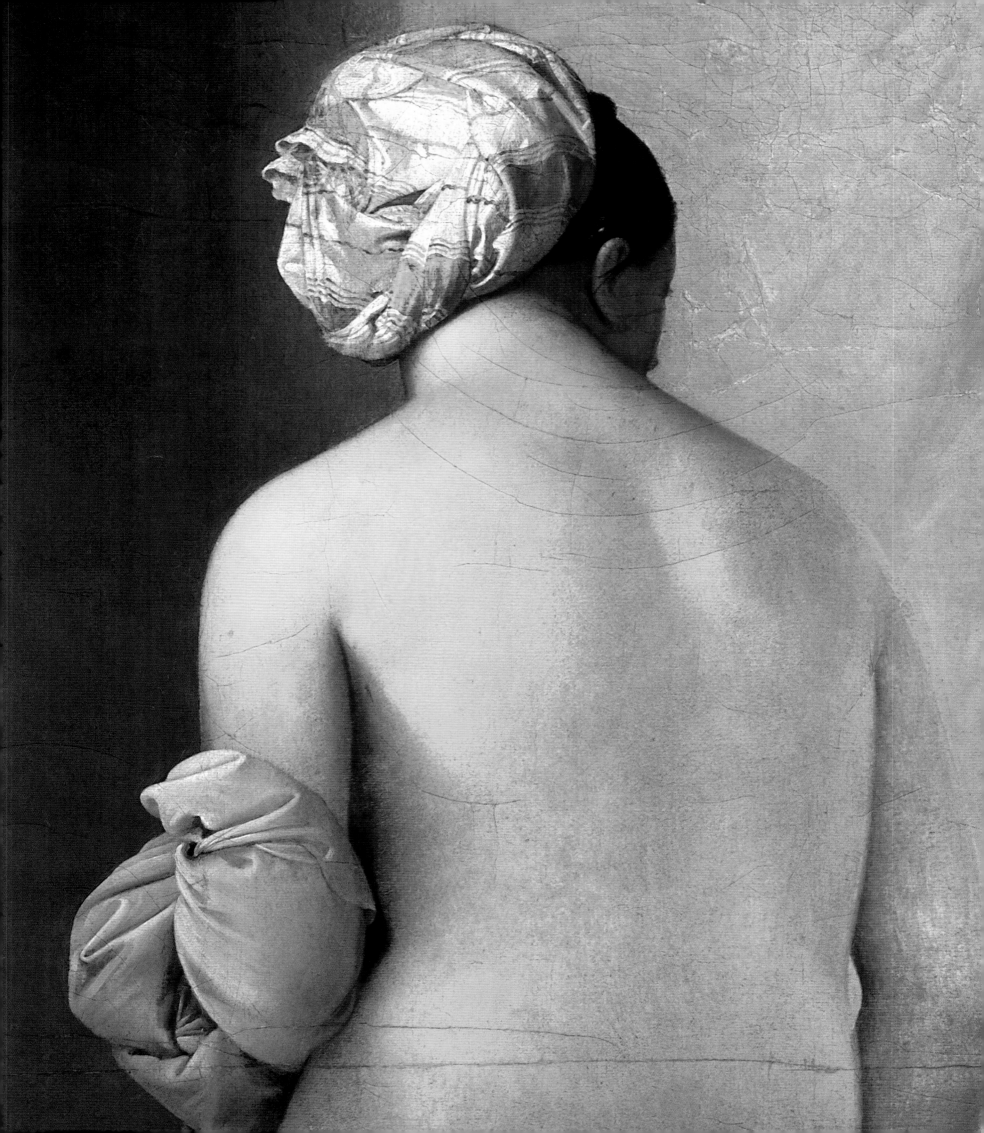

La Grande Odalisque
Oil on canvas, 35.8×64 in
1814
Louvre, Paris

La Grande Odalisque was commissioned from Ingres by Caroline Murat (Napoleon's sister and the wife of the famous French general); it was to be a pendant to the now lost *Sleeper of Naples*, a sleeping female nude which Ingres had painted some years earlier. In 1819 the canvas was exhibited in the Paris Salon, but it was not well received, coming under heavy criticism for the perceived "weakness" in the draftsmanship, the unrealistic chromatic palette and the anatomical incorrectness of the female figure. Yet these apparent "imperfections" were intentional: Ingres forfeited academic precision, naturalistic colors and meticulously studied anatomy in order to heighten the woman's beauty and sensuality. Her lack of proportion lend the image a sinuous, fluid rhythm and a refined elegance, and also echoes the similarly exaggerated forms of Mannerist art. Lying seductively on a bed or *chaise longue*, the *odalisque* fills the entire canvas; the few other elements in the painting all declare her "exotic" provenance; here Ingres anticipated the genre of Orientalism which would become extremely popular in French art. The simplicity of the composition is designed to highlight the nude body, which follows the horizontal lines of the canvas, interrupted only by the verticality of the half-drawn curtain; the device of the curtain in turn creates balance in the picture between the left and right hand sections. By forming a continuous line from the woman's right arm to the curtain she pulls, Ingres "encloses" the space in the foreground, enveloping the painting in a warm, welcoming intimacy which accentuates the sensual mood.

The Turkish Bath

Oil on wood, diameter 43.3 in
1862
Louvre, Paris

In 1717, Lady Mary Wortley Montagu, the wife of the British ambassador to Turkey, wrote in her *Letters* of her experiences in one of the country's famous baths or *hammams*: "*I believe, in the whole, there were two hundred women [...] first sofas were covered with cushions and rich carpets, on which sat the ladies [...] all being in the state of nature, that is, in plain English, stark naked, without any beauty or defect concealed. Yet there was not the least wanton smile or immodest gesture amongst them [...] There were many [...] as exactly proportioned as ever any goddess was drawn by the pencil of Guido or Titian, and most of their skins shiningly white, only adorned by their beautiful hair divided into many tresses, hanging on their shoulders, braided either with pearl or ribbon, perfectly representing the figures of the Graces.*" Stimulated by Lady Mary's captivating description, Ingres painted his own evocative scene, paying close attention to all the details mentioned in the *Letters*. There is a pure delight in the bodies of the nude women, carefully arranged within the *tondo* canvas in various states of abandon. Little detracts from the sea of sensual white flesh on which the light plays delicately: the few details, such as the coffee set in the foreground, the vases and simple architectural elements of the background, and the women's jewelry and headdresses, all serve to give context to the picture and amplify the exoticism. Many of these details were in fact added later by Ingres as he worked to improve and perfect the painting. A photograph of 1860 (commissioned by the artist himself) also shows that the canvas was originally conceived in a rectangular form. Ingres' decision to transfer it to the more unusual *tondo* format was a true masterstroke: the round frame highlighted the nudes' curved contours, creating a flowing, sensual movement which mirrored the mood of the painting perfectly. In the midst of the scene is Lady Mary herself, eyes languorously semi-closed in an expression of deep contentment as a pretty slave sprays her blonde hair with perfume.

AFRICAN MASKS

(AFRICA, 19ᵀᴴ-20ᵀᴴ CENTURY)

Like much African art, these masks operated in a "dual" world: by hiding and transforming the human face and body, they allowed the invisible spirits to manifest themselves. The rigidity of the masks' facial features, frozen in time, acted as a reminder of this "other" world. While the masks concealed facial expressions, they conversely allowed both wearer and observer to concentrate on the expressiveness of the body, often through dance, underlining the ambiguous duality of the masks: through their humanizing aspects, they were able to bring people closer to their spirits and divinities, yet at the same time they maintained a level of separation and mystical apartness from the human world. Some of the masks were made with moveable parts such as articulated jaws and arms, while others are barely recognizable when removed from their original context (the human wearer) and exhibited on gallery walls or in museum cabinets. This is particularly true of the helmet types, which are more like statues in appearance. These were actually worn on the head and attached to a costume which hid the face of the wearer and was an integral part of the mask itself. The function of the helmet-masks was to make the wearer look taller and even more awe-inspiring. To be fully understood and appreciated, the masks must be imagined attached to their costume and human wearer, who would animate them and bring out each individual spirit: the spirits that manifested themselves through the masks had their own characteristic range of expressions, which required songs, dance and music to be teased out. So, for example, among the Guro people of the Ivory Coast, the identity of certain masks changed in relation to the partner they danced with: the antelope mask *zamble* represented the wife or sister figure when teamed with the old man mask *zaouli*, while when *zamble* appeared with *gu*, the beautiful girl mask, it symbolized the husband. The use of masks continues to be widespread, and they are an important element of African culture. Their versatility means that they can assume a variety of identities – spirits, ancestors or mythical heroes – and be used for large public rituals such as funerals or agrarian rites, or worn in secret by members of different societies, or else used for rites of passage from youth to adulthood. The masks' central role in marking the crucial phases of human life and the agricultural cycle has in some places ensured their survival even in areas where Islam has been the dominant religion for some time, as is the case in certain parts of the Ivory Coast where ancient cults are still practised.

Bamileke Master of Bamendjo (Cameroon), Tsesah (Batcham) Mask
Wood, h. 26.4 in
Rietberg Museum, Zurich

This helmet-mask was worn on the head, while the face and body were disguised by a costume. The term *Batcham* is misleading, since it only indicates the place (the Batcham kingdom) where the German officer Von Wuthenow discovered the first example known in the West (by 1960 only two more had been found). The principle area of production of these masks (and perhaps where they originated) is thought to be a different Bamileke kingdom forty kilometers further south, namely that of Bandjoun. Here, they were used by members of the *Msop* secret society as instruments of social control. Very rarely, they were also used in ritual ceremonies (coronations and funerals), tied to the figure of the king or other court dignitaries. According to the Cameroonian scholar Jean-Paul Notué, in Bandjoun these masks represented the head of a hippopotamus emerging from the water, an animal which traditionally symbolized a high-ranking court official. Stylistically, the mask is articulated in two distinct parts: a horizontal plane corresponding to the lower half of the face, and a vertical one, consisting of two symmetrical projections divided by a median line depicting enormous eyebrows. The eyes join the two planes, and the fact that the pupils

are not bored, nor indicated by any other method, gives the mask a spectral quality; its expressiveness comes from the menacing appearance of the jutting eyebrows. Other elements are typical of art from the Cameroon Grasslands: the cheeks are puffed out, and the open mouth reveals a large row of teeth. The mask's strength is in the rhythmic interplay of the curved lines, the incisions and the volumes, which combine to form a unified whole, even though the individual facial features are deconstructed into pure geometric forms.

Male Kifwebe Mask

From Songye workshop of the Lusambo region (Democratic Republic of Congo)
Wood and pigments, h. 23.6 in
Rietberg Museum, Zurich

This type of mask belonged to the *bwadi ba bifwebe* society, whose scope was to control the power of the chiefs through the mystical powers of witchcraft. Similar masks were also used in other regions, by people such as the nearby Luba, whose versions were rounded. Although they were always worn by men, the masks represented both males and females, distinguished by their color and the more or less accentuated facial features. The white female masks, with features delineated in black, were associated with fertility and benevolent spirits, and their role in witchcraft was minimal. The male masks were much more fearsome and aggressive looking to reflect their different roles: they were used in battle, and worn by guards to patrol fields, roads and the areas where the circumcision initiation rituals took place. Their appearance expressed danger and they acted as a warning. The male *kifwebe* masks are characterized by a strong sense of dynamism and expressive power, projected by the protruding eyes, nose and mouth, which are much more contained in the female masks. The movement is emphasized by the forward directional thrust of the surface striations converging at the mouth, which (according to the Songye themselves) is depicted uttering a curse. The surface incisions have a symbolic value, recalling the subterranean areas from which the founding spirits of the *kifwebe* society rose, and, on a different level of meaning, the "womb" of the cave which produced the first humans. The male masks are also more elaborate in their use of color: red appears along with black and white. The polarity of black and white expresses the contrast between good and evil, life and death, health and disease, purity and impurity, while red acts as a mediating element and introduces a note of ambiguity between these sets of opposites.

Kifwebe Mask,
from Songye, Congo
(Democratic Republic
of Congo).
Private Collection.

JEAN-LOUIS-THÉODORE GÉRICAULT

(ROUEN, HAUTE NORMANDIE 1791 - PARIS 1824)

Géricault began his painting career within the Napoleonic tradition characterized by grand, military themes, which he interpreted with a Romantic spirit, also drawing on the Renaissance and Baroque masters for inspiration. Through his methodical study of the masterpieces in the Louvre he identified a number of favorite themes which would recur in his own art, such as the horse (*Horse Frightened by Lightning*, National Gallery, London). He enrolled in Louis XVIII's Musketeers for a time and became politicized, espousing liberal ideals which would later resurface in his work. From 1816-1817 Géricault was in Italy, where he focused his interests on antique statuary, Michelangelo, the Mannerist school and genre painting. Shortly after returning to France he executed his most famous masterpiece, the extraordinary *Raft of the Medusa* (Louvre, Paris), which was stylistically informed by Italian art and the chromatic palette of Rubens and Velázquez. The subject, however, was both contemporary and controversial: a recent infamous shipping disaster which had caused a furore and come to symbolize high-level government corruption and incompetence. Géricault's painting was thus regarded as a thinly veiled attack on the Bourbon regime. The artist's strong social conscience was also expressed in the lithographs he made in England between 1820 and 1821. Among his last works was a series of portrait studies of psychiatric patients (the most renowned being the *Woman with Gambling Mania*, Louvre, Paris), undertaken with his usual meticulous attention to detail and technical virtuosity. By this time his own mental and physical health was extremely fragile, and his last preliminary studies for epic compositions were tragically interrupted by his early death.

The Raft of the Medusa.

The Raft of the Medusa

Oil on canvas, 165×282 in
1819
Louvre, Paris

In 1816, the French frigate La Méduse foundered in the straits of Cap Blanc off Mauritania, even though contemporary reports claimed the conditions to have been calm. The officers saved themselves, taking all the lifeboats and leaving the rest of the crew and passengers to face an almost certain death. However, the desperate survivors managed to construct a makeshift raft measuring about 66×23 ft, onto which some hundred and fifty people scrambled and clung for their lives. After drifting in the ocean for thirteen days, the raft was finally picked up by the military ship Argus: only fifteen people had survived the horrendous ordeal. When news of the catastrophe reached home in France, a political scandal erupted: the old captain, an immigrant, was sentenced to a severe punishment, and his trial came to be considered by the majority of the French people as a "trial against immigrants". Following on the wave of popular public opinion, *The Raft of the Medusa* was seen as a pictorial condemnation of the oppression of the weak. The canvas depicts the moment when the final few wretched survivors realize there is a hope they might be rescued: the viewer's eye is drawn diagonally up across the ghastly scene to the two figures waving handkerchiefs and finally the tiny silhouette of the Argus on the horizon in the far distance. Géricault magisterially represents the mixed emotions of hope and despair, madness, terror and philosophical acceptance of this appalling human tragedy, adding intensity through the densely applied paint, strong lighting contrasts and dramatic composition. For the range of expressions captured in the faces of the survivors, the painter referred back to his many painstaking studies of the agonized and contorted faces of the ill, insane and even the dead, made during trips to asylums and morgues, which here lend the picture a disturbing level of realism.

Woman with Gambling Mania

Oil on canvas, 30×25 in
1822-1823
Louvre, Paris

This painting is one of a series of ten portraits of people with different psychiatric afflictions which were probably executed between 1820 and 1824. Following the controversy over the *Raft of the Medusa*, Géricault fell into a deep depression himself, and sought help from Dr. Étienne-Jean Georget. As a mark of gratitude, the artist offered the physician these ten studies, perhaps for use as teaching material in his pathology lectures. Each of the pictures portrays a person suffering from a specific mental condition (it is likely that they were patients at the Salpêtrière Hospital, where Georget practised). This particular work is the most famous of the series, and depicts an elderly woman with a gambling addiction. Some scholars have pointed out similarities between Géricault's painting and that of the Scottish artist David Wilkie, *Chelsea Pensioners Reading the Gazette of the Battle of Waterloo* (which Géricault had seen and admired during his stay in England), especially in the gambling woman's alienated expression. In fact, the realism of this painting, devoid of any hint of rhetoric or pathos, does reflect the influence of contemporary British art. On the other hand, Géricault's almost clinical detachment from his subject marks the work out as one of the earliest examples of the study of the physiognomy of the insane or, in particular, of criminals, a branch of medical science that was to arouse great interest over the course of the 19ᵗʰ century. In terms of artistic technique, the ten studies, carried out in the same spirit in which he had reproduced parts of the anatomy in the preparatory studies for the *Raft of the Medusa* some years earlier, represent one of Géricault's finest achievements.

EUGÈNE DELACROIX

(CHARENTON-SAINT-MAURICE, ÎLE DE FRANCE 1798 - PARIS 1863)

Delacroix came from a high bourgeois family, and after having completed his classical education he entered the studio of the Neoclassicist painter Guérin, before enrolling in Paris's prestigious École des Beaux-Arts in 1817. During his apprenticeship with Guérin, the aspiring young artist developed a passionate interest in the work of Antoine-Jean Gros and Théodore Géricault, with whom he would become friends (even posing for Géricault's *Raft of the Medusa*). Other important influences on Delacroix's artistic development included Michelangelo and Rubens, while technically he was also interested in watercolor painting and engraving, which he mastered during these years. 1822 saw his debut in the Paris Salon, where he exhibited *Dante and Virgil* (Louvre, Paris) which had been directly inspired by the *Raft of the Medusa*. The painting caused a sensation for its unusual subject and the intense drama of the composition. Two years later he painted the *Massacre at Chios* (Louvre, Paris), his first grand-scale Romantic work whose subject was a contemporary historical episode from the recent war of liberation of the Greeks against the Turks. In 1824 Delacroix traveled to London, where he avidly studied British painting and also saw several performances of Shakespeare plays, which he later drew on for a number of his paintings and drawings. After returning to France, he painted a series of *Odalisques* (1825), works whose deep sensuality was magnified by the sophisticated treatment of color. The painting most representative of his early period, however, is *The Death of Sardanapalus* of 1827 (Louvre, Paris): the king's horrific demise, along with all his concubines, horses and favorite dogs, is depicted with an exhilarating freedom and energy achieved through the application of vivid patches of color with rapid, deft brushstrokes. At the Salon of 1831 Delacroix presented *Liberty Leading the People* (Louvre, Paris), an ambitious canvas whose controversial theme was taken from the three-day revolution in Paris of the previous year. The artist's passion for exoticism led him to make a trip to north Africa in 1832, which was to prove crucial to the evolution of his painting in the latter half of his career: he filled numerous sketch books with notes and drawings describing the exquisite quality of the light and colors of the countries he visited, along with studies of the local people, their customs and behavior, which were subsequently used for celebrated works such as *Women of Algiers (in their Apartment)* and *Jewish Wedding in Morocco* (both in the Louvre, Paris). Back in France, Delacroix embarked on another period of intense activity, receiving important commissions to execute grandiose decorative cycles, including the *Allegories* in the Bourbon Palace (1833-1838 and 1838-1847), the decoration of the library in the Palace of Luxembourg (1840-1846), the central ceiling of the Apollo gallery in the Louvre (*c.* 1850-1851) and the frescos in the Chapel of the Angels in the church of Saint-Sulpice (1849-1861). During this period, the artist also painted a succession of canvases with historical and mythological themes, such as *Medea* (Musée des Beaux-Arts, Lille), the *Justice of Trajan* (Musée des Beaux-Arts, Rouen) and the *Entry of the Crusaders into Constantinople* (Louvre, Paris). In his latter years, Delacroix increasingly turned his attention to the natural world, depicting flowers, marine life and landscapes (*Sea from the Heights of Dieppe*, Louvre, Paris), and producing a group of animal studies towards the end of his life (1848-1861). His creative path is also documented in his journals, written by the artist from 1822-1824 and from 1847 until his death. Delacroix's art represents a true manifesto of Romantic painting, with its remarkable freedom of expression and predilection for political, literary and exotic themes, while his treatment of color and drawing technique were to exert a profound influence on the Impressionists.

Liberty Leading the People
Oil on canvas, 102×128 in
1830
Louvre, Paris

Having returned to the French throne after the Congress of Vienna, the Bourbons were overthrown in 1830 during the three-day popular revolt which came to be known as the "July Revolution". As a member of the national guard (an armed corps made up of citizens which opposed the regular national army on a number of occasions), Delacroix was an active participant in the insurrection, and his experiences on the tumultuous streets of Paris were transferred onto this impressive allegorical painting commemorating the historic event. The large canvas celebrated the courage and heroism of the French people, and the artist himself judged it "a modern subject" for its thematic and stylistic innovations. By choosing not to depict a specific episode, but to allegorize the revolution through the figure of Liberty, Delacroix elevated his picture to an idealized representation of the perfect Republican. When it was presented at the Salon of 1831, however, the painting met with a hostile reception: the critics were scandalized by the audacity with which Delacroix had treated the theme, and by the violence of emotion it expressed; but the artist was unapologetic, and felt proud to have created a work which celebrated the heroic virtues of his fellow nationals. Significantly, despite the sensation caused by the painting, it was quickly bought by the new government and hung in the Palace of Luxembourg, although (perhaps prudently) the general public was not permitted to see it for several months afterwards. *Liberty Leading the People* signaled an epochal turning point in European painting: it represented a solemn statement of intent for an entire new generation of painters, steeped in Romanticism, who were passionately experiencing their own times and reflecting this common experience in their art, leaving behind the traditional themes of "historical painting" taken from antiquity or a distant past they had no empathy with.

Women of Algiers (in their Apartment)

Oil on canvas, 70.8×90 in
1834
Louvre, Paris

In his journal, Delacroix described the moment he was finally admitted to a place few men are ever allowed to enter: another man's harem. Having walked down a dark corridor, full of anticipation for what he was about to see, he opened a door and stood for a moment "*intoxicated by the spectacle*" before his eyes, the languid, decadent "*women of Algiers*". The painter had managed to obtain an introduction into the house of a Turkish admiral through his influential connection Monsieur Poirel, chief engineer of the Port of Algiers. The encounter proved to be one of many life-changing experiences Delacroix had during his travels in north Africa, and he later declared that "*After my journey, men and things appear to me in a new light.*" Following his return to Paris, and three years after his trip to the harem, Delacroix decided to revisit the subject in this painting. In order to evoke the heady atmosphere of the scene with the utmost realism, he tirelessly studied the sketches he had made in Algeria, drawing on his own memory to recall the forms and colors, and even dressing his models in the exotic clothes he had brought back with him. The artist thus allowed the viewer a voyeuristic glimpse inside the harem, just as he must have witnessed it. In the smoky half-light of the room, three lavishly adorned women sit quietly while a servant on the far right pushes back the heavy drape to reveal the intimate scene. Silence seems to pervade the secret place, broken only by the deep exhalation of the beautiful woman in the white blouse holding the hookah pipe. The women's gazes are distant, indolent even, perhaps expressing their resignation to their monotonous life of segregation, or something altogether darker: since it is possible that the hookah may have contained opium.

FREDERIC EDWIN CHURCH

(HARTFORD, CONNECTICUT 1826-1900)

Known principally as a landscape artist, Church was one of America's leading Romantic painters and a central figure of the so-called Hudson River School. He began training under Thomas Cole, who was based in Palenville near New York, before being admitted into the National Academy of Design in 1849, where he continued his artistic education. While still at the Academy, Church began to make a name for himself as a talented young artist, and his early success was confirmed by the acquisition of one of his paintings by the prestigious Wadsworth Atheneum Museum of Hartford. On completing his studies Church moved to New York, where he took on his first pupil, William James Stillman. Every year during the spring and summer months he would undertake long journeys, often on foot, to visit and sketch landscapes, which he would then paint, exhibit and sell during the winter. He became renowned for his monumental, sweeping landscape paintings, depicted with analytical precision and realism despite their huge proportions, such as the colossal *Heart of the Andes* (now in the Metropolitan Museum, New York): measuring over 33 feet long by 16.4 feet high, it was sold at the time for the unprecedented sum of around $10,000, the highest price obtained to that date by a living artist. In 1860 Church bought a farm in Hudson, which inspired his magnificent views of the river. After the tragic death of his first wife Isabel Carnes, who was pregnant with their first child, the artist started a new family, with whom he traveled around Europe and the Middle East. On returning to his Hudson farmland in 1870 he built his beautiful, eccentric home "Olana", now a state historic site owned by the National Trust, whose eclectic architectural style assimilated and reinterpreted the exotic architecture which had captivated him during his lengthy travels. In

Twilight, "Short Arbiter 'Twixt Day and Night". Newark Museum, Newark.

this period the painter alternated between working on his trademark grand-scale landscapes and smaller views which were technically more sketch-like and spontaneous, representing the dawn light or sunset over the hill of Olana. Both home and away, Church always derived the greatest inspiration from his natural surroundings, as the breathtaking pictures of equatorial America, the Orient (Damascus and Jerusalem), Labrador and the Niagara Falls testify. Church's artistic philosophy also drew on the work of great landscapists from Lorrain to Constable, whose pursuit of the "sublime" reflected the belief that nature was an ineffable manifestation of the divine. During his successful career, he helped give birth to the Hudson River School, a loose collective of artists and writers such as Henry David Thoreau and Ralph Waldo Emerson who shared a deep passion for nature.

Twilight, "Short Arbiter 'Twixt Day and Night"

Oil on canvas, 48×31.9 in
1850
Newark Museum, Newark

The Newark Museum is home to a valuable collection of Romantic landscapes by artists of the Hudson River School, particularly Church, Cole and Bierstadt. *Twilight* is a quintessential example: a mesmerizing wide-angle vision of nature captured just after sunset, shot through with glimmers of changing light and color, and designed to induce the same feelings of wonder in the observer as Church himself must have experienced. This painting belongs to the series of landscapes executed by the artist between 1848 and 1850, when he spent the warmer months hiking and climbing through vast tracts of the North American wilderness, returning to his New York studio in the winter. *Twilight* is constructed with extraordinary skill: the craggy outcrop in the foreground to the bottom left creates a real sense of perspective, opening up the rest of the scene beyond; the eye is then fleetingly drawn to a tiny habitation, barely perceptible in the middle ground and entirely subordinate to the vast landscape which envelops it, acting as a reminder of humanity's insignificance before nature; finally, there are the lowering clouds which dominate the upper half of the picture, receding to the brilliant light of the sunset in the distance whose changing colors are reflected in the calm, mysterious waters of the stream. Conforming to the Romantic idea of the sublime, Church's painting exudes an aura of mysticism and rapture, intensifying the viewer's feelings of solitude and humility when confronted by the awe-inspiring beauty of nature.

Cotopaxi

Oil on canvas, 41.8×28 in
1855
Smithsonian American Art Museum, Washington, DC

Spurred on by his hiking expeditions in the wilds of North America, Church set off to explore the southern parts of the American continent between 1853 and 1855, inspired by the works of Darwin and the adventures of the great German naturalist Alexander von Humboldt, who had spent more than five months traveling through Colombia and Equador. The experiences produced more large-scale paintings, in which the observation of reality combines with a visionary mysticism, transfiguring the mountains, rivers and lakes through the interplay of light and color. As in much of Church's art, the presence of humanity is barely elaborated: landscape and light are, as always, the true protagonists, and details are illuminated as if to express the force of a higher, divine power. In this work, the snow-capped peak of the volcano Cotopaxi towers over the vast Equadorian horizon, indomitable as a god, and emits a thin yet faintly menacing plume of smoke into the blue morning sky. In the foreground is a small village, relatively distant from the slopes of the gigantic mountain yet close enough to feel its force and threat. Church's expertise as a colorist is demonstrated in the treatment of the sky, the clouds tinged by the rose morning light, and the large ominous shadows creeping slowly over the plain. Technically, the composition is tightly controlled, and organized with a rational sense of balance and harmony which manages to express depth without the crude use of lines but by the syntactic arrangement of the landscape through masses which gradually recede and fade towards the horizon.

ÉDOUARD MANET

(Paris 1832-1883)

Born into an affluent Parisian family, the young Manet was educated at the Rollin college; there, he became close friends with the future writer Marcel Proust, whose *Souvenirs* would later provide a precious insight into Manet's life and work. At sixteen he abandoned his studies to try and enter the navy as an officer; however, after failing the entrance exams he decided to board a merchant ship headed for Rio de Janeiro to train as a ship's captain. During the voyage, he started to draw caricatures of the crew, his very first ex-

periments in art. After failing a second time to enter the École Navale (naval school), Manet convinced his father to let him study art formally; and in 1850 he joined the studio of the academic painter Thomas Couture, where he remained for six years, despite violent differences in opinion with the master. Manet was convinced that truly modern painting must evolve out of the artistic tradition of the past, and set about studying the work of the great masters in the Louvre, underscoring the knowledge he gained by taking numerous trips to Holland, Ger-

many, Austria and Italy between 1852 and 1856. In particular, he was struck by the art of Giorgione and Titian and the Dutch masters of the 17th century, whose technique was centered on the handling of color. The great Spanish artists Goya and Velázquez also played a fundamental role in Manet's artistic development, and he was able to study their paintings in detail during his stay in Spain in 1865. His first major paintings, however, depicted scenes much closer to home, of Parisian life and people, partly inspired by another literary friend, the poet Charles Baudelaire (*The Absinthe Drinker*, Ny Carlsberg Glypotek, Copenhagen; *Music in the Tuileries*, National Gallery, London). *The Absinthe Drinker* was refused by the Paris Salon of 1859, despite being championed by Eugène Delacroix; this experience was to mark the beginning of a torturous relationship with the Salons, the critics of the French art establishment, and the general public. In 1861, Manet's *Spanish Guitar Player* (Metropolitan Museum, New York) would be one of few works of art to gain official recognition and approval. After making a series of paintings of a Spanish ballet company in 1862, Manet went on to execute two of his most renowned works, which would become a fundamental point of reference for the Impressionist and Post-Impressionist movements: *Le Déjeuner sur l'herbe* and *Olympia* (1863, Musée d'Orsay, Paris). Between them, the paintings created among the greatest scandals in the history of modern art, both for their subject matter and the anti-academic style in which they were treated. Manet abolished volumes, perspective, *chiaroscuro* and *sfumato*, applying color flatly within well-defined contours, juxtaposing dark and light tones to create daring chromatic contrasts. The absence of spatial depth derived from his

interest in Japanese prints, while the chromatic range and certain compositional elements were drawn from Spanish painting. Following his trip to Spain in 1865, the influence of Goya and Velázquez became even more marked, in paintings such as *The Young Piper* (Musée d'Orsay, Paris), the various versions of the *Execution of Emperor Maximilian* (the most interesting of these is in the Kunsthalle, Mannheim) and *The Balcony* (Musée d'Orsay, Paris). From 1863 Manet frequented the Café Guerbois and the Nouvelle Athènes groups, who were both instrumental in the genesis of the Impressionist art movement. However, in spite of his brief association with Impressionism (evident in works such as *Boating*, Metropolitan Museum, New York and *Claude Monet Painting in his Studio Boat*, Neue Pinakothek, Munich), Manet willfully distanced himself from the movement, refusing to participate in group exhibitions. Unlike the young Impressionist artists, Manet preferred painting figures to landscapes, and his handling of color, which largely suppressed transitional tones, was in complete contrast with the feathered, shimmering chromatic effects of the classic Impressionist style. His main friends remained the great literary luminaries Baudelaire, Zola and Mallarmé, who inspired a series of works with naturalistic settings such as the *The Bar at the Folies-Bergère* (Courtauld Institute of Art, London) and *Nanà* (Kunsthalle, Hamburg), which shortly preceded Zola's novel of the same name. Throughout his career, Manet also executed numerous portraits of friends and acquaintances, such as his famous *Portrait of Émile Zola* (Musée d'Orsay, Paris), depictions in which the painter preferred to express character through immediacy of representation rather than studied psychological penetration.

Le Déjeuner sur l'herbe

Oil on canvas, 81.9×104 in
1863
Museé d'Orsay, Paris

The Salon des Refusés had been set up at the behest of the Emperor Napoleon III as a parallel exhibition to the official Salon, in order to satisfy the numerous artists whose work had been excluded from the main exhibition. When *Le Déjeuner sur l'herbe* was unveiled at the Refusés in 1863, it aroused a tremendous amount of controversy among art critics and public alike. Huge crowds of people gathered in front of the painting, elbowing each other out of the way to get a look at the supposedly "obscene" image, and jeering at every detail of the scene. In his novel *L'oeuvre* (*The Masterpiece*) Émile Zola described the reaction: "*The rumor that there was a comical picture on show must have spread rapidly, because people were running in and out of the rooms, and groups of tourists, worried that they were missing something important, were pushing and shouting 'What?' – 'Over there' – 'It's incredible!' Witty comments were flying around, and they all referred to the painting's subject. Nobody understood it, everybody thought it mad, incredibly funny. 'See, the woman was too hot but the men were cold; that's why they are dressed.' 'No, that's not it! Can't you see that she's green? She must have been in the water for a good while before they dragged her out. That's why he's wrinkling his nose a bit.' 'Shame that that man was painted with his back to us, it makes him seem so rude.*" The emperor himself branded the painting "*an offence to modesty*", in line with the unanimous criticism which judged it to be indecent. What offended people the most was the stark realism of the nude female in the foreground, which was considered so different to the idealized nudes of the academic tradition; an irony, since it was clear (as Manet himself revealed) that the composition had been directly inspired by the Venetian masters of the Renaissance, even if it adopted a pictorial language which was thoroughly modern and unconventional.

Olympia

Oil on canvas, 51.1×74 in
1863
Musée d'Orsay, Paris

Following the scandal of 1863, Manet was reluctant to exhibit his *Olympia* (executed in the same year); but on the insistence of his friend Charles Baudelaire, he decided to show the painting two years later, at the Salon of 1865. It was a spectacular failure, and Baudelaire had to console the demoralized painter: his work seemed destined to excite controversy and censure, even though Manet himself had no intention of provoking the establishment. He always strenuously denied accusations that he wanted to be a revolutionary, yet despite taking his inspiration from acknowledged masters such as the Venetian colorists Giorgione and Titian, and the Spaniards Goya and Velázquez, Manet undeniably interpreted their work in an audaciously modern way. The painter was bitterly disappointed by the scathing reviews the *Olympia* received, even abandoning Paris for a time after this latest debacle. Comments by the art critic Jules Claretie are fairly representative of the general mood of hostility towards the picture: "*What is this Odalisque with a yellow stomach, a base model picked up I know not where, who*

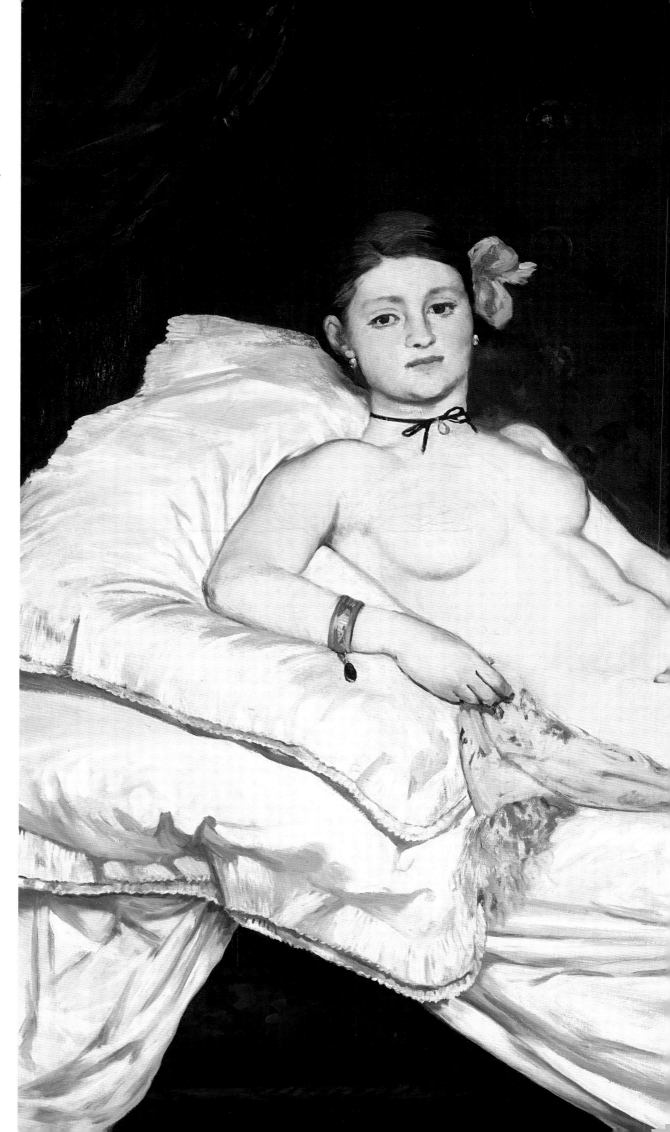

represents Olympia? Olympia? What Olympia? A courtesan, no doubt..."

The painting did have a fervant group of supporters, however, who believed it to be a work of unsurpassed modernity: and after a spirited public campaign by Claude Monet and other friends of the artist, it was eventually accepted into the Louvre in 1890 (before moving to the Musée d'Orsay), although it was only exhibited to the public in 1907, when the scandal was deemed to have died down. In Marcel Proust's *Remembrance of Things Past*, Princess Oriane de Guermantes describes her visit to the Louvre shortly after the painting was finally put on public show: "The other day we saw Manet's *Olympia*. It is not shocking any more. It has the same effect as Ingres."

Portrait of Émile Zola

Oil on canvas, 57.5×44.8 in
1867-1868
Musée d'Orsay, Paris

At the time Manet painted his portrait, Émile Zola was the rising star of the French literary scene: in 1867 he published his first naturalist novel, *Thérèse Raquin*, and he was just starting on his celebrated *Rougon-Macquart* cycle. Zola was also a harsh critic of the French establishment, a subversive polemicist whose incisive journalistic articles caused a sensation and aroused furious debates. His friendship with Manet and the Impressionist circle would be of huge importance to both parties: Zola repeatedly came to the defence of his artist friends, pitting himself against the conservative critics of the Salon who had ostracized them. The author even dedicated a pamphlet to Manet, which can just be seen in his portrait behind the inkpot on the desk. In it he wrote, "*Manet's place in the Louvre is assured, just like Courbet's, just like that of any artist whose personality is original and powerful.*" They were prophetic words: having been dogged by decades of controversy, Manet's works did enter the Louvre, confirming their iconic status. The painter here represents his friend as an intellectual absorbed in thought in the intimate setting of his study, echoing the great portraits of the 15ᵗʰ and 16ᵗʰ centuries of scientists and literary figures in their own *studioli*; a clear sign of Manet's debt to the old masters he had admired in the Louvre as an aspiring artist. Manet leaves more direct clues to his eclectic influences in the background of the picture: alongside a Japanese print and a sketch of *Olympia* is an engraving of the *Triumph of Bacchus* by Velázquez, an homage to the great Spanish painter whom Manet rediscovered on his trips to Spain.

JAMES ABBOTT McNEILL WHISTLER

(LOWELL, MASSACHUSETTS 1834 - LONDON 1903)

Originally from the United States, Whistler's family moved to Russia in 1843 when his father was employed to build a railroad connecting Moscow with St Petersburg. After his father's death in 1849, Whistler returned to the States, and from 1851-1854 he attended the West Point Military Academy; after his departure, he decided to devote himself to drawing and engraving. In 1855 he transferred to Paris and studied the work of the Realist masters Gustave Courbet and Henri Fantin-Latour, before finally moving to London, where he remained for most of his life. Shortly after establishing himself in the British capital, he met the Pre-Raphaelite circle of painters, forming a particularly close friendship with Dante Gabriel Rossetti. Whistler was to have a lasting impact on Rossetti's art, showing him how a sophisticated style of "high art" could be applied to everyday themes and subjects. The apparent simplicity of Whistler's paintings during this period belies their extreme complexity, leading some critics to compare his stylistic technique to music. The painter accepted this interpretation and subsequently entitled many of his works *Symphonies* or *Arrangements*, declaring that "just as music is the poetry of the ear, so painting is that of the eye". On visiting the London International Exhibition of 1862, Whistler was profoundly impressed by the Chinese and Japanese artworks on show; and his subsequent attempt at fusing the "exotic" style with the pictorial language of the Pre-Raphaelites gave life to a series of paintings in which he aimed both to synthesize and compare Oriental and Western cultures. Although the resultant works remained faithful to the traditional rules of composition, the use of color was highly innovative in Western art, approaching the two-dimensional chromatism of Japanese prints. In 1866 Whistler traveled to Chile to support the war of independence against Spain. Back in Europe, his encounters with the French Impressionists, in particular Edgar Degas and Edouard Manet, had a profound effect on his own painting, and he became the accepted leader of the British Impressionist movement. The artist then turned his interest to the Symbolists, in particular Charles Baudelaire and Stephane Mallarmé, whose poetry he deeply admired. In 1878 Whistler sued John Ruskin, one of his most trenchant critics, for libel, following Ruskin's ferocious attack on the artist's *Nocturne in Black and Gold: The Falling Rocket* (Detroit Institute of Arts, Detroit). The trial was tortuous and protracted, and although the court eventually found in favor of Whistler, the proceedings left him almost destitute. The set-back did not deter him from becoming a member of the British Artists Society in 1884, to which he was elected president from 1886-1888; and he continued to dedicate himself to painting, engraving, and the decoration of interiors until his death in London in July 1903.

Arrangement in Flesh Colour and Black: Portrait of Theodore Duret
Oil on canvas, 76×35.8 in
1883
Metropolitan Museum, New York

Theodore Duret (1838-1927) was a knowledgeable French art connoisseur and critic whom Whistler had met around 1880 through their mutual friend Edouard Manet. Duret also assiduously frequented Mme de Soye's private Parisian salon in the Rue de Rivoli, along with the Impressionists and those with a passion for refined exoticism. The critic's serious, imposing figure dominates the canvas: impeccably dressed in black

dinner suit and white tie, he holds an elegant fleshy pink silk scarf draped over his left arm, and a black top hat in his right hand. The delicate pearlescent gray tones of the background help to define and characterize the figure both stylistically and psychologically, creating a sense of understated melancholy. Music was, of course, supremely importance to Whistler, and this is a striking example of his more elegiac musical mood. The full-figure portrait has a solemn intensity, with the quick, light brushstroke technique and atmospheric luminosity typical of the Impressionist school; the complete absence of a descriptive background setting only serves to heighten the emotive power of the portrait itself. It was in these years that Duret, with his incisive art criticism, particularly his *Histoire des peintres impressionistes* (*History of Impressionist Painters*), examined and reevaluated the contribution of the Impressionist movement, with a special focus on the *plein air* technique, first suggested by Constable and Corot and resolved in the painting of Manet and Monet.

Symphony in White No. 2, 1864. Tate Gallery, London.

The Lady of the Lang Lijsen, 1864. Philadelphia Museum of Art, Philadelphia.

383

WINSLOW HOMER

(BOSTON 1836 - PROUT'S NECK, MAINE 1910)

One of the preeminent American painters of the 19ᵗʰ century, Homer taught himself to paint as a child. In 1855 he was apprenticed to a lithographer in Boston, and devoted himself to graphic media; and from 1857 he began to work as a freelance illustrator for a number of periodicals. His illustrations are characterized by figures drawn with clean outlines, simplified forms and intense contrasts of light and shade, qualities that would define his pictorial and graphic work throughout the rest of his career. Homer moved to New York in 1859, where he took a studio and continued to illustrate for various different publications, at the same time making his first experiments in painting. During the American Civil War the artist was sent to the front line several times, particularly to Virginia, to sketch battle scenes and daily military life. In the successive years Homer made a series of important oil paintings inspired by his experiences of the war, using his sketch books and notes as a reference. These early works were praised for their stark objectivity and powerful realism. In 1867 Homer traveled to Paris, where he stayed for a year: here he was captivated by the art of the Impressionists, with whom he shared an interest in natural light effects and painting from life, and the realism of Gustave Courbet. From 1873 Homer began to dedicate himself to watercolor painting, principally depicting idyllic rural scenes or popular vacation spots featuring elegant women and playing children, executed in a spontaneous, free style which was natural and immediate. His two-year stay in Britain (1881-82) on the Northumberland coast provided him with new subjects, and he was particularly fascinated by the lives of the fishermen, unsung heroes of the modern age. On returning to the United States in 1883 Homer established himself in Maine, where he painted his most famous seascapes. During the winter months he traveled extensively, visiting Florida, the Caribbean, Cuba and the Bahamas, all the while producing his engaging, emotive watercolors. In these works, Homer explored humanity's epic struggle against the forces of nature, exemplified by the representation of solitary men in small boats battling against the surging waves. The heroic, expressive potency of his mature works would have a profound influence on the succeeding generations of American realist painters.

A Basket of Clams

Watercolor on paper,
11.4×9.7 in
1873
Metropolitan Museum,
New York

The painting depicts two children carrying a basket of clams along the sand, in a small harbor with fishing boats shored up in the background. Every detail – the long shadows cast by the children, their simple clothes, the flotsam washed up on the beach, and the fishing boats and buildings in the background – is handled with persuasive realism. Perhaps the most striking feature is the extraordinary white marine light enveloping the whole scene, subtle but also bright and pervasive, exquisitely captured by Homer's delicate watercolor palette. Compared with his later works, where a greater focus falls on the strong narrative themes, here Homer concentrates on the pictorial rendering of the here and now in an everyday "slice of life". Homer's distinctive technique is informed by the realism of Gustave Courbet and the palette of the French Impressionists, two different artistic schools which had both deeply impressed him while in Paris. Blending aspects of both, he added his own original elements: in the *Basket of Clams*, the realism is transcended by the almost poetic atmospheric effects of the light. The *chiaroscuro* of the watercolors, soft and fluid, slightly blurs the forms, while the sight of the two children slowly making their way up the beach towards the observer reveals a typically American feeling for nature and humanity.

The Gulf Stream
Oil on canvas, 28×49 in
1899
Metropolitan Museum,
New York

Against the menacing backdrop of a turbulent sea and stormy sky, with sharks circling in the foreground, a solitary fisherman strains with every nerve to keep his small boat from capsizing, as the wind whips up and threatening clouds loom up above. The dramatic painting recalls Théodore Géricault's iconic *Raft of the Medusa*, which Homer would certainly have seen at the Louvre in Paris. Here, as in Géricault's work, man is shown at the mercy of nature, an effect heightened by the flashes of light falling across the canvas creating a *chiaroscuro* effect of light and dark patches. Homer uses reddish flecks here and there to break up the marine tones of the choppy waves, an unusual effect which brings to mind blood, adding to the sinister mood. The powerful pictorial style, both descriptive and narrative, reflects the taste in late 19th century American painting and literature, which offers a heroic representation of humanity buffeted by nature and destiny in situations often loaded with adventure, drama and pathos, to produce a sense of extreme emotional involvement in the observer or reader.

PAUL CÉZANNE

(AIX-EN-PROVENCE, PROVENCE 1839-1906)

The son of a wealthy banker, Cézanne studied at the Collège Bourbon in Aix-en-Provence, where he became close friends with the writer Émile Zola. At university in Aix he developed an interest in painting, and moved to Paris in 1861. From 1862-1869 he divided his time between Aix and Paris. Back in the French capital, Cézanne discovered the work of Eugène Delacroix and Gustave Courbet, visited the Salon des Refusés of 1864 and participated in the Café Guerbois meetings, where he met Camille Pissarro, who was to have a profound impact on his artistic theories. Cézanne's early work met with a hostile reception, and his pictures were systematically refused by the Paris Salons. In 1872-1873 he followed Pissarro to Auvers-sur-Oise, where his artistic development changed course: on the suggestion of Pissarro, he abandoned the literary and dramatic themes of his first period to concentrate on painting *en plein air* (open air). Cézanne focused increasingly on landscape painting, and abandoned the gloomy palette and subject matter of earlier works such as the *House of the Hanged Man* (Musée d'Orsay, Paris). Pissarro encouraged him to take part in the first Impressionist exhibition of 1874. In 1878 Cézanne withdrew to L'Estaque, a small town at the tip of the Gulf of Marseille, where he lived and worked in increasing isolation. All the while he continued to submit pictures to the Paris Salons, which were summarily turned down. Although Cézanne's work was still largely overlooked at this point, it had nonetheless generated a loyal following among a number of young Post-Impressionist painters such as Émile Bernard, Paul Sérusier, Maurice Denis and other artists belonging to the avant-garde group of Les Nabis. Gradually, interest in Cézanne began to widen, and the work he exhibited at the Salon des Indépendants of 1899 at last met with approval rather than contempt; in 1904, the Salon d'Automne devoted an entire room to him, and in 1907, the year after his death, a large posthumous retrospective was organized which finally marked his acceptance by the establishment, following his lifelong struggle for recognition. In terms of Cézanne's stylistic development, the concrete structural schemes of Courbet and the colorism of Delacroix both had a deep impact, as did the work of Honoré Daumier. These influences are evident in his early paintings, such as *Preparation for the Funeral (The Autopsy)* of 1867-1869 (Lecomte Collection); *Le Déjeuner sur l'herbe* (1870-1871, Private Collection); and the *Temptation of St Anthony* (c. 1870, Private Collection). His portraits and still lifes were more measured, yet still displayed considerable vigor and expressive force (*Still Life with Kettle*, 1869, Musée d'Orsay, Paris; *Portrait of Antoine Valabrègue*, c. 1871, J. Paul Getty Museum, Los Angeles; *The Black Clock*, 1869-70, Private Collection, Paris). Cézanne's successive works, painted under the guidance of his mentor Pissarro, began to move away from the Impressionist style, and were characterized by lighter tones and a rigorous compositional scheme. Cézanne affirmed that he wanted to make of Impressionism "something solid and lasting", aspiring to a formal synthesis involving the extreme simplification of natural elements to their essential values, which used color to build and model form and create volume. His Aix period (1883-1887) is marked by an ever tighter compositional control over the representation of nature. During those years, Cézanne tenaciously pursued his radical line of pictorial enquiry, obsessively revisiting the same subjects again and again, such as his many *Views of L'Estaque* (Art Institute of Chigago and Musée d'Orsay, Paris), the *Château noir* (National Gallery, Washington) and the *Mont Sainte-Victoire* (Musée d'Orsay, Paris; Kunsthaus, Zurich). His intention was to elaborate a new mode of visual representation which moved away from naturalism to concentrate on the pure, essential forms within nature, the "cylinder and the sphere". In 1890 Cézanne painted a grandiose series of still lifes (now in various international museums), along with portraits of his wife and several different versions of the *Card Players* (Musée d'Orsay, Paris; Courtauld Institute, London; Metropolitan Museum, New York). The painter continued his feverish activity into his final years, exemplified by the many variations on the theme of *Bathers*: first painted in 1885-1887 (Kunstmuseum, Basel), he developed the subject to monumental proportions, with a growing abstraction of natural form.

The Smoker

Oil on canvas, 36.2×28.7 in
c. 1891
Hermitage, St Petersburg

The theme of the smoker, popular in genre painting of the 17th century, was enthusiastically taken up by Cézanne, who returned to it numerous times. Here it is used both as a pretext for in-depth psychological analysis, and for the painter's ongoing stylistic investigations. The person portrayed was probably Alexandre Paulin, a peasant who worked for the artist at his beloved countryside family estate at Bouffan, where Cézanne lived in peaceful isolation from 1886-1899. The scene appears to be set in the artist's studio, since hanging on the wall in the background behind the smoker are two of his own paintings, just visible. The first, a *Still Life with Bottle*, is a youthful work now in Berlin, while the second has been identified as the *Bathers in the Open Air* (Hermitage, St Petersburg). According to one interpretative hypothesis, these "pictures within a picture" introduce important thematic elements into the main painting, in addition to adding color: their subjects would here allude to the worldly temptations the artist has shunned in order to seek the interior harmony necessary to preserve the authenticity of his inspiration. It is perhaps for this reason that the man has an abstract, faraway look, effectively rendered by the representation of his eyes as two small black cavities, as if the smoke had created a mist of oblivion between him and

everyday life. Stylistically, the subject allowed Cézanne to study, deconstruct and reconstruct reality, according to his clear vision of the world as composed of solid, geometric forms and volumes, which can be observed in the robust, "constructive" brushstrokes used to paint the face and closed fists of the smoker.

The Card Players
Oil on canvas, 18.8×22.5 in
c. 1890-1895
Musée d'Orsay, Paris

Cézanne justified his self-imposed exile to Aix-en-Provence, after the period spent in Paris, by declaring: "*I had decided to work in silence until the day in which I felt myself able to defend the theory behind the results of my research*". In his youth, however, the artist had led a more sociable life, often appearing at the Impressionist meetings in Parisian cafés, when he would even draw attention to himself with his purposely uncouth manners, exaggerated southern accent and deliberately shabby appearance. During that time Cézanne's work came under constant criticism, particularly for its perceived clumsiness, which broke every rule of academic painting and reflected the artist's controversial yet fundamental philosophical stance: he aimed to "*start all over again*", railing against tradition, almost as if painting had not existed before him, and resolving the problems of color and composition in an entirely individual and innovative way. After the initial dismissal of Cézanne's paintings, from 1899 they began slowly to fetch respectable prices in Paris; yet down in Aix the painter continued to be seen merely as a rich banker's son who daubed inconsequential little pictures and lived in his own eccentric fantasy world. His solitary life was increasingly interrupted, however, by visits from his growing band of followers, who came to regard him as a kind of "noble savage" who had managed to forge his own distinct and autonomous path in the world of painting. He famously advised the young Émile Bernard to "treat nature by means of the cylinder, the sphere, and the cone, with everything brought into proper perspective"; and he confided to another young painter his own aim "to render perspective only through color". This, effectively, is how the tension between color and structure is resolved in paintings such as the *Card Players*, where the vibrant light and the geometric forms of the figures find a balance thanks to the characteristic firm, "constructive" brushstrokes.

Mont Sainte-Victoire Seen from Gardanne

Oil on canvas, 24.8×32.7 in
c. 1897
Kunsthaus, Zurich

The Provençal mountain, which had already featured in some of Cézanne's youthful works, became the main object of his analysis in the last years of his life. At least eighteen variations on this theme are known. We can almost feel the effort made by the aging painter as he attempts, with extreme rigor, to go just a little deeper in his investigation of chromatic relations, where every single brushstroke impacts on the whole. The mountain is depicted from different points of view and at different times of day, in a quest, inevitably never quite fulfilled, for a representation of nature that attains to the truth of the object, faithful to the vision of what has been defined as the artist's "inner eye". Cézanne set himself a goal he knew to be extremely difficult to achieve, and that would inescapably lead to the discarding of the conventions that held good before him. In 1903 he wrote to Ambroise Vollard: "*I work tenaciously, I see the promised land before me. Will my fate be that of the great leader of the Jews, or shall I be able to enter? […] I have made some progress. Why so late and with such difficulty? Could*

it be that Art is in reality a priesthood that demands of the pure that they belong to it entirely?" And, two years later, to Émile Bernard: "*Yet since I am now old – almost seventy – the color impressions conveyed by the light are in my case the cause of abstractions which neither permit me to cover my canvas entirely nor to pursue the delimitations of objects when their points of contact are fine and delicate; the result is that my image or painting is incomplete. On the other hand the planes are placed one on top of the other.*" The version of the *Mont Sainte-Victoire* in Zurich, reproduced here, is one of his last (painted between 1904 and 1906), and illustrates the painter's words perfectly. Classical spatial perspective has ceased to exist, distance seems to have been canceled out, and the green of the fields has the same value as the color used to represent the clouds. The rendering of the atmosphere, according to Cézanne's pictorial principles, required a chromatic and volumetric analysis no less thorough than that of the mountain itself. Some parts of the canvas which are left unpainted take on a luministic function and at the same time contribute to that sense of inevitable incompleteness and lack of limitation of the forms that characterized the artist's late work.

Auguste Rodin
(Paris 1840 - Meudon, Île de France 1917)

Rodin was born into a working-class family in Paris, and became interested in art from an early age, enrolling himself into the École Spéciale de Dessin et de Mathématiques where he took courses in drawing with H. Lecoq de Boisbaudran. Having failed the entrance requirements for the École des Beaux-Arts, he started to earn a living as a craftsman and ornamenter, all the while developing a passion for sculpture. In 1864 he submitted his first work to the Paris Salon, *The Man with the Broken Nose* (Musée Rodin, Paris). It was refused, however, because the jury considered it to be "unfinished", a quality which would characterize much of Rodin's later work: as well as recalling the *non finito* of Michelangelo's sculptures, Rodin's "unfinished" style also drew on the contemporary artistic investigations of the Impressionists into the effects of natural light. The same year, Rodin joined the studio of the famous sculptor Carrier-Belleuse, for whom he worked until 1870, producing models for *objets d'art* and collaborating on the decoration of the Brussels Stock Exchange. Like many aspiring artists before and since, Rodin made an important trip to Italy in 1875, which was to play a fundamental role in his subsequent artistic direction. There he was able to deepen his knowledge of Michelangelo's work, whose influence can be seen in all of Rodin's work, especially in his predilection for nudes robustly modeled with vigorous plasticity. He would subsequently write to his fellow sculptor E.A. Bourdelle: "It is Michelangelo who has freed me from academic sculpture." Rodin's first major figure, a virile nude male entitled *The Age of Bronze* (1876, copies in the Victoria & Albert Museum, London, Nationalgalerie, Berlin and Musée d'Orsay, Paris) clearly shows the impact of Michelangelo; yet despite its obvious debt to the master, the sculpture was seen to be so innovative in its realism as to arouse the suspicion that it was a fake, and Rodin found himself accused of *surmoulage*, the practice of casting from a live model. Undeterred, he remained faithful to his own artistic philosophy, and the next year sculpted *The Walking Man* (Musée

Rodin, Paris), a much more radical departure from academic tradition for its rough, unpolished surface and the decision (albeit inspired by classical sculpture) to create a human figure in fragmentary form, without a head and arms. Only with the *St John the Baptist Preaching* of 1880 (various versions in international galleries, including the Museum of Modern Art, New York) did Rodin finally shrug off the controversy which had dogged his early work. The sculpture was awarded a prize at the Salon of 1880 for its dynamic realism and painterly modeling which again found parallels in the contemporary Impressionist school. Following this success Rodin received an extremely prestigious public commission from the French government, to sculpt an entrance doorway for the planned Musée des Arts Décoratifs in Paris, a museum which was never built. Rodin's work, inspired by Dante's *Divine Comedy* and called *The Gates of Hell*, was never finished, yet some of the individual figures made for it represent the pinnacle of his artistic achievement (*The Thinker*, *Ugolino*, *Fugit Amor* and *The Kiss*, all in the Musée Rodin, Paris with copies elsewhere). Another important commission came in 1884, resulting in his masterpiece *The Burghers of Calais* (Musée Rodin, Paris). Although Rodin's success and status within the artistic establishment had been confirmed, his work and techniques continued, periodically, to be misunderstood: the dramatic *Monument to Balzac* (one of his many portraits; Musée Rodin, Paris), was refused by the Salon because (just like the *Man with a Broken Nose*) it was considered unfinished, and when it was exhibited at the Salon of 1898 it caused an outrage. By 1916, however, the true worth of Rodin's sculpture was recognized, and his entire body of work, including the pieces which had previously incited such savage criticism, was accepted by the French state; Rodin's Parisian atelier became the Musée Rodin.

St John the Baptist Preaching,
1878-1880.
Museum
of Modern Art,
New York.

The Kiss

Marble, h. 72 in
1886-1898
Musée Rodin, Paris

Although *The Kiss* is now an iconic, stand-alone sculptural group, it was originally conceived for the *Gates of Hell*, and in fact depicts the fateful moment in Dante's *Comedy* when the doomed lovers Paolo and Francesca steal their first passionate kiss. Later, Rodin decided not to insert the group into the *Gates*, since he deemed it to be at odds with the more forceful dynamism of the other figures sculpted for the *Gates*. Instead, he created a second, very different version of the couple for the bottom left hand portion of the doorway (now known as *Fugit Amor*), this time representing them tragically clinging on to each other as they are buffeted by the winds of the second circle of Hell ("the Lustful"). The first version was exhibited by Rodin with the simple title of *The Kiss* in an exhibition held at the Galerie Georges Petit in 1887, and was an instant success, so much so that the French state commissioned a larger marble version for the kingly sum of 20,000 French Francs, unprecedented for a sculpture which had not even been exhibited, let alone awarded a prize, at the official Salon. When the great marble sculpture was eventually shown at the Salon of 1898, along with the *Balzac*, it had long since lost its association with the original context it was sculpted for, especially since its title, like those of many of Rodin's pieces, was merely descriptive and provided no clue as to the real identity of the two lovers and their literary origins. Naturally, then, the public assumed *The Kiss* to represent an ordinary,

contemporary couple, which created a stir both for the nudity and unusually large proportions of the figures, elements normally reserved for heroic, commemorative sculpture. The group nonetheless confirmed Rodin's fame as an erotic sculptor, able to transform an intimate, fleeting moment between two lovers into a work of tragic monumentality unknown to late 19th century society. The exposition of the large *Kiss* at the Salon of 1898, followed by its entry into the Musée du Luxembourg and its presence at the Universal Exhibition of 1900 won Rodin a series of prestigious international commissions to produce more marble replicas of the group. The most important of these requests (for which Rodin received the conspicuously high fee of 25,000 French Francs) came from the respected British archeological collector Edward Perry Warner, who wanted a single piece of contemporary sculpture to add to his impressive collection of antique statuary and artifacts. The contract for the commission specified that "the genital organs of the male figure must be rendered in full detail", so as not to appear different from the frank representation of the male anatomy of the Greek and Roman statues it was to be displayed alongside. The revolutionary Rodin was thus, by the turn of the century, considered to be the legitimate heir of the classical sculptural tradition even by those connoisseurs who were not experts in modern sculpture.

CLAUDE MONET

(PARIS 1840 - GIVERNY, NORMANDY 1926)

Monet's family moved from Paris to the port of Le Havre when he was still a child, and it was here that he started making his first forays into art, beginning with caricature drawings. Around 1858 the young Monet met Eugène Boudin, who was to have a crucial effect on his artistic education, introducing him to *plein air* (outdoor) landscape painting from life, after the Dutch tradition. In 1859 Monet left Le Havre for Paris, where he saw the work of Jean-Baptiste-Camille Corot and Charles-François Daubigny at the Salon; he also began to frequent the Académie Suisse, and met fellow student Camille Pissarro. After being called up for military service in Algeria in 1861, he returned to Le Havre the following year, before moving back to Paris. Here he came into contact with Pierre-Auguste Renoir, Alfred Sisley and Jean-Frédéric Bazille, with whom he stayed for a period in the forest of Fontainebleau (1863-64), painting landscapes from life in the manner of the Barbizon and Daubigny schools. In 1865 Monet met another leading light of the French artistic scene, Gustave Courbet, whose influence can be felt in paintings such as *Camille (Woman in Green)* of 1866 (Kunsthalle, Bremen), one of many works depicting Monet's future wife, Camille Doncieux. Like other young artists in his circle, Monet was also deeply impressed with Édouard Manet's *Le Déjeuner sur l'herbe* (1863), which had reopened the debate on how figures should be rendered in open air settings. Monet's own interest in this fundamental aspect of pictorial representation surfaced in his painting of the same name (*Le Déjeuner sur l'herbe* of 1865, fragments in the Musée d'Orsay, Paris) and also in the *Women in the Garden* (Musée d'Orsay, Paris). However, it is in the landscapes and cityscapes painted by Monet during these years (particularly of the River Seine) that we can trace the gradual evolution of the revolutionary new style of painting he would soon become synonymous with: Impressionism. His study of the way light reflected on the water in *La Grenouillère* of 1869 (Museum of Modern Art, New York), a bathing lido on the river just outside Paris, was breathtakingly innovative. A trip to London in 1870 proved to be another pivotal moment in the development of Monet's pictorial language, where he experienced firsthand the work of John Constable, and most importantly, Joseph Mallord William Turner. When, in 1874, Monet exhibited *Impression. Sunrise* in the photographer Nadar's shop, an art critic seized on the painting's title and the term "Impressionism" was coined. Even though it was first used in a derogatory sense, the term was quickly adopted by the group of young artists who were its prime exponents. Monet's growing interest in the depiction of light and atmospheric conditions at different times of the day led to him to paint a number of monumental series all based on a single theme. The first of these was dedicated to the station of *Saint-Lazare* in 1877, in which the painter focused repeatedly on how the light was affected by the smoke from the locomotives. The series on *Rouen Cathedral*, painted in the years preceding 1894, consists of some fifty canvases depicting the cathedral at various points throughout the day, and in various light conditions. In 1883, Monet moved out of Paris to a villa in nearby Giverny, where ten years later he created the now famous pond of water lilies. Between 1909 and 1926, the year of his death, he painted the lilies over again, pushing his pictorial research to the very limits of the non-representational.

Poppies
Oil on canvas, 19.7×25.6 in
1873
Musée d'Orsay, Paris

Émile Zola described the public's reaction to the first independent group exhibition of the young "Impressionists", which was held between April 15 and May 15 in the shop of photographer Félix Nadar: "*The ladies stopped trying to stifle their laughs in their handkerchiefs, and the men's bellies puffed in and out as they guffawed with laughter [...] They were all elbowing each other out of the way and craning their necks to see [...] every canvas was judged, the people were calling out to each other, witty comments were flying around the room*". The catalogue had been curated by Edmond Renoir (brother of the painter Pierre-

Auguste), who had lost his
patience with Monet for
sending too many pictures,
all of which had monotonous
titles: *Entry into the Village;*
Exit from the Village; Morning
in the Village... When

Edmond complained, Monet
calmly told him "*Just put*
'Impression'": the subject of
the picture hardly mattered
to the painter, since his
primary interest was in
relaying his visual perception

of nature in all its immediacy,
in other words, the
"impression". The term was
so apt that the group
accepted it as the very
definition of their style and
school, even though it had

started out life as a pejorative
jibe by critics who judged
their work to be vulgar and
superficial. *Poppies*, one of a
number of paintings
presented by Monet in this
seminal exhibition, was his

attempt to express the effect of brilliant afternoon sunshine on a landscape through the handling of color. It was not the simple subject matter that the public found shocking; it was the radical new technique, which flouted the rules of academic painting that stated that color must be subordinated to draftsmanship; and one of the jokes that circulated about the Impressionists was that they loaded a pistol with paint and shot it at the canvas, signing the results.

Rouen Cathedral, Midday
Oil on canvas, 39.3×25.5 in
1894
Pushkin Museum, Moscow
(below on the left)

Rouen Cathedral, Early Sun
Oil on canvas, 41.7×28.7 in
1894
Musée d'Orsay, Paris
(below in the middle)

Rouen Cathedral, Full Sunlight
Oil on canvas, 42.1×28.7 in
1894
Musée d'Orsay, Paris
(below on the right)

Rouen Cathedral, Evening
Oil on canvas, 39.7×25.5 in
1894
Pushkin Museum, Moscow
(opposite)

These paintings belong to a series of works depicting the façade of Rouen Cathedral, which Monet executed between 1892 and 1894. Each picture captures a specific time of day, so each day the painter must have worked on several canvases contemporaneously, going back to them the next day at roughly the same time. This is confirmed by the annotations, such as "*late afternoon, around six*", found on some of the paintings. Each work is thus different from the next because of the variations in the light and atmospheric conditions, but forms part of a whole that can be divided into other groups: pictures painted by the light of morning, in full sunlight or around sunset. The patterns of light and shade constantly shift as they are caught on the white, highly reflective marble surface of the cathedral and refract off the elaborate decorations and splayed portals: so, for example, in some canvases the pale blue tones of dawn predominate, transitioning to the white shades of the morning light, the golden reflections of noon, and the reds and oranges of the afternoon. Monet himself experienced different states of mind while painting the pictures, as his letters reflect. At times he seems to have been overcome by despondency, as in one he wrote on March 30, 1893 to Paul Durand-Ruel: "*My stay here goes ahead: this does not mean that I am close to finishing my cathedrals. Alas, I can only repeat: the more I see, the worse I get at rendering what I feel; and I tell myself that anyone who says he has finished a canvas is tremendously arrogant. Finished, meaning complete, perfect; and I work at full stretch without getting anywhere, seeking, groping, without achieving much, but to the point of exhaustion.*" In 1895 the painter showed twenty or so of the pictures he had painted at Durand-Ruel's gallery. Not everyone appreciated the paintings and the reasons for the discordant views can be sought in part in what the painter Camille Pissarro wrote to his son Lucien: "*It is the unhurried work of a strong will, which pursues the tiniest nuances of effect and which I have not seen done by any other artist. There are those who deny the need for such research when is taken to this point.*"

*Water-Lily Pool,
Harmony in Green,*
1899. Musée
d'Orsay, Paris.

*The Artist's Garden
at Giverny,* 1900.
Musée d'Orsay,
Paris.

403

PIERRE-AUGUSTE RENOIR

(LIMOGES, HAUTE-VIENNE 1841 - CAGNES-SUR-MER, ALPES MARITIMES 1919)

Renoir was born into a working class family, and at the age of just thirteen went to work as an apprentice in the Parisian porcelain factory of the Levy brothers, where he was able to develop his talent for drawing by decorating the fine pieces of china. He remained there until 1858, and in 1862 enrolled in the École des Beaux-Arts; during this time he also started frequenting the studio of the painter Marc Gabriel Charles Gleyre, where he became friends with Claude Monet, Alfred Sisley and Jean-Frédéric Bazille. Together, the group of young artists spent a period in the forest of Fontainebleau (1863-1864), dedicating themselves to the study of nature and landscape from life. Renoir also met the landscape artist Diaz de la Pena around this time, who encouraged him to lighten his color palette and paint outdoors. His first works executed on returning to Paris reveal the influence of the realist artist Gustave Courbet (in *The Inn of Mère Antony* of 1866, for example, National Museums of Fine Arts, Stockholm). In 1974 Renoir participated in the first, epochal group Impressionist show, exhibiting one of his finest Impressionist masterpieces, *The Theater Box (La Loge)* (Courtauld Institute Galleries, London): this work combines two of his principle interests, everyday scenes of Parisian life and the study of light. Two years later Renoir painted what was to become one of the archetypal works of the French Impressionist movement, the *Dance at the Moulin de la Galette* (Musée d'Orsay, Paris); and the large canvas *Mme Georges Charpentier and her Children* of 1878 (Metropolitan Museum, New York) finally confirmed his iconic status as one of the leading French artists of his era. However, by this time Renoir was already beginning to grow impatient with the limits of the Impressionist style, and in 1881 he made a number of foreign trips in search of new inspiration. After a brief, disappointing journey to north Africa, he traveled to Italy, where he was reinvigorated by the Renaissance art and the ancient frescos of Pompeii, which led him to reevaluate his entire artistic philosophy. The resultant change in direction was defined by Renoir himself as his *manière aigre* ("harsh or sharp style"), while the critics perhaps more accurately described it as "ingresque", since it was clearly indebted to the Neoclassical master Jean-Auguste-Dominique Ingres as much as to Italian Renaissance painting. The works of the *aigre* period, such as *The Bathers* of 1884-1887 (Museum of Art, Philadelphia) are characterized by a pure formal precision, a painstaking attention to draftsmanship, and the sober, austere treatment of color. Towards the end of the century Renoir developed a serious form of rheumatoid arthritis which left him wheelchair bound. In spite of the excruciating pain, the artist continued to work, devoting himself mainly to portraits and female nudes whose treatment of color recalls Titian and Rubens. From 1900 he began to spend long periods on the French Côte d'Azur, finally settling in Cagnes-sur-Mer in 1903. His late paintings returned exclusively to one of his favorite subjects, the monumental female nude (such as *Bathers* of 1918-1919, Musée d'Orsay, Paris), depicted with soft, fluid brushstrokes which perfectly harmonized the figures within their setting.

Dance at the Moulin de la Galette

Oil on canvas, 51.6×68.9 in
1876
Musée d'Orsay, Paris

Every day in the spring of 1876, Renoir's friends helped him to carry the canvas that he was working on from his Rue Cortot studio in the Parisian district of Montmartre to the nearby Moulin de la Galette. Renoir had purposely taken the studio to be within walking distance of his subject, but it was still a considerable undertaking to move a picture of this size, and proof of his dedication to the concept of open air painting from life. At that time the Moulin was a popular meeting place for the local bourgeoisie and artists alike, who would regularly gather there to dance, gossip, and have a good time in congenial surroundings. Renoir too clearly reveled in the buzzy, festive atmosphere of the place, and his painting captured all the *joi de vivre* of the carefree crowd, providing a snapshot of contemporary life, *la vie moderne*, which the poet Charles Baudelaire had eulogized. An infectious air of optimism infuses the scene: these are the new heroes of modern, contemporary society, affluent members of the *beau monde* who have come out to chatter, dance, pose and enjoy themselves, to see and be seen in their finery; and the canvas is a riot of fashionable hats, hairstyles, cravats, bustles and patent leather shoes, sweeping into

the distance as far as the eye can see, and picked out by the dappled light characteristic of Renoir's Impressionist style. The painter cast a positive eye over the world he belonged to, and his work seems to exorcize the problems and banality of everyday life. Critics would come to define his style as "Romantic Impressionism", both for its

brightly poetic tone, and for the subjects he chose to represent: lovers and groups of friends at dances, in gardens, or in Bougival or Chatou just outside the city, popular countryside haunts where the Parisians would flock to spend a lazy Sunday. Both technically and thematically, the *Dance at the Moulin de la Galette* is a quintessential Impressionist

work, with forms dissolving into one another: paint is applied in small, richly highlighted patches of color with daringly loose brushstrokes, a technique which the critics found incomprehensible, along with the results.
The painting was ridiculed, particularly for the dancing figures arranged on an inconsistent plane which did

not conform to the rules of perspective, "*on a surface similar to the violet-purple storm clouds which gather in the sky on a stormy day*".
Of all the critics, only Georges Rivière understood the true value of the work, writing enthusiastically that it was "a piece of history, a precious moment of Parisian life depicted with rigorous accuracy".

The Umbrellas

Oil on canvas, 71×44.9 in
1881-1886
National Gallery, London

A bustling crowd of people is caught in a sudden downpour in a Parisian public park: instantly, a large mass of black umbrellas are opened up to cover the space above them. At the center of the picture, a young woman in profile looks anxiously up towards the sky as she wrestles her own umbrella open, while in the top right corner a man in a top hat tries to avoid the people dashing here and there by holding his umbrella above the rest. In the midst of all this frenetic activity, the little blonde girl in the foreground seems almost to belong to a different painting: her stillness and serene expression is a direct counterpoint to the rushing adults around her. Time appears to stand still around her, and even the stylistic treatment of her colorful hat, hair, clothes and hoop, rendered with the familiar shimmering contours of dappled Impressionist light, contrasts with the more formal, solid outlines of the other figures. In fact, this painting marked a crossroads between the carefree, joyful themes and style of Renoir's earlier period with their radiant rainbow color and light effects, and the radically different *aigre* or "ingresque" style which was to follow. As Renoir later told his first biographer, the art dealer Ambroise Vollard, "*Around 1883 a sort of break occurred in my work. I had got to the end of Impressionism and had reached the conclusion that I could neither paint nor draw. In a few words, I was in a blind alley.*" Renoir's trip to Italy around this time helped him out of the crisis: he was able to admire the work of the old Renaissance masters and regain his artistic inspiration, temporarily putting down his brush to take up the pencil and charcoal; and when he finally came to finish *The Umbrellas* in around 1886, his work had already turned a corner from the classical Impressionist style expressed in the figure of the little girl.

ILYÁ YEFÍMOVICH RÉPIN

(TSUGUEV, UKRAINE, 1844 - KUOKKALA, FINLAND 1930)

Répin was a Russian painter and sculptor whose parents were tied to the military establishment. From the very outset, his work was characterized by a strong psychological and expressionist vein, as he sought to explore the tensions exposed by a rapidly changing social order. In the 1920s Répin was held up as a beacon of progressive Soviet realism; the state even encouraged emerging artists to follow his lead in the hope that the "Socialist Realist" movement would spread from the USSR across Europe, to counter the nascent desire for autonomy from pure form and latent abstractionism. Répin began his education at the Peredvizhniki school of art in the Ukraine. In 1866, after a brief apprenticeship with an icon painter, he moved to St Petersburg, where he was admitted to the Imperial Academy of Arts. From 1873-1876 he visited Italy and also spent time in Paris, where a number of his paintings were exhibited alongside work by the Impressionists. However, Répin's style was more heavily influenced by the old European masters, particularly Rembrandt. In 1878 he returned to his native Ukraine, joining the Association of Peredvizhniki Artists, nicknamed "the Itinerants" or "the Wanderers". Starting shortly before the assassination of Tsar Alexander II in 1881, Répin executed a series of paintings on the theme of the Russian revolution, works which became exemplars of the Russian national style for their biting analysis of social disparity, set against a background of traditional religious beliefs and the new movements which were emerging at the time. In 1882 the artist decided to move back to St Petersburg, where he continued to elaborate his pictorial language, culminating in one of his most dramatic paintings, *Ivan the Terrible and his Son* of 1885 (Tretyakov Gallery, Moscow): the raw depiction of emotion in the horrified, devastated face of Ivan the Terrible, clutching his dead son to his breast, caused a stir, and ushered in a new genre of historical painting with a strong emphasis on realism and psychological penetration. Répin was equally celebrated as an excellent portraitist, and his subjects read like a roll-call of Russia's leading figures, including the writer Leo Tolstoy, the scientist Dmitri Mendeleev, the composer Modest Mussorgsky, the collector Pavel Tretyakov, and the Ukranian poet Taras Shevchenko.

They Did Not Expected Him, 1884.
Tretyakov Gallery, Moscow.

Portrait of Pavel Tretyakov

Oil on canvas, 38.6×29.5 in
1883
Tretyakov Gallery, Moscow

The Muscovite Pavel Tretyakov was a patron of the arts, dealer and industrialist who collected works of art throughout his life, buying them directly from the artist (as in the case of Répin), or seeking them out from second-hand market stalls and small private galleries. Initially, the collection was kept in Treyakov's own house, but by 1870 it had expanded so much that it had to be transferred to a new, larger space (the building it is currently housed in was built later, in 1902). A few years before his death, Tretyakov donated his entire collection to the city of Moscow; at that point, it numbered 1,287 paintings, 518 drawings and nine sculptures, all dating to the 18th and 19th centuries. Répin painted two portraits of Tretyakov, depicting him in both paintings surrounded by works from his own precious collection. Here, the golden tones highlight the subject's serious, thoughtful face, as well as illuminating the ornate gilded frames of the paintings behind him. Répin offers an intense psychological profile of the great patron, whose calm, contemplative gaze expresses the deep satisfaction of one who takes enormous pleasure and pride in his art.

THOMAS COWPERTHWAIT EAKINS

(PHILADELPHIA, 1844-1916)

One of the most important and versatile American artists of his era, Eakins was a painter, photographer, sculptor and educator, and an exceptionally talented exponent of late 19th century realism. From 1861 he studied drawing and anatomy at the Pennsylvania Academy of the Fine Arts, developing a scientific interest in the human body which led to his taking further courses in anatomy at the Jefferson Medical College between 1864 and 1865. He continued his education in Europe from 1866-1870, notably in Paris under Jean-Léon Gérôme. Back in Philadelphia in the early 1870s, he began to focus more intently on painting from life, often depicting ordinary people in everyday situations; in parallel, he produced a large series of portraits of contemporary scientists, intellectuals, artists and medics, earning himself a reputation of the portrait painter *par excellence* of the American intelligentsia. During these years Eakins added to his repertoire with a series of paintings featuring the male figure in a variety of different settings: young nude bathers, boxers training and in the ring, gymnasts and sporting nudes surprised in mid action, mostly captured in strong daylight. He was also fascinated by the rapid evolution of photography in both America and Europe, conducting his own experiments with the medium: he introduced the camera into the artist's studio, and after seeing Eadweard Muybridge's photographic motion studies, he even pioneered his own technique for capturing movement on film through sequential multiple exposures. Eakins was equally influential in the field of teaching, and attracted a wide following among the new generation of American artists, in spite of the fact that his personal reputation was seriously damaged by a number of unfortunate incidents and scandals surrounding his controversial teaching methods and working philosophy. Ever interested in new ways of expressing movement, his artistic investigations gained three-dimensionality in his sculptural work. A trip to Spain, where Eakins was able to admire the work of Velázquez and Ribera, was decisive in galvanizing his highly individual realist style. Eakins returned to the Pennsylvania Academy to teach in 1876, becoming its director in 1882. Taking a radically modern approach, he discouraged his students from the slavish imitation of antique statuary, emphasizing instead the value of studying the human body and movements from life, an artistic philosophy he adhered to throughout his own long and varied career.

The Artist's Wife and His Setter Dog

Oil on canvas, 30×22.9 in
c. 1884-1889
Metropolitan Museum, New York

The painting depicts the artist's young wife, Susan, in his Philadelphia studio at 1330 Chestnut Street, where he moved to in 1884 (the year of his marriage and, presumably, the year he started the portrait). Eakins' realist sensibility is apparent in the way he has lingered on every particular, from the main subject, Susan, to the smallest background element. The room is richly decorated and furnished in a style which draws from both the decadent and aesthetic movements popular in the late 19th century manner: details such as the Persian rug, the chair Susan sits on, the desk behind her, the Oriental curtain and the suggestion of a Japanese print to the right of the painting all add to the highly individual atmosphere. The red tones of the studio space contrast sharply with Susan's brightly lit blue dress, to put her in relief. Her young, slightly drawn face expresses both wistfulness and intellect; the immediacy of her pose, captured in an instant as she lays her open book in her lap and tilts her head towards the observer, recalls the genre of interior portrait photography practised at the time. Susan Eakins was the daughter of Hannah Macdowell, a respected Philadelphia artist who specialized in engraving and printmaking, and instilled a passion for art in both Susan and her sister Elizabeth. Susan had met Eakins in 1876, and that same year she decided to study art herself, enrolling in the Pennsylvania Academy of the Fine Arts where she continued taking classes until she married. Her husband painted her portrait a number of times; this example is one of the most intense and characterful.

Paul Gauguin

(Paris 1848 - Atuona, Marquesas Islands, French Polynesia 1903)

Gauguin spent his early childhood in Lima, Peru, before returning to France where he studied in Orléans and Paris. In 1865, at the age of seventeen, he enlisted in the navy as a cadet, and spent five years at sea. Back in Paris, he found a job at a bureau de change and began to paint and sculpt in his spare time. He eventually became close friends with Camille Pissarro after having been introduced to the Impressionist circle, taking part in their group exhibitions between 1879 and 1886. This period also saw Gauguin leave his full-time job to dedicate himself completely to his painting. Over the next few years, the artist suffered a number of financial and family crises which forced him to move out of Paris. In 1885, he went to Pont-Aven in Brittany, northern France, for the first time, where he met fellow artists Émile Bernard and Laval; and in 1887 he traveled with Laval to Martinique. The following year he returned to Pont-Aven, and also stayed in Arles, where his friendship with Vincent van Gogh came to a dramatic and violent end. These years were crucial to the evolution of Gauguin's artistic philosophy: he abandoned Impressionism and developed a new style, defined as "Synthetism", which was essentially anti-realist and symbolist in nature. The first work associated with the Synthetist style is the *Vision after the Sermon* of 1888 (National Gallery of Scotland, Edinburgh). A number of widely different influences contributed to the conception of Synthetism, in particular, primitive Breton art, Japanese prints and the research carried out by Gauguin and his friends Bernard and Anquetin on the symbolic meaning of color. The unconventional formal solutions elaborated by Gauguin would have a strong impact on the subsequent development of the Symbolist movement, of which the artist is considered to be one of the founders. During his Brittany period, Gauguin painted a number of celebrated portraits (*Madame Ginoux*, 1888, Pushkin Museum, Moscow; *The Beautiful Angel*, 1889, Musée d'Orsay, Paris) as well as executing a series of paintings characterized by a striking mystical quality, such as the remarkable *Yellow Christ* (Albright-Knox Art Gallery, Buffalo, NY). At the same time,

Gauguin experimented with other modes of artistic expression, such as wood sculpture, with which he recreated forms appropriated from primitive art (*Be Mysterious*, Musée d'Orsay, Paris). Gauguin's activity in Brittany led to the forming of the so-called Pont-Aven school, which included, among others, Bernard, Séguin and Sérusier. After a brief return to Paris, where the artist became a leading light in the literary meetings of the Café Voltaire, he left for Tahiti in 1891, in search of a civilization which he felt to be pure and uncorrupted. Enchanted by the beauty of the land and people, he devoted himself to their study with an almost ethnological assiduity, portraying the locals' daily lives and customs and jotting down his impressions in several travel journals (*The Ancient Maori Cult*; *Noa Noa*). Among the more celebrated works completed during this first Tahitian trip are *Tahitian Women (On the Beach)* (1891, Musée d'Orsay, Paris); *Te matete (We Shall Not Go to the Market Today)* (Kunstmuseum, Basel); and *Ia orana Maria (Ave Maria)* (Metropolitan Museum, New York). After returning to Paris in 1893 Gauguin became seriously depressed, partly as result of his growing alienation from Western society and values. His Tahitian experiences continued to inform his painting during this phase, resulting in works such as *Mahana no Atua (Day of God)* (Art Institute, Chicago) and a series of wood engravings which reworked the magical evocatory power of the Tahitian idols. In 1895 Gauguin was drawn back to his beloved Tahiti, but by this time the artist was increasingly isolated, in debt and depressed; his disturbed state of mind expressed itself through vast compositions which allegorized the destiny of humanity, such as the moving *Where Do We Come From? What Are We? Where Are We Going?* of 1897 (Museum of Fine Arts, Boston), a masterpiece regarded as the artist's pictorial testament. To the very end of his life, the women of Tahiti remained a favorite subject and an endless font of inspiration: *Rupe Rupe (Fruit Gathering)* (Puskin Museum, Moscow); *Two Tahitian Women* and *Red Flower Breasts*, both in the Metropolitan Museum, New York.

IA ORANA MARIA

**Ia Orana Maria
(Ave Maria)**

Oil on canvas, 44.5×33.8 in
c. 1891-1892
Metropolitan Museum,
New York

In a letter sent by the artist on
March 11 1892 to his friend

Daniel de Monfreid in France,
Gauguin described a painting
he was working on in detail,
even providing a sketch. The
canvas, he wrote, measured
around 44.5×33.8 in and from
the drawing it is clear that the
work was conceived
horizontally. It has been

confirmed beyond doubt that
the painting is the one now in
the Metropolitan Museum, yet
the fact remains that Gauguin's
initial description does not
match the size or orientation
of the current canvas. A
number of tests undertaken on
the surface of the painting

have revealed a white
background applied onto a
previous version of the
composition, and it has also
been observed that the green
patch at the top right of the
current picture corresponds to
the grassy area of the original
version: it is therefore likely

that Gauguin, dissatisfied with the first version of the picture as described in his letter to Monfreid, turned the canvas through 90° and started again, retaining only the compositional concept of the first attempt. In *Ia orana Maria* ("*Ave Maria*" in Tahitian dialect), an angel points out the exotic-looking Virgin and Child in the foreground to two native women, who join their hands in prayer to worship the sacred figures. Gauguin's scene is a veritable paen to rich color and tonal contrasts, from the multi-colored wraparound skirts of the women and the Virgin, to the exotic bananas in the immediate foreground, the greens of the lush vegetation, and the delicate pinks and blues of the angel, who is as light and ephemeral as the other figures are solid. Before choosing Tahiti as his second home, Gauguin had considered other exotic places, many of which he had visited during his years in the navy, such as Martinique, Java and Madagascar. But on the eve of his departure to Tahiti, he wrote: "*Madagascar is still too close to the civilized world. I will leave for Tahiti and hope to end my life there*".

Tahitian Women (On the Beach)

Oil on canvas, 27×35.8 in
1891
Musée d'Orsay, Paris

Gauguin wrote in his memoirs, "*If I were to tell you that one of my maternal ancestors belonged to the Borgia family of Aragon and was the viceroy of Peru, you would accuse me of lying and being pretentious*". There is some truth in this statement, however: the artist was indeed descended from a noble Peruvian family on his mother's side, and spent his early years in Lima before moving back to Paris with his parents. The need to search for his origins, real or mythical, was probably at the root of his eternal restlessness, and throughout his life he traveled tirelessly between France and the exotic lands of Martinique and Tahiti. In 1891, the successful auction of a number of his paintings enabled Gauguin to take his first trip to Tahiti. There he was bewitched by the indolent beauty of the local women, with their strong shoulders and powerful hips, and he painted them repeatedly in varying poses and settings, without ever bestowing them with individual identities, since he was not interested in producing realistic portraits or delving into their inner personalities. In this canvas, the strong facial features of the two women recall primitive masks, or indeed the ceramic masks and small wooden idols Gauguin himself made during this time. In the so-called "primitive" cultures and art of Tahiti, Pre-Columbian Mesoamerica, Brittany and Japan, the artist sought a visual candor which he believed to have been lost in Western art, enslaved (as he saw it) to academic conventions, spatial perspective and the realistic representation of the world. He thus created a new kind of "religion", the cult of exoticism: by isolating the two women (who are in fact one and the same model in different poses) on a flat surface with vivid chromatic contrasts, he gave them an impassive monumentality, transforming them into two primitive goddesses, sitting on the fertile soil of a new Eden.

417

SACRED ART
OF NEW IRELAND

(MELANESIA, 19TH CENTURY)

The art of New Ireland is known principally through the objects collected between the late 19th and early 20th centuries, a period in which the introduction of metal tools led to an artistic production of exceptional quality. Three main styles of New Ireland art have been identified: the first, known as *malagan* (or *malanggan*), comes from the north and north west of the island; the second is associated with the *uli* cults practised by the communities of the interior; and the third (*kulap*), from the south of the island,

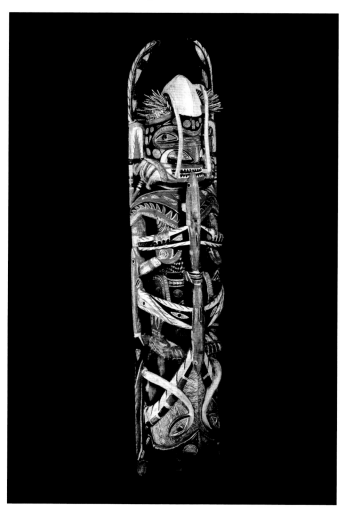

is characterized by commemorative figures of relatively small sizes sculpted in chalky stone. The term *malagan* refers both to the set of rites performed to honor the dead, and the masks and sculptures used in these rites. The *malagan* style produced various types of masks and decorations, generally pierced and bored, in which anthropomorphic motifs (stylized bodies or human heads) combine with zoomorphic elements (birds, snakes and fish). These works were assembled to create vertical pillars similar to totem poles, or horizontal frieze decorations whose images overlapped or appeared side by side in sequences, surrounded by connecting laths, which were also carved and sculpted, further embellisheding the sculpture as a whole. The brightly painted *malagan* sculptures achieved an expressive power rarely equaled in the art of Oceania. The *tatanua* masks assumed a crucial role in the *malagan* rituals: made from wood, bark and other natural materials such as leaves and bird feathers, they incarnated the spirits of the dead and the other beings which populated the afterlife. The communities who lived in the interior of the island practised cults (*uli*) involving highly elaborate ceremonies, which symbolically expressed the duality between the female (whose role was to create and feed), and the male (who controlled the energy unleashed during the ritual). Wooden sculptures (*nalik*) were also used for these celebrations, and at the end of the rites they were placed on the seats of the men in the ceremonial building, at the front of which the women solemnly laid yams, the symbol of life. As in the case of the *malagan* these celebrations were organized to commemorate the death of a prominent member of the community, whose skull was exhibited after having been carefully washed in the sea, remodeled and finally decorated.

Malagan Figure, 1882-1883.
British Museum, London.

Tatanua Mask

h. 16 in
19th century
British Museum, London

Originating from north and central New Ireland, this type of helmet mask, unique to the art of this island, is known as *tatanua* after the male dance in which it was used, a part of the funerary ritual to honor the dead. The masks were prepared exclusively by the men of the community. Although they may at first appear strikingly similar, each one has distinctive features which reflect different meanings and symbolic associations. The upper part of the masks generally consists of a crest on a cane framework held together with plant fibers and covered with bark or, in more recent examples, textiles imported from Europe. The decoration of the crest mimics the hairstyle worn by young men during the mourning period, when the head was partially shaved and coated with whitewash. The sides of *tatanua* masks are decorated in different styles, using materials such as feathers, wool, shells, short wooden sticks or seeds; the crest is normally made from plant fibers of a yellow or reddish brown color. Usually, the face is carved from soft limewood (*Alstonia*) and decorated with black, white and reddish brown pigments. In this example, which came to the British Museum from the late 19th century collection of Hugh Hastings Romilly, blue pigment has been added (a European product), to enhance the brilliance of the whitewash. The eyes are set with pieces of painted shell (*Turbo petholatus*), while the earlobes are elongated and pierced, and the open mouth displays two rows of sharp teeth. A description of the kind of ceremony in which these masks were used was published in 1907 by Richard Parkinson, following his visit to New Ireland.

VINCENT VAN GOGH

(GROOT-ZUNDERT, NORTH BRABANT 1853 - AUVERS-SUR-OISE, ÎLE DE FRANCE 1890)

Much of Van Gogh's life and artistic activity is known to us through his intense correspondence with his beloved brother Theo, which provides a rich insight into both his artistic development and psychological state of mind. The son of a Protestant minister, Van Gogh grew up in Groot-Zundert, a small village in the province of Brabant in southern Holland. After completing his studies in 1869, the fifteen-year-old Van Gogh was taken on by the art dealer Goupil & Cie in The Hague, a position he obtained through his Uncle Vincent ("Cent"). He was successively transferred by the firm to their London branch, and then to Paris, where he became increasingly resentful at the treatment of art as a mere commodity, and was subsequently dismissed in 1876. Back in Holland, Van Gogh made various attempts to find work before enrolling on a course at the Protestant missionary school in Laeken, near Brussels, and in 1879 he got a temporary post as a missionary worker in the Belgian mining region of Borinage, where he spent a difficult period which saw his mental health deteriorate. In the autumn of 1880 Van Gogh finally gave up the missionary life, and at the suggestion of his brother Theo, began to devote himself to art, moving to Brussels where he produced a series of drawings and watercolors over the next two years. At the end of 1883 he withdrew to Nuenen, the isolated country village in Dutch Brabant where his parents had recently moved from their previous home in Etten. The two years Van Gogh spent in Nuenen had a profound impact on his artistic development: inspired by the memory of his experiences among the miners of Borinage, he began to draw and paint the places and people of the area, in particular poor peasants and weavers, either at work or in rare moments of rest (*Peasant Woman Near the Hearth*, Musée d'Orsay, Paris, and the famous *Potato Eaters*, Rijksmuseum Kröller-Müller, Otterlo). In 1886 he joined his brother Theo in Paris, marking the start of his French period, which was interrupted only by a brief trip to Antwerp at the end of the same year. Van Gogh's Parisian stay (1886-1888) was a fruitful one: the burgeoning artistic environment was inspirational, and he even began collecting Japanese prints. Most importantly, he discovered Impressionist painting, coming into contact with fellow artists Henri de Toulouse-Lautrec, Claude Monet, Pierre-Auguste Renoir, Georges Seurat, Paul Signac and Paul Gauguin, with whom he formed a close friendship which was later to have dramatic repercussions. It was in Paris that Van Gogh began to experiment with vivid color, stimulated by the work of the Impressionists and the technique of Pointillism. In 1888 Vincent left Paris for the south of France, settling in the Provençal town of Arles. Captivated by the strong light and

bright colors of Provence, he went on to produce some of his most important masterpieces, including the *Bedroom in Arles* (1889, Musée d'Orsay, Paris) and the series of *Sunflower* paintings (1888-1889) which would become iconic. Throughout this time, however, he continued to suffer from mental health problems, leading to one of the most infamous episodes in his life: at the end of 1888, during a violent quarrel with Gauguin (who had been staying at Arles on Vincent's insistence), he attacked his friend and ended by cutting off part of his own earlobe, painting a memorable self-portrait shortly afterwards (*Self-Portrait with Bandaged Ear*, Courtauld Institute Galleries, London). Increasingly prey to dark bouts of depression, Van Gogh was taken to Arles hospital several times, before finally being committed to the psychiatric clinic of Saint-Paul, in Saint-Rémy de Provence. Here, during moments of lucidity, he painted with passionate fervor, creating work characterized by swirling vortices of thickly applied paint and an ever more intense color palette, as exemplified by one of his best-known paintings, *The Starry Night* (Museum of Modern Art, New York). In the spring of 1890, Van Gogh left the clinic and moved to Auvers-sur-Oise near Paris, where he was cared for by Dr Paul Gachet and his unflinchingly loyal brother Theo. During his final few months Vincent continued his frenetic painting activity, concentrating especially on landscapes and portraits (*Portrait of Dr Paul Gachet*; *The Church at Auvers-sur-Oise*, both in the Musée d'Orsay, Paris; *View of the Plain near Auvers*, Neue Pinakothek, Munich; *Wheatfield with Crows*, Van Gogh Museum, Amsterdam). At the end of July, Van Gogh shot himself, and died two days later.

Memory of the Garden at Etten

Oil on canvas, 28.8×36.3 in
1888
Hermitage, St Petersburg

In the spring of 1881 Van Gogh went to visit his parents at their house in Etten, where he stayed for several months. Inspired by the surrounding landscape and the local peasants, whose faces were etched with the signs of hard work and poverty, he produced a series of incisive drawings along with a few watercolors. When Van Gogh came to paint this canvas a number of years later, his parents had long since left Etten (moving to Nuenen in 1883); and the sleepy village appears filtered through the artist's memory and transfigured by the light and color of Arles, where he was then living. Provence embodied all that Vincent admired and held dear: the vivid "Moroccan" colors of Delacroix, the simple, severe mountainous landscapes of Cézanne, the rich chromatic fusion of Adolphe Monticelli, the painter who had influenced some of the still lifes Vincent had executed in Paris, and the clean, clear outlines (created by the dazzling sunlight) reminiscent of his beloved Japanese prints. *Memory of the Garden at Etten* also represents the point in Vincent's career when his work most closely approached that of Paul Gauguin, who stayed with him in Arles from late October 1888 until their fateful argument in December of the same year. Stylistically, Vincent's painting demonstrates a decisive move away from Impressionism and towards Gauguin: the elements of the composition are disarticulated in favor of clean lines, whole patches of color are applied flatly to the surface, and the sinuous arabesque linear rhythms are typical of the style Gauguin elaborated as founder of the Pont-Aven school in Brittany. Above all, however, Gauguin's influence can be felt in Vincent's uncharacteristic decision to paint from memory, relying on imaginative recall, rather than directly from life. Gauguin himself often returned to the exoticism of the South Seas in the paintings he made in Brittany, and conversely, when in Tahiti, he would sometimes load his pictures with European references. After the two painters had broken off their relationship, Vincent's art took a different direction, recreating reality through startling chromatic effects, anticipated by the bold color juxtapositions in this painting.

L'Arlésienne (Portrait of Mme Ginoux)

Oil on canvas, 35.9×30 in
1888
Metropolitan Museum, New York

After a turbulent life punctuated by disappointments, failure, depression and unrequited love, Vincent sought peace in the south of France, and for a time at least, he was relatively content there. He moved into the famous so-called "Yellow House" in Arles (unfortunately destroyed by bombing during World War II), and made friends with the owners of the local café, the Ginoux. Vincent here depicts Mme Ginoux (who was also painted by Gauguin) in pensive mood, with a faraway look, perhaps taking a moment to reflect on a passage of the book she is reading. The abstract setting

and incongruous perspective introduce an unreal, almost dream-like quality to the picture. The portrait, of which there is a second, darker version in the Musée d'Orsay, Paris (*Madame Ginoux with Gloves and Umbrella*) is one of the most touchingly expressive examples of Vincent's art, exuding a melancholic yet dreamy quality.

Self-portrait
Oil on canvas, 25,6×21,3 in
1889
Musée d'Orsay, Paris

Vincent – as he liked to sign his work – dreamed of forming a southern French school of painting with Paul Gauguin, a school which would rebuild art from its very foundations and take the principles of Impressionism to their extreme conclusion. The dream vanished in the violent breakdown of his friendship with Gauguin, and the further deterioration of his mental health led to his being admitted into the asylum at Saint-Rémy. Here he continued to paint fervently, and in September of the following year, in the absence of other models, he portrayed himself several times. From Arles, he wrote to his brother Theo: "*The emotions are sometimes so strong that one works without knowing one works, when sometimes the strokes come with a continuity and a coherence like words in a speech or a letter*". During these periods of manic activity, Van Gogh's brushstrokes flowed like a writer's pen across paper, unleashing his emotions and the full power of his creative energy onto the canvas. The self-portraits are also self-interrogations, in which he tracks the progression of his own illness: here, his thin, sharp face and frowning brow frames a penetrating gaze, which seems to scrutinize his own image. The strong, swirling brushstrokes of the splendid blue background, like eddies in a storm, express the artist's internal torment. This represents the most innovative aspect of a pictorial vision where color and form is instinctively transformed by the sensibility of the artist.

The Starry Night, 1889.
Museum of Modern Art,
New York.

CREDITS

431